For Hél

With muc

Enjoy !

J

x x x

Palgrave Studies in Political Leadership

Palgrave Studies in Political Leadership seeks to gather some of the best work on political leadership broadly defined, stretching from classical areas such as executive, legislative and party leadership to understudied manifestations of political leadership beyond the state. Edited by an international board of distinguished leadership scholars from the United States, Europe and Asia, the series publishes cutting-edge Research that reaches out to a global readership.

More information about this series at
http://www.springer.com/series/14602

Leadership and the Labour Party

Narrative and Performance

John Gaffney
Professor of Politics, Aston University, Birmingham, UK

palgrave
macmillan

Palgrave Studies in Political Leadership
ISBN 978-1-137-50497-5   ISBN 978-1-137-50498-2   (eBook)
DOI 10.1057/978-1-137-50498-2

Library of Congress Control Number: 2016938712

Cover image © Mark Thomas / Alamy Stock Photo

Printed on acid-free paper

This Palgrave Macmillan imprint is published by Springer Nature
The registered company is Macmillan Publishers Ltd.
The registered company address is: The Campus, 4 Crinan Street, London, N1 9XW, United Kingdom

For Cressida and Luke

CONTENTS

ACKNOWLEDGEMENTS

In previous publications, I have thanked two or three colleagues and the editorial team. Here the list of people to thank is long and doubtless incomplete. Academic colleagues, politicians and press secretaries, journalists and political cartoonists, think tankers, party workers, people not interested in politics, and many others have taken an interest in my research in a range of ways and have commented, criticized, granted interviews, attended and contributed at various presentations of my work at seminars and conferences, and given me critical encouragement. I want to thank them all. I also wish to thank the Leverhulme Trust for the grant that funded this research. It enabled me to employ a research assistant and have a 2-year teaching buy-out. Those two busy research years (August 2012–August 2014) gave me an enormous sense of privilege. The two individuals I owe most to are Amarjit Lahel who over the Leverhulme grant period was my research assistant, and Marley Morris who helped me with background research in the spring and summer of 2015. Their input and advice have been outstanding, and my debt of gratitude equally so. Stewart Wood and Marc Stears, close advisers to Ed Miliband, were very helpful, even though I must have got them (and Peter Hain and Jonathan Rutherford) into trouble with the boss with unhelpful and deliberate misreporting of my press releases and interviews. Their integrity and understanding in this was exemplary, especially given that the election campaign was about to begin. This and several other media distortions taught me how dangerous and difficult to negotiate the media can be – near-impossible if you are a central political actor like Ed Miliband, especially given the violence of the rightist media, but equally some of the media within the Labour Party itself which quite took me aback; so there are several journalists I will not be thanking here. But I really would like to thank other journalists, politicians, observers, and many others whose interest and support has made writing this book so enjoyable. Here they are; thank you to all: Richard Angell, Judi Atkins, Gavin Audley, Philip Ball, Kate Bandeira, Gary Barker, Mark Bennister, Phillip Blond, James Bloodworth, Peter Brookes, Patrick Burns, Philip Collins, Jon Craig, Andrew Crines, Jon Cruddas, Mark D'Arcy, Eva Descause, Anneliese Dodds, Katherine Dommett, Robert Elgie, David Farrow, Mark Ferguson, Catherine Fieschi, Alan Finlayson, Mark Fuller, Cressida Gaffney, Mark Garnett, Gary Gibbon, Maurice Glasman, David Goodhart, Simon Griffiths, Peter Hain, David Harley, Ludger Helms, Laura Hood, Sue Jamieson, Simon Jenkins, Peter Kellner, Julia King, Neil Kinnock, James Landale, Mathew Lawrence, Neil Lawson, Kayte Lawton, Quentin Letts, Jonathan Lewis, Simon Mares, James Martin, David Moon, Rick Muir, John Newbegin, Jackie Newbury, Reema Patel, Nick Pearce, Arlen Pettitt, Sally Puzey, Emma Reynolds, Rachael Richards, Emily Robinson, Martin Rowson, Jonathan Rutherford, Hopi Sen, Hélène Stafford, Joel Suss, Paul Taggart, Paul t'Hart, Louise Thompson, Polly Toynbee, Caroline Wheeler, Michael White, and Ben Worthy.

Whoever read my book proposal for Palgrave Macmillan made a set of extremely helpful comments and suggestions and I was very grateful for these when writing the book; they had quite a dramatic effect upon the range of my research suggesting, for example, more comparative analysis with France and French politics and leadership.

Colleagues in the Politics and International Relations Department at Aston University, in particular Ed Turner and Nat Copsey, were very helpful with views and comments (in the case of Ed, often the opposite of my own views). My own academic institution was also very supportive throughout the Leverhulme research period. My students on my Political Leaders courses at Aston University and at Sciences-Po Lille and Sciences-Po Rennes have not only been great fun to teach, their input into my own thinking about political leadership has been enormous and much appreciated. I remember one seminar on Weber's definition of charisma (see Chapter 1) where they demolished his definition almost word by word, phrase by phrase, *non-dit* by *sous-entendu*; showing how intellectually rewarding it can be just being attentive to examples of language and text; so to them thanks.

The staff at Palgrave Macmillan and the editorial team of the Political Leadership series have, as ever, been supportive and helpful – indeed, without them I would not have a contract.

You will of course have noticed, dear reader, the name missing from this eminent list is, of course, Ed Miliband himself. In the early stages of the research I intended to meet him (a train trip with him to his constituency in Doncaster was envisaged which would have been great fun). I then realized, as I argue in Chapter 1, that the real focus of my research as it evolved, and the real value to the study of politics, was to analyse not the man and his thoughts and ideas, but the rhetoric and performance of his leadership of the Labour Party as a 5-year sequence of public events: 'Ed Miliband' rather than Ed Miliband. I needed to capture the 'persona' not get to know the person. If my approach is correct, to do so would have been like meeting Colin Firth in order to understand George VI. I realized Miliband was the one person I should not meet. I decided, therefore, to leave any meeting until after the research was done and the book written. It is, so I look forward to meeting him! My thanks to all concerned. All the mistakes and inaccuracies are of course my own.

ABBREVIATIONS

CDU	*Christlich Demokratische Union Deutschlands*
CLP	Constituency Labour Party
CWU	Communication Workers Union
EEC	European Economic Community
ERM	Exchange Rate Mechanism
ESRC	Economic and Social Research Council
EU	European Union
GDP	Gross Domestic Product
GOP	Grand Old Party (US Republicans)
HMRC	Her Majesty's Revenue and Customs
ILP	Independent Labour Party
IPPR	Institute for Public Policy Research
LCC	London County Council
MP	Member of Parliament (Westminster)
NEC	National Executive Committee
NHS	National Health Service
NI	National Insurance
NLR	*New Left Review*
NUM	National Union of Mineworkers
OBR	Office for Budget Responsibility
Ofgem	Office of Gas and Electricity Markets
OMOV	One Member One Vote
ONS	Office of National Statistics
PLP	Parliamentary Labour Party
PMQs	Prime Minister's Questions

PPE	Philosophy, Politics, and Economics
PR	Public Relations
PS	*Parti Socialiste*
QMC	Queen Mary, University of London
SDP	Social Democratic Party
SNP	Scottish National Party
SPD	*Sozialdemokratische Partei Deutschlands*
TUC	Trades Union Congress
UK	United Kingdom
UKIP	United Kingdom Independence Party
VAT	Value Added Tax

LIST OF FIGURES

CHAPTER 1

Political Leadership, Rhetoric, and Culture: Aristotle Good, Max Weber Bad

RATIONALE OF THE BOOK

There are two organizing principles to this study. The first is that political leadership generally, and within the left particularly, is poorly theorized and as a consequence inadequately understood; and that this inadequate understanding impacts significantly not only upon scholarly understanding, but also upon the fortunes of political parties generally and of the UK Labour Party in the 2010–2015 period in particular. On this point, it became clear to me researching this book how little the Labour Party understands this phenomenon. The second is that a proper understanding of party leadership and, in this instance, the Labour Party in the period 2010–2015 led by Ed Miliband, depends upon an analysis of leadership's evolving relationship to party discourse and the public 'performance' of leadership, and that for leadership, practically, and for us, analytically, aligning these two with other factors – organization, public perceptions, policy elaboration, doctrinal issues, critics and supporters, and other political developments ('events') – offers insights into leadership performance and how the Labour Party functioned in the 2010–2015 period; and also how that period informed subsequent developments.

The focus of our analysis, therefore, will be upon developments in the party in the period under review, upon the textual emergence and deployment

© The Author(s) 2017
J. Gaffney, *Leadership and the Labour Party*, Palgrave Studies in Political Leadership, DOI 10.1057/978-1-137-50498-2_1

of the One Nation narrative, and each of these in terms of the latter's interpolation by the party leadership, and its effects upon Miliband's leadership image. The evolution, therefore, of the party narrative, an 'arc of rhetoric' 2010–2015, will be the focus of our study, along with an appraisal of Ed Miliband's leadership. In narrative terms, this rhetorical arc had two authors, the party and the leader, who 'mediated' their interacting narratives. This rhetorical arc also had an evolving external context – for example, the party in the polls, One Nation's critics (often very vocal/articulate), Miliband's leadership 'performances', the relationship with trade unions, party organization, and the media.

This book is not a chronicle of the Labour Party's fortunes in the 2010–2015 period, the 'Miliband era'. Chronicles of the Labour and Conservative Parties over the last 20 years abound. Indeed such immediate histories, particularly before and after national elections, have become widespread across Europe, in particular in France where *histoire immédiate* of political parties, movements, and individual leaders has become a boom industry. As regards the Labour Party (and the trade unions and Labour movement generally), it probably enjoys more shelf space than all other UK political parties put together, and for over 100 years every nanosecond of the party's life, even the many decisive unminuted moments in smoke-filled rooms supplied with beer and sandwiches, has been recorded (often compellingly so).

This study, therefore, is not a chronicle but an analysis, and for several important reasons. If we take the 'post-mortem' by academics, commentators, and Labour activists, strategists, and 'Team Miliband' itself – after the initial shock and awe of such an unexpected scale of defeat in May 2015 – generally speaking, a series of (mainly uncontentious) reasons for the defeat were identified.[1] And there was general agreement on the elements constituting the list of reasons; in fact, it was a litany (apart from a view from some that defeat was due to not being left-wing enough, which laid the foundations for Jeremy Corbyn's leadership campaign). Among the main reasons identified were: the 'incumbency advantage' of sitting MPs (although this no longer applied, in particular in the South-west or in Scotland); fears of an unholy SNP–Labour coalition; the inaccurate polls; the decline of the Labour Party's public sector vote (and the decline of its allegiance); Labour's not countering Conservative accusations of overspending before 2010; the Conservatives doing better than expected against the Liberal Democrats; the Labour Party's fighting not on three

---

[1] For example 'After Miliband' conference 5 June 2015, University College Oxford.

fronts like the Conservatives (Lab/Lib Dems/UKIP), but (at least) five (incompatible) fronts (Lib Dems, UKIP, Conservatives, SNP, and Greens); 'messaging' not getting 'out',[2] and the failure to 'follow through' on rebuilding from the 'base' (e.g., Arnie Graaf leaving the overall project in March 2014), or else spending too much time trying to do so. All of these were clearly pertinent factors. The two most significant reasons for Labour's defeat, held as being true by all observers, were that the party was not trusted on the economy and that the party leader, Ed Miliband, was not considered prime ministerial.[3] Each of these, I have no doubt, was a factor (although, ironically, this 'received view' was often based entirely upon the polls which were themselves so misleading and wrong). And there is a third 'main reason' agreed by many, understood by fewer than many, and best articulated by the Labour MP for Dagenham and Rainham, Jon Cruddas, that the party failed to develop a 'narrative' suitable for a party in the grip of redefining itself after the major defeat of 2010 and the exigency of a new direction, while situating itself in the context of the party's history. This 'failure' is, in fact, central to the whole of my analysis, and I shall deal with this throughout this study. I do not unreservedly share Cruddas' view of what the narrative was or should have been, nor even what constitutes a narrative; but that the party's narrative or narratives of itself, as it were, its voice, were crucial to the party's identity and its performance in the public arena. We shall come back to this last point below.

Before that, I wish to return to the question of the two main received reasons for the defeat (and the reasons for this book) – the lack of an economic narrative (here, a doctrine and convincing policies) and an 'un-prime ministerial' leader. The argument of this book, and a point taken up by very few observers, although I suspect most of them implicitly think it, is that the two – the 'narrative' and the 'performance' of that narrative by the leader were inextricably linked. For me, this is the key. To a greater or lesser degree depending upon both the narrative and the leader – and the situation – for better or worse, one became the other: the leader became the voice of the party, and 'enacted' and performed the party's identity and direction. This was not just about 'getting it right', but about understanding something profound about a political party like the Labour Party.

---

[2] This was the view of Marc Stears, Miliband's special advisor. See 'After Miliband' Conference, 5 June 2015, University College Oxford.
[3] Or that he lacked 'charisma', a near-universally held view.

The relationship between narrative and leadership, between rhetoric and performance, between doctrine and its voicing, are crucial to party politics, and are crucially underrated, by both practising politicians and scholars. This study will demonstrate *that* this is the case and *how* this is the case, and what this means for a new approach to understanding and analysing politics. I can say, therefore, that my analysis is as much about the theory and practice of leadership as it is about the Labour Party. Or rather it is about both of these, but doctrine, narrative, leadership, and performance are part of one entity whose elements interact with one another all the time. That is the central thesis of this book.

Performing the Party

In terms of my own appraisal of the Labour Party and the performance of leadership from the aftermath of the 2010 General Election and until the unexpected (a near 100-seat difference between Labour and the Conservatives!) defeat of 2015, I should make several points here, some of them to myself as well as to the reader. The first is that I am very aware of the possibly even unconscious temptation to be right after the fact. I have the alluring luxury of appraising Ed Miliband's leadership *after* he failed to bring his party to power. There is a duty therefore upon me of academic integrity, to not let the party's defeat *itself* demonstrate my analysis. I have constantly to ask myself whether my research findings (the vast bulk of which were made before May 2015) would withstand intellectual scrutiny if Miliband had become the UK's Prime Minister in May 2015, and whether in light of the fact he did not, I might be tempted to make my analysis a teleology. I elaborate upon my approach – particularly the contexts of performance, and particularly in the theoretical part of this chapter. And there are, if not teleological elements then formative origins to subsequent performance. For example, it has always been my – and others' – view that the manner, conditions, and contexts of Miliband's election to the leadership in 2010, not least the 'two brothers' aspect of the contest and its aftermath, played heavily in subsequent developments. I shall revisit this in detail in the Conclusion. But my view on this and upon the idea of me imposing a teleology is that, as the French mystical philosopher Simone Weil wrote, not anything can happen, but nothing is determined. Some of the points I make now should perhaps wait until the Conclusion of this book, and I shall revisit them, but it is worth addressing the issue briefly here in terms of my approach to this whole period, and my research on the 2010–2015 period. My own view in May 2015 was that there might be a hung Parliament, and a possible minority Labour government. I did, however, believe this because the polls kept asserting it (and I am a political scientist not a fortune teller). This possibility, an assumed conviction held by most at the time, seemed, however, to go against the thrust of my own research; and for a month or so during the election campaign, I was perplexed as to how I would square my findings with the assumed forthcoming reality; and, therefore, how I would write this book. It did not happen, but I remain aware that my research was not an oracle, nor is it other than one perspective. I do assert, however, that my findings – many of which are interpretive and therefore contestable, like a theatre critic who may be wrong – reflect and in part explain the defeat. Miliband's 2010–2015 performance was no masterpiece – although Stravinsky's *Rite of Spring* and Joyce's *Finnegans Wake* were lampooned and vilified, so interpretations are themselves often subject to great error. Political performances of this type today, moreover, normally only get one chance to succeed. However, Miliband's leadership performance, probably justly, does not deserve the epithet of a work of art, although there were some brilliant performances, as we shall see. What our analysis demonstrates, however, is that narrative and performance themselves are crucial to an understanding of the overall political process. So, bearing this in mind, let me briefly say here what I shall come back to in the Conclusion: in spite of the catastrophic beginning in 'leadership' terms of Ed Miliband's election to the leadership of the party, until halfway through the legislative term, early 2013, it was still very possible that subsequent developments could have been different. In fact, I would go further and say that the fortunes of the leadership and the party can be identified in a series of performances made and not made, or decisions taken and not taken, narratives deployed or abandoned in a developing series of discursive, rhetorical, or other 'events' in the second half of the legislature up until May 2015. It is true to say, however, that my view, then as now, was that many performances and the deployment of leader 'image' (which we shall put into context practically and theoretically) were often poor or at least lacking in both rhetorical consequence and a convincing performance.

Within this context, the fortunes of the party and the party leadership can be apprehended as a series of performed discursive or rhetorical events. A musical analogy is illustrative. We can imagine the period 2010–2015 as a musical composition played in particular surroundings where the role and the quality of the orchestra and the role and identity of its key performers – for example, first violin, conductor – are crucial to good performance; as are the venue, the acoustics, the general *mise en scène*; the weather outside and air conditioning inside; the nature of the audience and its reception of the piece; the quality of the piece, and its structure and performance. Part of my Conclusion will be an appraisal of whether it was a successful piece (performatively and politically), or if not, why that was the case and, theoretically, what are the role and dynamics of leadership performance in the wider political culture.

THE CONDITIONS OF PERFORMANCE AND PERSONA

A political leader's persona is a construction that performs – rather like an actor – in the political space. The research question here is: what is the architecture and what are the modalities of leadership persona construction and performance in contemporary politics? I need, therefore, to provide a theoretical framework for the analysis of the mediated persona of the 2010–2015 leader of the Labour Party, Ed Miliband. My analysis is multidisciplinary, involving theories, methods, and approaches in political science, as well as rhetorical, media, cultural, and performance studies. Bringing these approaches together, I hope to establish the discursive, iconographic, and stylistic conditions for the elaboration, mediation, and performance of contemporary political leadership persona. In terms of interdisciplinarity, Chapter 1 draws upon political and rhetorical theory, Chapter 2 upon Labour Party history and leadership studies, Chapter 3 upon narrative theory, Chapter 4 upon performance studies, Chapter 5 upon chronological analysis, and Chapter 6 again upon political and rhetorical theory (and a bit of psychoanalytic speculation and semiology). For clarity, I shall deal with the literature relevant to my analysis in each of the chapters.

The 'conditions of performance' constitute severe challenges to the presentation of leadership, for both leaders and their support teams. Political leaders and their entourages now find it as necessary as it is difficult to elaborate, mediate, and control their projected persona, in great part because the media and the media's demand for constant leadership presence make managing leadership persona different from before. Two dramatic recent changes have been the pervasive extension of the media generally and social media in particular, and what we can call the 'publicization of the private', so that the 'character' of the leader, his or her persona, is now of major significance in the political process. For better and worse this entry of the (imagined) private into the public space has created what we can call the 'personalized political' whereby each of the two elements can affect the other positively or negatively. In one sense, however, there is nothing new under the sun. Leadership persona has always 'performed', whether in the Athens Agora, or on the radio via 'This is London calling ...' during World War II, or during the collapse of French authority in Algeria in 1958, and de Gaulle's *Je vous ai compris!*, in every 'moment' where leadership is tested. Hence, although I shall focus upon the rhetorical and performative changes of the very recent period and in one political party, my research will, I hope, further research in the study of leadership performance generally.[4]

A political leader is not the person we see but a persona projected by the real person and his or her entourage – advisors, spokespersons, speech-writers; a persona that is fashioned, mediated, received, perceived and mis-perceived, 'imagined', and constructed by the party and the public, and all this within a given set of cultural, historical, and institutional conditions which inform – in a range of ways – the actors involved. The duality person/persona is difficult to analyse (but no less necessary for that). As I have pointed out elsewhere (Gaffney 2016), in the 2011 film, *The King's Speech*, Colin Firth is not George VI; in the 2012 film, *The Iron Lady*, Meryl Streep is not Margaret Thatcher, but they appear to be. As regards a 'real' political leader, the methodological and analytical difficulty in 'real life' is that the 'actor' and the enacted persona are the same 'person' (and the 'person', indeed, contributes to the 'persona'). The 'suspension of disbelief', therefore, feels unnecessary (although it is still taking place). So, for the analyst, a method has to be found to dissociate and demon-strate the two, in order to identify the conditions, enactment, and receipt of persona performance. Moreover, for the last 30 years, at least, politics has been mediated via the acute personalization of politics. And more recently (from around 2000), because of 'celebrity politics', itself a kind of adaptation of celebrity culture generally, leaders have become or aspire to become 'incarnations', embodiments of their party and its ideas, and a conduit for the expression of the party's image, which is consciously shaped to try and express or respond to non-party 'national' opinion, as well as 'give voice' to its own evolving doctrine, values, and beliefs. This dual exigency is no easy task. The type and style of the representa-tion of leadership persona have also changed, particularly as regards the

---

[4] For a wider theoretical discussion of this see J. Gaffney (2016).

(constructed) idea of proximity and the place of emotion in character and in relationships (Goldie 2002; Marcus 2002). This means that the leader embodies or tries to embody the party and, to a certain degree, 'offer' it, even in its diversity, through his or her persona to the wider electorate.

Leadership persona, therefore, is both crucial and fragile. Tony Blair's premiership (1997–2007) was formative of the contemporary state of leadership in the UK. His image, from 'Bambi' in the early 1990s (before he became Prime Minister), and then fresh young leader of a new generation come to power, to the later notion of deceitful complicity in planning the Iraq war, and the dark arts of spin more generally, was fundamental to the political process in the UK and to public perceptions of contemporary politics (in Chapter 2, we shall return to this issue of leadership and the Labour Party, particularly after 1994, and its relation to the contemporary situation).

The leadership persona and 5-year 'performance' of Ed Miliband (offering a large, yet controllable amount of material) was an appropriate study because he was of a new political generation, operated within the context of rapidly evolving media, and in the period under study as Leader of Her Majesty's Opposition was a potential Prime Minister, this latter increasing dramatically attention paid to his potential prime ministerial 'character'. I identify, (re)construct, and 'gather' Miliband's persona. I set the scene for my analysis of him being 'made' and remade, and 'performed', and analyse the effects of this in the public space, as well as the responses to his performing persona.

One of the defining characteristics of who he was between 2010 and 2015 was what he said (and wrote, and was reported to have said). Another is what others said of him. Language and its place in 'persona-construction' and deployment are, therefore, central. My approach combines elements of discourse analysis, rhetorical analysis, and the analysis of style, image, and performance in order to construct and appraise leadership persona as a discursive or rhetorical event (or ensemble of discursive events). I shall also, as pointed out above, develop, from the disparate literature, a framework for establishing the 'image' of the persona, that is, the 'imagined person'. The (re)construction of persona, therefore, involves an interdisciplinary approach, which I shall elaborate in more detail below. In order to do this, I have divided the book into six chapters: (1) This introductory theory chapter; (2) Leadership Lessons from the Past; (3) The Arc of Rhetoric and the Leader as Author; (4) Rhetoric and Performance: Miliband's Finest Hour; (5) Narrative Collapse and the Teller without a Tale; and (6) Conclusion: Narrative, Rhetoric and the 'Personalized Political'.

THE CENTRALITY OF ETHOS

Chapter 1: Below I look at the 'discursive' and the 'imagined' (the two constitute the architecture and mechanics of persona and performance), and argue that these interact all the time, but that for our purposes their separation will facilitate methodological and conceptual clarity. From Hellmann's original work on John F. Kennedy, which I shall use in my own approach in a minor way (Hellmann 1997), the discursive persona and the imagined person are in a dynamic, dialectical relationship, and their construction is contributed to by the actual person (sometimes, and crucially, unconsciously – I shall return to this in my Conclusion). The role of each, however, will be addressed separately for methodological reasons. Centrally, we shall adapt the Aristotelian categories of *ethos*, *pathos*, and *logos* to contemporary purpose, as the untranscendable Aristotle is central to our understanding leadership. We shall also argue against Weber, and examine narrative, and suggest a diagram for the understanding of 'performance' and its conditions, one of them being narrative itself.

RELUCTANT LEADERS, BAD LESSONS

Chapter 2: This is an account of leadership developments within the Labour Party, and the way in which party leaders have inflected party thinking and the parameters of its thinking and direction. For much of its hundred years and more of existence the Labour Party is a case study in the failure to understand the nature, exigencies, and consequences of leadership, both partisan and national. In many ways, the contemporary period was one in which the Labour Party reacted to and eventually came to terms with, paradoxically, the persona of Margaret Thatcher and the radically new conditions of political performance from the 1980s onwards. I shall examine here what leaders have brought to the party in terms of shaping its leadership narrative and relation to party identity, often unknowingly given the party and the left's generally problematic attitude and relationship to leadership itself.

THE PARTY'S STORY

Chapter 3: Here, I identify what I have called the 'arc of rhetoric', the architecture as it were of the Labour Party and leader's narrative from 2010 to 2015. After the party's (historic) defeat at the 2010 General Election and the resignation of Prime Minister Gordon Brown, the party or many within it entered a period of reflection and self-examination. This coincided with the long 2010 leadership campaign. Upon his election as the new leader, Ed Miliband called for a Policy Review. This is a normal and traditional party political reflex. However, what the party underwent was not only a Review but a wealth of intellectual and textual production constitutive of an ideological revisionism. By applying narrative theory to the party political texts emerging within the Labour Party after 2010, which together constructed and constituted the corpus of One Nation discourse, we can grasp the underlying significance of this ideational revision of Labour Party and left thought generally. Through an identification and analysis of the sequence of texts and their constitution as a 'story' that interpolates an underlying 'plot', we can see how a revision of Labour's 'tale' offered to leadership a new party discourse appropriate to it, mediating – if not reconciling – the problematic duality of narrative authorship by both party and leader.

THE LEADER'S STORY

Chapter 4: Here I analyse Ed Miliband, the party leader, and his use of the rhetoric of One Nation and the construction of his leadership persona. I shall analyse Miliband's performances at the Labour Party Conference of 2012, and in particular his 'One Nation' conference speech. My analysis identifies how, through performance of 'himself' and the deployment of an alternative party narrative centred on 'One Nation', Ed Miliband began to revise his 'received persona' and that of the party itself. By using a range of rhetorical and other techniques, Miliband began to adapt the Labour narrative to the 'personalized political' and the theme of One Nation.

LOSING BOTH VOICE AND AN ELECTION

Chapter 5: This is an analysis of the 2013–2015 period and of the May 2015 General Election from the perspective of the performance of leadership and party, particularly *vis-à-vis* leadership and the presentation and deployment of policy proposals and the Party Manifesto and, in the examination of the period leading up to the General Election, an appraisal of the performative and rhetorical choices made (and not made). Within the framework of our overall theoretical discussion, this part of the chapter includes analytical comment on the General Election campaign itself. The thrust of this chapter is the analysis of Miliband's leadership performance during the election campaign and his relationship to public opinion.

NARRATIVE AND THE 'PERSONALIZED POLITICAL'

Chapter 6: This is my concluding chapter and is a discussion of, first, the 2015 General Election and its aftermath from the point of view of all the elements of leadership performance and, second, the theoretical implications of the research. I shall comment here upon the rhetorical, strategic, organizational, and leadership development of the party from 2010 to 2015. I shall also comment on and appraise the 'performance' of both the party generally and Ed Miliband in particular during the 2015 election campaign itself. I shall critically appraise: (a) persona construction by the team (and leader); (b) persona co-construction by the media; and (c) persona reconstruction by the recipients of the image and persona. All of my analysis will relate the constructed persona back to my overarching research questions: how does persona-construction and performance take place and what is its role in the political process?

Given my emphasis upon the interdisciplinary nature of my analysis, I shall, as I have said above, discuss and draw upon theories underlying several analytical approaches, *inter alia* rhetorical and discourse analysis, performance studies, 'celebrity politics' research, and narrative theory. Even psychoanalytic and semiotic considerations where appropriate will be helpful. Ed's choice of records, and its effects upon his image in his *Desert Island Discs* broadcast in November 2013 are a rich resource for analysis (see Chapter 6). We shall address many of these issues at various points throughout this study, rather than try to create an unworkable Theory of Everything here. Having said this, I do see the overall 'performance' of leadership within and upon a party narrative as integral to the political party as a whole. There is a tendency in political party analysis, as we saw above, as regards for example the 2015 Labour Party defeat, to constantly separate out elements of interpretation: the economic narrative was deficient, the leader was 'uncharismatic', party organization and policy were defective, and so on. These inadequacies of interpretation continued well after the election and into the 2015 leadership contest; and demonstrated a continuing inadequate grasp of the performative conditions of Jeremy Corbyn's leadership challenge. For us, all of these are related, in fact are part of the same thing: the 'performance' of the Labour Party in its various expressions through time. We need therefore to see all these conditions and elements of performance (even bad performance) in a holistic and dynamic way.

THEORETICAL CONSIDERATIONS

In this introductory chapter, we need to have two important discussions for my approach to be properly understood. The first involves making the case for the importance of a rhetorical approach to contemporary politics. Broadly, I subscribe to Aristotle's approach (I'm a fan) but we need to (a) modify his categories and (b) address the question of the contemporary conditions of rhetorical production; in the case of (a) the noble 'standing' of the speaker is no longer assumed, and in the case of (b) the Agora has changed somewhat.... We also need to address the normative question of our (i.e., both the researcher's and the audience's) relationship to rhetoric's function; in a phrase, that Aristotle's distinction between oratory and demagoguery is a false one; they are identical in intention, namely to persuade (and today markedly to enhance *ethos*). Our second discussion is probably even more important as a clearing the ground exercise, involving refutation rather than modification. Max Weber is one of the most important thinkers in twentieth-century social and political science, and his definition of 'charisma' has been one of his most influential contributions to scholarship (and latterly journalism, café conversation and *The X Factor*...). It is also as wrong as it is influential. I need, therefore, to address this issue and set out my own idea, as to what I truly mean by 'charismatic leadership'.

In my main case study, I wish to analyse how Ed Miliband performed as a leadership persona, and the conditions and consequences of this. In an age of 'celebrity politics' – see in particular Chapter 4 – analysing the persona who interpolates the rhetoric, who is the rhetoric's 'voice', raises methodological but also normative issues which inform us, such as 'what do I think of this (imagined) person?' In this way, normative and moral concerns are at their most acute when it comes to the deployment of the character of the speaker. Our norm-based emotions (and our curiosity?) about the character of the speaker are part of the context of our analysis of the speaker's treatment (the rhetoric) of the audience's norm-based emotions.

In leadership rhetoric, therefore, as an analyst I (and, dare I say, you as a reader or observer) make a distinction regarding the person, or rather the imagined persona of the speaker. Although the 'secular' analysis of rhetoric is our aim, moral and other dimensions (e.g., psychological) of the teller of the tale inform our view of the tale told, and are linked to the idea that the rhetoric's purpose is to tell us about the speaker, as well as about the speaker as an agent in the process of persuasion. This is why, in the case of Ed Miliband, his relationship to his brother David, the leadership favourite in 2010, became a problematic factor in the projection, at times, and receipt, often, of Ed's persona. This 'Cain and Abel' aspect of his persona was never properly dealt with, and if Labour had won in 2015 would probably have been transformed into a positive, at least formidable, character trait. With defeat, and of course retrospectively, it took on Shakespearean and Freudian proportions. Circumstances and events change the significance of things and our perceptions of them; we should bear this in mind.

In the context of the Labour Party and its leadership 2010–2015, this means that one of the performative 'conditions' of Miliband's performance and reception by the wider public was 'who he was'. He was a 'professional politician', and a 'North London intellectual' (this author was never quite sure if this expression had an anti-Semitic nuance – although his secular Jewish environment probably was a factor in the construction of his persona (Cesarani 2014; Hershman 2015)), was one of a generational cohort of PPE graduates from Oxford, and so on. These may be constraints, but should rather be seen – or rather, sadly, should have been seen by Team Miliband – as the *conditions* of leadership performance. Each of these issues was seen as a problem and to be 'avoided' – although not by the right-wing press of course – rather than being seen as a condition of performance, a difficult condition but which if seen in this way may have been turned to advantage. As Sartre said of the poet Paul Valéry, 'Yes, Paul Valéry was a petit-bourgeois intellectual, but not all petit-bourgeois intellectuals were Paul Valéry' (Sartre 1960: 80) (yes, Ed Miliband was a PPE graduate but not all PPE graduates are Ed Miliband...). So the persona of a political leader is informed by the person they are and would have themselves as being. I want now to look at the 'framework' that persona construction and performance take place in.

INSTITUTIONS, CULTURE, AND PERFORMANCE

For the purposes of analysis here, we can take institutions to mean the conventions and places which pertain to, by framing, leadership 'acts'; for example, the presidency, the government, the party, the public, the media; or processes – conventions and traditions, a dominant leadership mythology. These can each be seen as a contextual and consequent institution (although could be argued as being culture; let us say here strongly culturally fashioned institutions). A President, for example, will 'perform' in a different configuration of institutions to a Prime Minister. Leadership performance, for example, will normally – not always – be different in 'the House', from the performance to the party, or from performance to the public. It was clear, for example, that Prime Minister's Questions (PMQs) imposed a particular rhetorical form upon Miliband (point scoring, noise, personality attacks, aggression, rowdiness); and yet it was also clear he disapproved of such, and knew it was negative in character terms. What is less fathomable is why, knowing this, he made little rhetorical effort to modify his – and therefore everyone else's – behaviour, and their attitude to him or to his persona (Corbyn's attempts from September 2015 to change this, however, had their own set of disadvantages).

I want briefly to look at institutions and culture in a little more detail as two of those conditions of performance. The institutional context of leadership performance is a condition of the performance itself, from the conventions, to the nature, conditions, and protocols of, say, executive office, to political parties (history, organization, doctrine), the media, the education system; or institutions which have, more elusively, contributed to the fashioning of the real character, psyche, and emotional life of the leader – family, education, class. These amount to the contexts of the 'lived experience', in Sartre's terms, the *vécu* (interview with *New Left Review (NLR)* (1/58) in November 1969) which, we should stress, was a dynamic, dialectical experience, was not just 'the past'. Performance, character, and persona will be conditional upon 'who they actually are' physically, psychologically, and so on, as well as 'who the audience is/are'. In a more direct way, more immediately, the institution-as-condition is also physical: the television studio, the convention hall, the Congress, the House, the Agora, and so it could go on: sites and practices which, over time, become *where* performances take place.

And there will be a myriad of institutions within the institutions, and a further myriad of expectations and conventions of an office. The *circumstances* of the institutional configuration, moreover, will have influence or will be influenced because of the role and effects of the status quo, or because of deviation from the status quo (e.g., a 'crisis' or, at a pedestrian level, applauding in the House of Commons). At their most extreme, dramatic circumstances inform the institution or configuration of institutions dramatically, as in war or a collapsing regime (a collapsing set of institutions and the configuring of new ones). Institutions that change 'easily' (e.g., are less stable), moreover, differ from ones that do not and the mutability of institutions is always related to history and culture.

In terms of Miliband this means that we need to consider whether (and why and how) the 'institutions' of the Labour Party in their widest sense were and are 'mutable' organizationally, doctrinally, and in terms of leadership persona (and party identity), and what the ramifications of such mutability were or might be for leadership authority and influence.

DRAMA AND MEMORY

I mentioned collapsing regimes. The circumstances surrounding de Gaulle's coming to power in 1958 (Rémond 1983) – the collapse of a regime, a possible military coup – were *dramatic* and, as it were, called forth dramatic leadership, his own. From the de Gaulle case, we can see that leadership performance and the subsequent reconfiguration of institutions were sharply influenced by drama and dramatic circumstances, and we should interpret the former (performance) while bearing in mind the latter (drama). However, we could take this a helpful stage further (or back) as regards culture and say that 'drama' is part of the political culture of French politics, hence the recognition when in dramatic crisis of the (need for) dramatic crisis leadership; and also, in the case of de Gaulle, the 'recognition' of the Cassandra figure (who had *warned* them all in 1946 by stating the new Constitution would not work) and the 'saviour' (who had earlier *saved* them all in 1944, the returning 'First Resister' of 1940). These elements are part of the culture in which the institutions (and the leader, and the leader's performance, and the audience) are embedded. Drama is a cultural artefact, as well as constituting the contingent circumstances of political action and leadership performance. Drama takes different forms and has different aspects and character in different political cultures, but it is always there 'somewhere' even as a memory. It will be a constant or constant potential in some cultures (France), a rarer occurrence (economic crash, terrorism, social upheaval, riots, break-up of the UK, Brexit) in others (UK). This will have, dare I say, dramatic consequences for leadership. If drama is itself not just facilitative of (allows for or gives opportunity to) providential leadership, but is also part of the culture that gives rise to it, it will also inform the nature of the leadership and its opportunities, and will be a cultural prerequisite to this type of leadership, that is to say, will be the kind of leadership which flows from drama and crisis (perceived or 'real'). Some cultures, moreover, have more influence upon leadership, and this for two reasons. The contextual reason is the intensity of the 'memory' within the community. In France, for example, there is a very active memory (often inaccurate, often partial, but this does not reduce its strength) of French history, of the upheavals within it, and of the individuals who have played a part (and who often 'embody' a tradition – whether revolutionary, reactionary, adventurous, foolhardy, or salutary; references to figures such as Nye Bevan or Keir Hardie play a similar role in the UK Labour Party). This will throw into relief the perceived relationship of individuals to events.

What does this mean for the UK context? First, this dramatic 'illusion' is much less pronounced, but there remains a 'memory' of strong leadership in crisis – Churchill of course, but also, though less so, Thatcher later; then Blair in happier times (Kosovo, but then Iraq). These 'types' 'hover' over all leadership personae, and have more influence in perceived crises or dramatic circumstances. The 2010–2015 period in the UK was a period of 'crisis' in many ways (e.g., the continuing fallout from the 2008 crisis, and from the Iraq war of 2003, deep cuts in public services, deficit reduction, a faltering NHS); the question was the degree to which these were perceived as such and by whom, and how the Labour leadership responded rhetorically to them, and how the public in turn responded to the Labour leadership.

ARISTOTLE

In order to pursue this aspect of rhetoric, we need to focus upon three issues: first, how the persona of the speaker/leader is rhetorically constructed and deployed; second, what are the institutional and cultural contexts of rhetorical performance and audience response; third, bringing these two together, how rhetoric can be understood and analysed both as a performance (involving a whole range of experienced and negotiated emotions) that involves fundamentally the speaker–audience relationship, and as one that is enacted upon the basis of its institutional, cultural, and normative contexts or 'conditions'. In order to do this, our essential focus will be upon reworking Aristotle's notion of *ethos* (and to a lesser degree *pathos* and *logos*) and situating this, as a performance, in its institutional and cultural contexts.

Unlike Aristotle, however, we are less interested today in the standing of the speaker and whether or not he (then, only he) is worthy or the like. But the role of the speaker in the rhetoric and, therefore, *ethos* as a *relational* term (to *pathos*, *logos*, and to the audience and *itself*) are crucial to contemporary analysis. I would argue that today it is the most important rhetorical element because *ethos* is so often the *aim* now of rhetoric: the imagined persona of the speaker as an active, enacting part of the rhetoric, and his or her imagined or perceived relationship to normative issues, to emotion, to argument and, especially, to the audience; these are the keys to contemporary rhetoric. In the political party today this is how, performatively, the leader aspires to 'embody' the party, by using *pathos, logos,* and narrative to project the leader (and vice versa). There is also a kind of developmental approach to rhetoric that I question. Generally speaking there is an assumption that *ethos* establishes the speaker, *logos* deploys the speaker's argument, and *pathos* (particularly towards the end) gives the argument its élan. For me, these three are in a more dynamic relationship, with often, as I shall demonstrate, any two rhetorically 'serving' the third at any point. Underlying these ideas is the notion of the comportment and character of the speaker: his or her 'personality', projected in the rhetoric as well as imagined outside it (as it is with Aristotle). My point is that the *ethos* of the speaker informs everything, and in leadership studies the function of analysis is to show how argument and emotion serve the purpose of enhancing the relationship between speaker (leader) and audience. I am as concerned with what the leader/speaker made the audience feel about the leader/speaker as I am about what he or she made the audience feel about the issues. Here we can see that the *distinction* often made between 'personality' and 'policies' is a false problem; in fact, it is a complete misreading of how politics functions.

CHARISMA

My analysis will demonstrate how this (composite) character – structured by themselves and others – informs, underlies, fashions 'our' (the listener's) reception of the character of the leader, and how 'we' in turn fashion it; and whether (and if so how) this imagined character *precedes* as well as is deployed *in* the rhetoric of leadership (and imagined as acting after it, e.g., leading us). This raises the question of the nature and modalities of our relationship to such 'characters'; and this raises the question of charisma. So, before coming back to Aristotle, we need to do a detour via Max Weber.

In spite of a century of theoretical difficulty with Weber, his notion of 'charisma', elaborated in *The Theory of Social and Economic Organization* and in 'Politics as a Vocation' (Weber 1964 [1920]; 2004 [1919]) still dominates. Inside academia, it prevails. Outside academia it is universal, both in journalism and broadcasting, as well as in everyday exchanges. The continuing emphasis upon and use of (a version of) charisma is one of the reasons for all our other dilemmas and confusions regarding the leader's qualities and their expression in rhetoric and the interpolation of persona within it. This is Weber's definition:

> A certain quality of an individual personality by virtue of which he is set apart from ordinary men and treated as endowed with supernatural, super-human, or at least specifically exceptional powers or qualities. These are such as are not accessible to the ordinary person, but are regarded as of divine origin or as exemplary, and on the basis of them the individual concerned is treated as a leader. (Weber 1964: 358)[5]

It is a long definition but it is not just long, it is unclear, while being tentative and assertive at the same time, and is, in fact, contradictory. It is as if Weber is trying to identify charisma rather than define it. So what is it? From the definition it is extremely difficult to pin down *what* it is because it is difficult to pin down *where* it is. It is based on *several* phenomena not one ('qualities ascribed'), and upon both qualities (plural) and ascription. This raises the question, can the qualities be possessed if they are not ascribed? In fact this question has haunted Weberian studies as has its near-opposite: might the qualities ascribed not be possessed? It also does not make sense: for it is a 'quality' which endows 'qualities'; and not just qualities, but qualities *and* powers (magical powers or other?); are powers synonymous here with qualities? And *which* powers, which qualities? And what are the qualities of 'ordinary men' that the charismatic individual is set apart from? And if the qualities of the charismatic individual are not 'accessible' to the 'ordinary' (*x2*), how do they recognize them? And are qualities '*regarded* as of divine origin' or are they actually divine or simply falsely assumed as being so (by deluded 'ordinary men')? Are the

---

[5] 'Charisma' soll eine als ausseralltäglich (ursprünglich, sowohl bei Propheten wie bei ther-apeutischen wie bei Rechts-Weisen wie bei Jagdführern wie bei Kriegshelden: als magisch bedingt) geltende Qualität einer Persönlichkeit heissen, um derentwillen sie als mit über-natürlichen oder übermenschlichen oder mindestens spezifisch ausseralltäglichen, nicht jedem andern zugänglichen Kräften oder Eigenschaften oder als gottgesandt oder als vor-bildlich und deshalb als 'Führer' gewertet wird. Wie die betreffende Qualität von irgendei-nem ethischen, ästhetischen oder sonstigen Standpunkt aus 'objektiv' richtig zu bewerten sein würde, ist natürlich dabei begrifflich völlig gleichgültig: darauf allein, wie sie tatsächlich von charismatisch Beherrschten, den 'Anhängern', bewertet wird, kommt es an. (M. Weber (1964) *Wirtschaft und Gesellschaft*, vol. 1, Köln: Kiepenheuer & Witsch, p. 179)

terms 'supernatural', 'superhuman', and 'exceptional' synonymous or do they constitute a *hierarchy* of charisma (from the sacred to the profane perhaps)? Is the charismatic individual 'set apart' (as if 'naturally') by the qualities or are they set apart by the ordinary men (as an 'act' in their minds)? And if so how far apart? And what is an 'individual personality'? Is this a tautology or does it mean an 'individual's personality'? I could go on. If we are talking about where the charisma is, is it in the ascribed or the ascribing? And 'where' is each of these?

For the purposes of analysis here let us see 'charisma' (I shall stop using this term soon) not as qualities, powers, or ascribed qualities, but as an *event* that takes place, and where the performance of, here the leader – on the basis of its institutional, cultural and other conditions of performance – will be of a particular type, quality, and resonance, and whose effects may include emotions such as admiration, attraction, and so on. We need, therefore, to understand the act or *enactment* and *voicing* of 'charismatic' leadership as an act *performed*, an act enacted, but with specific qualities and skill in its deployment. In this way, the 'determinants' cease to be such and become the *context* or conditions of performance.

Aristotle Again

Back to Aristotle, and his three categories (Aristotle 1991). We can leave *pathos* relatively intact. For me, as traditionally, *pathos* is the means of persuasion and a resource by which a whole range – perhaps *the* whole range – of emotions is evoked and exploited. That said, the *logos* too of policy elaboration in the Labour Party began to be informed (2012 and into 2013) by the *pathos* of compassion, moral outrage, and other emotions: decency, a sense of justice, protection of the young. It then collapsed into a kind of unremarkable 'retail offer'. I shall come back to this in Chapter 5. *Logos*, rather than being the logical argument of the speech wherein facts and examples are given, in order to persuade with supporting evidence (although, as we shall argue, for Aristotle *logos* is indeed also used to enhance the status of the speaker, as well as being, crucially, for him and for us, not simply logical but logical in terms of and for the purposes of the rhetoric, through *enthymeme*); I see *logos* not only as the argument but also as the architecture, the structure of the whole speech as it is performed, the score of the performance.

What is of most concern to me here, however, is the rhetorical category of *ethos*, addressed in contemporary rhetoric but generally more in business studies and marketing where it is synonymous with 'credibility', which explains little (although it means this too). I shall take *ethos* to mean the persona of the speaker both *in* (rhetorically and performatively) and imagined (before, during and after) *outside* the speech. *Ethos* refers to all the aspects of the character and performance of the speaker which contribute to the speech's reception and the speaker's image. The character will be a composite constructed by both the speaker (which might itself be a composite of himself or herself and speechwriters and advisors) and the audience (which itself is, by definition, composite).

NARRATIVE AND PERFORMANCE

Having abandoned one cliché, charisma, I want to embrace another, narrative. It is true this term too has, over the last 10 years, invaded academia, everyday exchange, national perceptions, and political culture. It is, however, central to my analysis because it is the central condition (and result) of rhetorical performance. So I need to be clear what it means in this book. The narrative of the Labour Party is first, at a very straightforward level, what the party – and arguably commentators' and critics' contributions – says, writes, and thinks. And its central ideas are arguably identifiable as grouped around 'ideational clusters' (Freeden 1998) which give it coherence and distinguish it from other narratives. Beyond this it is the conscious 'story' that the party and movement 'would have itself' or themselves. In the 2010–2015 period the main author/proponent of this in the party was Jon Cruddas, the Chair of the Policy Review. As I shall demonstrate in Chapter 3, for me narrative also has a deeper structure which, if not dictates, then informs the story. My mentors here are the Russian Formalists (*inter alia* Propp 1968) and the tradition (*inter alia* Bakhtin, Medvedev, Voloshinov (Morris 2003; Martin 1986; McQuillan 2000)) that flowed from them, as well as the related, accompanying development of semiotics (*inter alia* Barthes 1957) and the search for the 'true', 'underlying' or 'other' meaning of things. In the case of narrative such as One Nation I shall demonstrate how its evolution corresponds to a deeper structure – perhaps requirement or function are better terms – of narrative, namely 'plot'.

We have looked at culture and its refracted influence upon leadership performance; we should also look at circumstance as being fundamental to grasping the significance of political performance, and of institutions; and, conversely, we must examine performance itself. But we hope to have established the conditions of production of leadership performance: institutions, culture, and circumstance. When looking therefore at the Labour Party 2010–2015 and Miliband's 'performed' leadership, we need to be sensitive to a range of factors: the culture of the party (and of leadership within it), the organizational aspect of Labour Party leadership, the attitudes of both party and public, the narrative traditions of the left, and the performance of leadership itself. Figure 1.1 below is not a complete explanation at all, but it may be helpful in conceptualizing the way in which culture and institutions inform narrative, rhetoric, and performance.

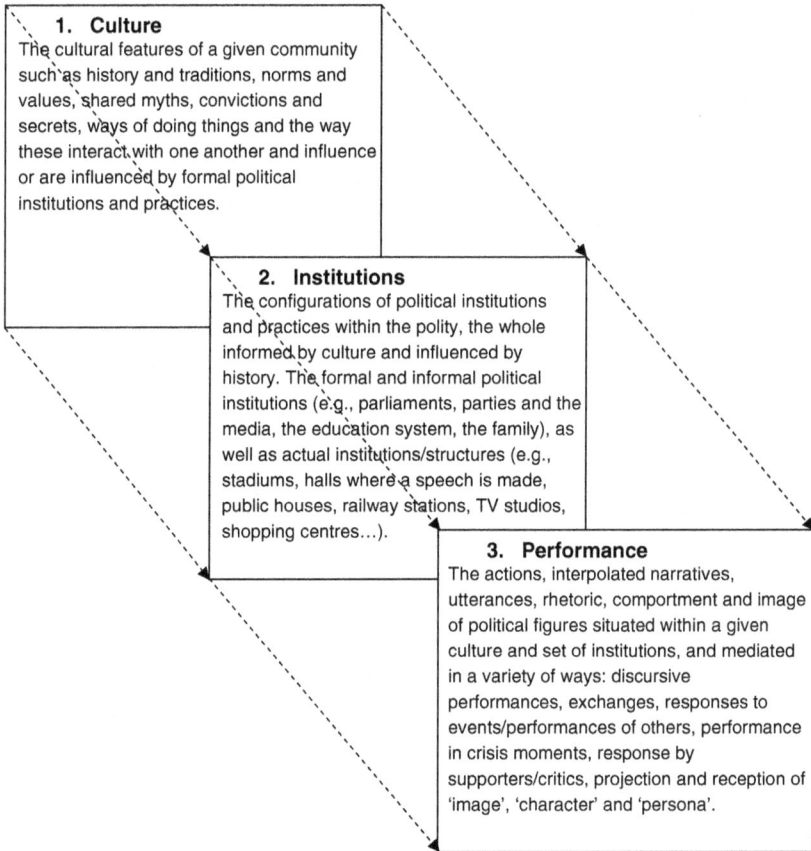

1. Culture
The cultural features of a given community such as history and traditions, norms and values, shared myths, convictions and secrets, ways of doing things and the way these interact with one another and influence or are influenced by formal political institutions and practices.

2. Institutions
The configurations of political institutions and practices within the polity, the whole informed by culture and influenced by history. The formal and informal political institutions (e.g., parliaments, parties and the media, the education system, the family), as well as actual institutions/structures (e.g., stadiums, halls where a speech is made, public houses, railway stations, TV studios, shopping centres...).

3. Performance
The actions, interpolated narratives, utterances, rhetoric, comportment and image of political figures situated within a given culture and set of institutions, and mediated in a variety of ways: discursive performances, exchanges, responses to events/performances of others, performance in crisis moments, response by supporters/critics, projection and reception of 'image', 'character' and 'persona'.

Fig. 1.1 A framework for the study of political leadership performance

CHAPTER 2

Leadership Lessons from the Past

The left generally has both a rudimentary and reluctant relationship and attitude to leadership (the right's attitude – fetish – is inadequate in a different way). Ideologically, the left knows little of personal leadership because such is seen as a counter to its belief in egalitarianism. Leftism posits an *impersonalism*, like republicanism, where *la chose publique*, the *res publica* is concertedly collective. The left's other attitude, linked to deep myths (and truths) about tyranny and misrule, is not one of ignoring leadership but of actively opposing it. In the history of the Labour Party this informed attitudes from very early on. As we shall see, there actually were no leaders until Ramsay MacDonald and he, in the eyes of his supporters-turned-foes, was of the worst kind to the point where he eventually abandoned the party and it him. From then onwards and with its already established doctrinal disapproval of personal leaders the party was as if inoculated against it. As we shall see, Attlee, for example, became leader precisely because he was considered if not weak then unassertive. Assertive leaders have invariably been at odds with their party, and at worst are portrayed as betraying socialist principles. This problematic attitude, a mixture of denial and hostility, and occasional acclamation, means that leadership within the party is problematic and ill-understood. It also has the paradoxical effect of seeing personalized challengers emerge, usually from the left: Bevan, Benn, Corbyn. In the case of MacDonald no attempt was made after 1931 to

© The Author(s) 2017
J. Gaffney, *Leadership and the Labour Party*, Palgrave Studies in Political Leadership, DOI 10.1057/978-1-137-50498-2_2

understand the phenomenon, only deny or oppose it. And the move from Blair to Brown was a monumental misunderstanding of the springs and role of leadership persona. This means that the effects of leadership issues can be all the more capricious, the post-Miliband leadership contest of 2015 being a classic example.

And yet it is quite clear, as I shall demonstrate in this chapter, that the party leader has enormous influence upon the direction and success, or lack of, of the party. And it is clear that the character traits, interpersonal relations, and public prominence of Labour Party leaders have had far-reaching effects upon the party's fortunes. Party leaders also 'represent' and 'give voice to' a range of doctrinal strains within the party. This is generally recognized – at its simplest the leader is spokesperson for the left or the right or centre-right, and so on, of the party. However, as I have argued in Chapter 1, doctrine and its rhetorical interpolation is far more consequential than is generally assumed, and doctrine, ideology, and left 'thought' generally are far more mutable than doctrine would have itself as being. This is fortunate because this is how persuasion takes place and doctrine and ideas evolve depending upon opportunities and circumstances (and the nature of language itself). This 'rhetorical mutability' was at the heart of, for example, Attlee's ability to reconcile opposing views, Wilson's 'manipulation' of left and right doctrinal sources, Kinnock's rallying the party against Militant, and Blair's persuading the party to follow the New Labour path. Over and above this, moreover, as I shall show, the style, image, character traits, and performance of leaders are an integral part of this overall leadership phenomenon. MacDonald, Henderson, Lansbury, Attlee, Gaitskell, Wilson, Callaghan, Foot, Kinnock, Blair, and Brown, are all classic examples of the use or misuse or non-use of 'self' and performance to leadership effect.

The irony here is that these considerations, although of great consequence, are rarely integrated into party thinking with any sophistication. The clichés surrounding leadership, even today – the 2015 and 2016 leadership campaigns being a perfect illustration – are evidence of this. Regarding the 'character' of leadership itself, understanding rarely moves beyond claims to 'vision' or a 'sense of direction' or, more contentiously, someone who will tell the party some 'home truths', or perhaps even more contentiously, the leader who argues that personality politics has nothing to do with leadership. This is little more perceptive than a business studies seminar on leadership. And in the case of the 2015 leadership campaign – as in most – the concentration (by candidates and observers, and especially the party's own various media, blogs, and so on) upon 'policy' and where each candidate 'sat' on the doctrinal spectrum, rather than also upon, for example, the rhetorical effects of Yvette Cooper 'performing' her gender and motherhood, Andy Burnham his modest roots, Jeremy Corbyn his outsider status and political integrity, Liz Kendall her plain speaking, and so on are indications of how rudimentary understanding is.[1]

The role of the 'rhetorical self' in the political process is also severely under-researched in the social and political sciences generally. With the recent scholarship of researchers like James Martin (2014) and Alan Finlayson (2014) and a growing revival of interest in political rhetoric, we can see the beginnings of change (see the references throughout this chapter). In Chapters 3 and 4 I shall examine Ed Miliband's rhetorical self and persona, and their (or its) performance in the public space. In this chapter, in order to demonstrate the effects of leadership upon the party and its fortunes, let us look at the former leaders, their character traits and strengths and weaknesses, as well as their performances, in order to show (a) how Labour leaders have influenced the identity and direction of the party and (b) how the 'spectrum' of Labour Party leadership has evolved, that is to say how a range of leadership 'types' and their attendant character traits and personalities have fashioned the party's view of itself and of leadership. I am not providing mini-bios here but looking at what Labour's leaders have brought to the way the party sees leadership itself. And it is clear that when taken together we can see, as I point out in the second part of this chapter, that the various leaders have created, not a 'type' of leader, but a paradigm of leadership traits and perceptions of leadership.

In parenthesis, although it lies outside a study of this length, a further line of rich enquiry would be an analysis of other potential candidates for leadership. What would have been the effects on the left and the political culture itself of Shirley Williams becoming the first female party leader and Prime Minister of a Labour government (and Prime Minister *before* Margaret Thatcher)? What might have been the effect of Herbert Morrison's leadership rather than Attlee's? What were the effects – negative and positive – upon the party's perceptions of leadership of figures such as Nye Bevan, Roy Jenkins, Denis Healey, David Owen, Tony Benn, David Miliband (and Oswald Mosley...)? I now turn to the ancestral gods and lesser mortals.

---

[1] See Gaffney (2015).

KEIR HARDIE 1906–1908

Technically the first official leader of the Labour Party was Ramsay MacDonald (good start!) who occupied the post from 1922. Before this, the Chairman of the Parliamentary Labour Party (PLP) was the unofficial leader. Six men held this post between 1906 and 1922: Keir Hardie (1906–1908), Arthur Henderson (1908–1910), George Barnes (1910–1911), Ramsay MacDonald (1911–1914), Arthur Henderson again (1914–1917), William Adamson (1917–1920), and John Robert Clynes (1920–1922) (Laybourn, cited in Jeffreys 1999: 3); each for just 2–3 years, and in most cases not really seeing themselves as leaders of the party as a whole, which in reality was still coalescing into a coherent movement. Out of these, Henderson and MacDonald became official leaders later in Labour history; Barnes, Adamson, and Clynes were relatively minor figures. Here, then, we focus on the 'leadership' of Keir Hardie and then the subsequent significant leaders and what they bring to notions of leadership.

While a leading figure of the early Labour Party, Hardie appeared to have little interest in being Chairman of the PLP, preferring to focus his time and energy on his personal political passions – such as the issue of women's suffrage. In a speech at the Independent Labour Party (ILP) conference in 1914, Hardie admitted: 'I have my own work to do, but any appearance of 'boss' does not come naturally, not to me. I think I have shown that I can be a pioneer, but I am not guided so much by a consideration of policy or by thinking out a long sequence of events as by intuition and inspiration. I know what I believe to be the right thing, and I go out and do it.' (Laybourn, cited in Jeffreys 1999: 15)

Hardie still plays an important role in Labour mythology as 'Labour's greatest hero'. He is described by Kenneth O. Morgan as a 'unique popular crusader' who argued in favour of a range of major causes: for the minimum wage, colonial freedom, gender equality, and world peace. He is also described by Morgan as a man whose 'greatness is reflected in the simplicity of his lifestyle' (his personal life was slightly less simple). Hardie then, encapsulates particular Labour principles such as modesty and fearlessness – and his reservations about leadership are part of this story. The mythology of Hardie suggests a running theme: that to be a great Labour figure one must reject careerism and personal ambition – perhaps any desire to be leader whatsoever (Morgan 2008). We shall come back to this. It also raises the idea that there is such a thing as the 'greatest hero'. We shall come back to this too.

Ramsay MacDonald 1922–1931

One of Labour's most controversial politicians, MacDonald stands out as the leading, most impressive figure of the early period, becoming Prime Minister in two Labour-led governments, and then of a 'National' government. MacDonald's political dominance and skilful oratory were fatefully accompanied by his need to 'micromanage' and his inability to delegate, a condescending attitude towards his colleagues, and a penchant for perceiving himself as a martyr to the cause (Wrigley, cited in Jeffreys 1999: 30–32). To illustrate this last point – in response to a request from Ernest Bevin on steel quotas in 1928, MacDonald responded, 'My dear Bevin, do you remember a tribe of Judah named Issachar which was likened to an ass upon whose shoulders innumerable burdens were heaped? I am that tribe' (Morgan 2006: 119).

Unlike other Labour leaders of the period, MacDonald did not have much of a trade union background (Wrigley, cited in Jeffreys 1999: 21) (although he was unquestionably 'working class', his mother a maid and his father a farm labourer). He advocated a kind of Utopian gradualism and was determined to show that Labour was a responsible party that could govern the country; explaining his decision to form a minority government in 1924, MacDonald said:

> When the opportunity came, so far as I was concerned I never had a moment's hesitation as to what we should do. To have shirked responsibility would have been cowardly, and this country does not like cowards; it would have put us into a bad Parliamentary fix. Altogether it would have shown the spirit of shivering fear rather than that of trustful gallantry and the latter is the spirit of the Labour Party. (MacDonald 1924)

Yet his periods as Labour Prime Minister were marked by political instability, economic mismanagement, and were followed by economic disaster, which later informed notions of leadership action (Wrigley, cited in Jeffreys 1999).

In the early pre-World War I years of the Labour Party, MacDonald pursued an electoral strategy for Labour based on an agreement with the Liberals to stand down candidates where it would risk dividing the anti-Conservative vote, alongside Lib–Lab cooperation and working together in Parliament. This culminated in the Liberal Asquith minority government of 1910–1915 which survived with support from Labour MPs. The strategy was criticized for in effect turning Labour into a subsidiary of the Liberals, but MacDonald believed that in the long term Labour would replace the Liberals as the leading progressive party (Pugh 2010).

While MacDonald was a 'shrewd tactician', he was also a man who cared about the doctrinal underpinnings of the Labour Party and did his best to shape a party narrative that extended to and captured the different wings of the party, even those he was opposed to. He did this in books such as *Socialism and Society*, *Socialism and Government*, and *The Socialist Movement*. These works emphasized collectivism, and social evolution as opposed to revolution. But they lacked a convincing account of *how* the Utopian society presented could be achieved as, sadly and perhaps tellingly, did his actions in government (Marquand 1977).

MacDonald's political views were influenced by a conception of society as a living organism – the different parts of society working together in harmony, thus entailing a rejection of both individualism and sectional interests (including trade unionism and especially syndicalism) in favour of state socialism. MacDonald was also a strong advocate of liberal representative democracy and disliked majoritarianism. His attitude to voters too – particularly women – could be dismissive, even scornful (describing female voters in his own constituency as 'the sad flotsam and jetsam of wild emotion' after his defeat in 1918 (Morgan 2006: 107–112)). We can add in parenthesis that the dominance of men and their attitudes to gender adversely affected the party throughout the century (Baxter 2006).

As an opponent of British involvement in World War I, MacDonald fell out of favour with the political mood in the country and with the Labour movement – resigning as Chairman of the PLP and then losing his seat in the 1918 General Election (Wrigley, cited in Jeffreys 1999: 27–28). In the 1920s, when public opinion began to shift away from approbation of the war, MacDonald was well placed to return to the centre of public life (Pugh 2010: 164–166); the Cassandra myth is one of the most powerful in many political cultures. He became the first official leader of the Labour Party in 1922. In 1923 and 1924, he made tours of the country and his platform speeches were met with what can only be described as adulation. He was commended for his graceful manner and his expressive voice: 'capable of every range of expression, from a whisper to the great bass notes of an organ' (Morgan 2006: 101. John Beckett also spoke of his 'organ-like voice' (Pugh 2010: 166)). Still, even at this early stage Labour was behind the times: while MacDonald performed platform oratory, Baldwin was making effective use of the wireless (Morgan 2006: 102; see also Baldwin 1933).

Foreshadowing modern-day leaders such as Blair, MacDonald was criticized from within the party for cosying up to wealthy elites and Liberals in London society – not least the socialite Lady Londonderry (Morgan 2006: 103–104) – and the King, George V, liked him. The defining moment for MacDonald was of course his decision, in the midst of an economic crisis and the collapse of the Cabinet over a disagreement on unemployment benefits, to form a National Government with the Conservatives and the Liberals in 1931. The Labour Party saw this as a traitorous decision and expelled him from the party. MacDonald's decision became pivotal to Labour's wider narrative of leadership's quality of betrayal. It has remained an important piece of Labour history and has fuelled accusations of betrayal ever since (notably the comparison with Blair but also with the Social Democratic Party (SDP) 'Gang of Four' (Wrigley, cited in Jeffreys 1999: 32–34). MacDonald's central role – Labour's first leader and first Prime Minister – therefore fed into the party's mythology regarding disdain for leadership itself.

Arthur Henderson 1931–1932

Like most of the other early leaders, it is not entirely clear whether Arthur Henderson had much interest in leading the Labour Party, a position he held three times (although he was only officially leader in 1931–1932; on the previous occasions, Chairman of the PLP). Henderson took the lead in party organization and played an important role in supporting MacDonald as leader. While Henderson was interested in exercising power – indeed fellow politician John Hodge (himself no shrinking violet) described him as dictatorial – he preferred a backseat role, more like that of a Chief Whip (which he was between 1925 and 1927) to being the face of the party (Haworth and Hayter 2006: 85). Henderson saw MacDonald as a capable leader – in great part it should be noted because of MacDonald's considerable oratorical skills, and also because he shared Henderson's moderate views (Haworth and Hayter 2006: 87). Relations between MacDonald and Henderson (then Foreign Secretary), however, started to deteriorate during the second Labour minority government over disagreements on foreign policy – in particular, Henderson's election as President of the World Disarmament Conference in Geneva, which angered MacDonald. MacDonald also feared Henderson wanted to be leader, though this was not the case at all – Henderson was interested in a peerage and felt that he was too old and unwell to seriously consider the leadership for himself (Thorpe 1988: 119–120). I mention this here because it illustrates the point that personal relationships and therefore – especially – personal misunderstandings had, and have still, major political consequences.

Unlike MacDonald, Henderson was greatly concerned about trade union support and ensuring party unity; indeed, on the critical 1931 vote on unemployment benefits, Henderson went against MacDonald and voted to reject the cuts for fear of provoking the TUC and splitting the party (Pugh 2010: 213). Still, even as late as 1931, Henderson described MacDonald as 'absolutely irreplaceable' (again a myth of leadership that has 'secretly' informed the party ever since), and when MacDonald decided to form a National Government hoped that he would return to lead Labour (Riddell, cited in Jeffreys 1999: 49–51).

It would be severe to say that Henderson's leadership of the Labour Party in the aftermath of MacDonald's decision to form a National Government was the worst in Labour history; he was, after all, operating in extremely difficult conditions and was seriously ill for part of it. Henderson was unwilling to become leader on account of his age, but he was the obvious candidate, given his apparent heroic role in the party for taking Labour out of the government. Also, there was no real alternative – Clynes, the other possible person, declined the opportunity (Thorpe 1988: 123–126). But during his leadership Henderson was an isolated figure, depressed about Labour's chances at the next election and worried that his opportunity to take part in the disarmament conference in 1932 had been lost (Thorpe 1988: 129) (here is another example, as with Hardie and many others, of how the leader's real interests lay outside the party). Like MacDonald before him, he was particularly concerned about Labour appearing 'responsible' in power, but this was not in keeping with the rest of the party, which had become radicalized after leaving office and wanted a tougher response to the National Government. His speeches focused on personally justifying his role in the previous Labour government rather than looking forward (Riddell, cited in Jeffreys 1999: 52). His tactics were criticized by members of the PLP, including Ernest Thurtle, George Lansbury, and Susan Lawrence (Thorpe 1988: 131–132). Rumours (another developing and consequential feature of the party) that Henderson was considering taking Labour into an alliance with the National Government did little to help party unity. Henderson was unable to assuage Labour's anger towards MacDonald, resulting in the former leader's expulsion (Thorpe 1988: 132–134). Henderson struggled in the 1931 campaign – particularly as he faced a serious challenge to his own seat. His campaign speeches were dull (although he was generally well received, mainly because he only ever went to Labour heartlands), he was deeply pessimistic and often unwell, and he struggled with the rhetorical shift towards attacking former colleagues like Snowden and MacDonald (Thorpe 1988: 135–137). Labour was crushed in the 1931 election, winning only 46 seats in contrast to 556 for the National Government. Henderson himself failed to retain his seat (Riddell, cited in Jeffreys 1999: 54). We can see just from these anecdotes about Hardie, MacDonald, and Henderson how consequent were the acts and personal attitudes of leaders within a party and movement which barely understood the phenomenon of leadership itself and, to the extent that it thought about it, was generally hostile to it. We can see also that 'types' of leader were emerging and a range of perceived character traits and qualities – such as attractive, dull, compelling, adored, effective, treacherous – and that these traits and dispositions had real effects upon the fortunes and evolution of the party.

George Lansbury 1932–1935

Like Hardie and MacDonald, George Lansbury was a strange kind of Labour leader who appeared to prioritize causes over and above his duties as head of the party – in his case, foreign policy. As the leader of the PLP and of the Opposition to the National Government Lansbury was spirited and determined (Thorpe 2008: 66–67); but as leader of the wider party he struggled to mark his authority. The National Executive Committee (NEC) was dominated by figures like Bevin, Dalton and Morrison who marginalized Lansbury and left him little room for political manoeuvre. In part, this was, as we have seen, because former leader MacDonald was seen as having become too powerful in the party; the feeling was that the leader's role needed to be curtailed (Thorpe, cited in Jeffreys 1999). This too became a central feature of Labour's attitude to leadership.

Lansbury came from a 'radical' tradition in Labour of 'Poplarism', a form of activism where local councils were deeply implicated in the well-being of their community. As the Mayor of Poplar in the 1920s, Lansbury and his Labour colleagues in the council refused to pay the 'precept' to the London County Council in order to address unemployment and make the rates system in London fairer and less burdensome on the poor; the councillors were imprisoned for a short while but then released with their demands granted. These notions of integrity and courage greatly strengthened his reputation in the party (Thorpe, cited in Jeffreys 1999: 62; Foot 2005: 253–259) and gave to leadership itself some of the character traits of the wider movement like courage and determination. Lansbury's 'downfall', however, was his pacifism; as fascism spread across Europe, he declared support for ideas such as unilateral disarmament and the sharing of the world's resources. Lansbury's Utopian vision jarred painfully with the times and soon with the wider party. Ernest Bevin's speech at the Labour Conference in 1935, in Dalton's words, 'hammered [Lansbury] to death' as he tore into Lansbury's pacifism and accused him of MacDonald-like betrayal (already a rhetorical motif). Lansbury refused to compromise with the party and was forced to resign shortly after Bevin's speech (Schneer 1990; Thorpe, cited in Jeffreys 1999: 69–75; but see also Shepherd in Clarke and James 2015: 163 for a more nuanced view).

More recently, Lansbury has undergone a reappraisal from Blue Labour (see p. 84) and other figures. Lansbury has been described by Jon Cruddas as 'arguably the greatest ever Labour leader'. In a speech in 2011 in Bow to commemorate Lansbury, Cruddas argued that Lansbury's ejection as Labour leader marked a turning point in Labour history, where the party's rich intellectual and romantic tradition was overcome by 'pragmatists and political operators'. He gave a similarly laudatory lecture at QMC in November 2013. Cruddas extolled Lansbury's Christian socialism (he was one of the founders of the Christian Socialist League in 1906), his commitment to combatting poverty, his humility, and his localism (Poplarism). Cruddas described him as an English radical, combining the magical and the thoroughly ordinary (Cruddas 2013b). By the 1930s, however, we can see that, whatever their other merits and personal courage, Labour's leaders were an odd lot and really not the most impressive group of leaders or exemplars for other aspirants in the party.

CLEMENT ATTLEE 1935–1955

How did Clement Attlee ever become Labour leader? This extraordinarily shy, unassuming figure, described at university as a 'level headed, industrious, dependable man with no brilliance', seemed to tip-toe his way to the top of the party. He was certainly a beneficiary of the mass Labour cull in the 1931 election (Pearce, cited in Jeffreys 1999: 81). This too became a feature of Labour leadership – potential leaders who lose their seat at a crucial moment in their political trajectory, and unexpected advantage being given to others. The first middle/upper class Labour leader (who hated the thought of port being passed the wrong way around the dining table), Attlee was not a leader who imprinted a wider political vision on Labour (thus not a 'Romantic' in Cruddas' terminology), but he did have a firm commitment to the principles of socialism of the William Morris variety, developed during his time as a social worker in Stepney (Pearce, cited in Jeffreys 1999: 81–83). While Attlee certainly had a good deal of luck in becoming Labour leader, he was also committed and hard-working, playing a vital role in Opposition to the government in the 1931–1935 period (Pearce, cited in Jeffreys 1999: 85). Rather than assuming MacDonald's cavalier attitude to colleagues, Attlee adapted to party opinion: 'Attlee would be the leader who followed or at least advanced alongside his party' (Pearce, cited in Jeffreys 1999: 85). Attlee became MP for Limehouse in 1922. Lacking 'charisma' (sorry) and struggling to make much of an impact on constituents, he quite lacked the 'common touch'. His campaign to win the seat relied critically on the help of his agent John Beckett, who would drive him around the constituency to meet and give advice to voters. Beckett noted that Attlee would 'exchange friendly greetings' with constituents while 'looking extremely unhappy' (Pugh 2010: 142–143). This dichotomy between being cultivated and being 'ordinary' would also become a permanent issue within the party, particularly as regards leadership.

Attlee's greatest achievements were of course during his post-war premiership. But prior to his time as Prime Minister, he was actually seen by other Labour figures as a liability, a 'caretaker' figure with seemingly few leadership or public speaking skills (Pearce, cited in Jeffreys 1999: 86). Even during the wartime coalition government, Attlee's substantial role received little exposure (Pearce, cited in Jeffreys 1999: 88). According to Pugh, Herbert Morrison was the natural candidate for leader after the 1935 General Election, but the PLP leant towards Attlee. This was not despite but because of his shy, unassertive manner – Labour MPs were apprehensive about having another strong-willed figure (i.e., another MacDonald) at the helm (Pugh 2010: 241).

In 1945, the British public surprised Attlee and everybody else by delivering the party its first overall majority in a shock landslide. It is instructive to look at Attlee's victory speech in 1945, at that stage (perhaps at this stage too…) the party's high point. In his address he stated in a subdued, staccato tone which utterly failed to match the extraordinary political moment:

> The sweeping victories throughout the country mark an epoch in the political life of this country. Never before have the electors shown clearly their desire that there should be in this country a Labour government carrying out Labour's full policies. I am certain that this election has been one in which

the electors have thought deeply on the fundamental questions of the future, and they realize that Labour is a party of the future, and that Labour's policy is the only policy that can lead us to peace abroad and social justice at home. The Labour Party's great victory shows that the country is ready for a new policy to face new world conditions, that it believes that Labour has the right policy, and that it also has the men to carry it out. (Attlee 1945)

Following on from 5 years of Churchill's rhetoric, Attlee's speech came across as straightforward, utterly pragmatic, and empty – he used the words 'policy' or 'policies' five times, emphasized the rational thought process of voters, and highlighted the competency of Labour's senior figures. But with all the changes in social attitudes in the war years, and the army (literally) of returning soldiers in 1945, it was a cultural revolution that swept Labour to power. A little more lyricism for this electoral victory and the country's deliverance, even for posterity, would have been welcome. He did, however, also identify Labour as a party of the future just as his most successful successors Wilson and Blair would, despite their different rhetorical styles, the one redeeming feature of the speech.

As Prime Minister, Attlee brought about extraordinary changes – not least the initiation of key components of the welfare state. He also ran his Cabinet effectively – in sharp contrast to MacDonald – playing a powerful mediator role regarding his often warring Cabinet members (Pearce, cited in Jeffreys 1999: 89–90). Despite the presence of major figures, major 'characters' in the Cabinet – Bevin, Dalton, Morrison, Cripps – Attlee was the uncontested leader during this period (Pearce, cited in Jeffreys 1999: 89–93), forming a powerful axis with Bevin and blocking the leadership ambitions of an exasperated Morrison (Jeffreys 1993: 10–11). He was determined to avoid the mistakes (in large part the *inactivity*) of the MacDonald administrations and was committed to social change (Pearce, cited in Jeffreys 1999: 91–92). But Attlee's vision is still hard to pin down – he was a 'practical idealist', interested in getting the job done (Pearce, cited in Jeffreys 1999: 94). And he was certainly not interested in political games – indeed, his decision to not delay the 1951 election on account of King George VI's trip abroad was a simple matter of courtesy but helped to lose Labour the election, given its poor timing with the economic state of affairs in the country (Pugh 2010: 300). The irony is that the man many refer to – increasingly – as Labour's greatest Prime Minister would arguably not be up to the task today. Not only did he pay no attention to the press (Pearce, cited in Jeffreys 1999: 94), he was a poor campaigner, trapped – like many Labour leaders – in old-fashioned methods (e.g., travelling around the country giving platform speeches) and completely out of tune with the mood of the wider party (Pugh 2010: 300).

HUGH GAITSKELL 1955–1963

Hugh Gaitskell is traditionally seen as on the Labour Party's 'old right', an early revisionist who presided over a period of considerable Labour infighting and who, unlike Attlee, was not afraid to get into arguments. Gaitskell's leadership was characterized by three internal disputes: over Clause IV, unilateral disarmament, and the Common Market (Heppell and McMeeking, cited in Crines and Hayton 2015: 31; Brivati, cited in Jeffreys 1999).

The 1959 election was the first where television played a significant role and highlighted the importance of political leadership and performance in electoral success (Heppell and McMeeking, cited in Crines and Hayton 2015: 41). Gaitskell was not a distinguished public orator, and Harold Macmillan often got the better of him at both PMQs and on television. Gaitskell faced regular interruptions in his jousts with Macmillan and some wondered whether his leadership had been irretrievably damaged due to his substandard performances in Parliament (Heppell 2012: 41, quoting Williams 1979). This also raises the interesting question of the status of a leader being in part defined by that of their main adversary. Macmillan said that Gaitskell's mistake in PMQs was to ask too many questions at once, allowing Macmillan to choose to answer only the ones that were manageable (Heppell and McMeeking, cited in Crines and Hayton 2015: 35). Gaitskell was most definitely a rationalist, not a romantic, and known for his numerical skills. His speeches often lacked emotional punch (but not always; see, e.g., his 'fight again' speech) and instead relied on the logic of the argument to persuade listeners (Heppell and McMeeking, cited in Crines and Hayton 2015: 43). Sometimes this strategy met with great success (e.g., his parliamentary speech about Lord Home's appointment to the Foreign Office, where he accused Home of being a 'puppet' of Macmillan (Heppell and McMeeking, cited in Crines and Hayton 2015: 35), or his Common Market conference speech in 1962, 'the end of a thousand years of history'), but often it lacked passion and benefited his opponents. Gaitskell's commitment to unrelenting reasoned argument whatever the cost also encouraged his reputation as a divisive figure – his association with the right of the party at times led to heckling and abuse during his speeches (Heppell and McMeeking, cited in Crines and Hayton 2015: 42).

According to Brivati, Gaitskell's legacy to the party was 'a style of confrontational leadership and a political approach of brutal frankness' (Brivati, cited in Jeffreys 1999: 113). Gaitskell's 'fight and fight and fight again' Party Conference Speech (1960) on unilateral disarmament is a case in point. Amid considerable commotion in the audience, he at one point cried:

> You know: I have been subject to some criticism and attack. I am entitled to reply!' He then went on to state: 'Do you think we can become overnight the pacifists, unilateralists, and fellow travellers that other people are? (*Pause during clapping, booing*) How wrong can you be? *How wrong can you be?* As wrong as you are about the attitude of the British people! (*In response to commotion in audience*) A noise of that kind only shows you don't want to hear the arguments! (Gaitskell 1960).

The aggressive, finger-pointing body language, the provocative interactions with the audience, and the sharp rhetoric all gave the impression that Gaitskell was doing battle with his party rather than delivering a typical political speech (and this rhetorical use of Conference has echoed down the years with other leaders – for instance Kinnock's famous 'Labour council' speech at the 1985 Conference, using a similar tactic against a small element within the party, albeit with much more 'Conference' support behind him).

Gaitskell's failed attempt to rid the party of Clause IV through a change in the constitution has been compared unfavourably to Blair's success in doing it in the 1990s – of course they were operating in vastly different contexts, with the unions far more powerful during Gaitskell's leadership (Brivati, cited in Jeffreys 1999: 107–108). Gaitskell faced opposition on Clause IV from key figures such as Harold Wilson and Anthony Greenwood, as well as vocal antagonism from the left-wing magazine *Tribune* (*The Guardian* 1985 [1960]). But Gaitskell could also be charged with not appreciating the emotional attachment to Clause IV for Labour or offering an emotionally moving alternative – instead, pursuing the logic of his argument regardless of the consequences within the party (Heppell and McMeeking, cited in Crines and Hayton 2015: 42). For Gaitskell, changing Clause IV was part of a broader programme of revisionism, as developed by Labour politician and writer Tony Crosland. The key insight of revisionism was that public ownership was a means of achieving socialist ideals, not an end in itself. Changing Clause IV was therefore central to the revisionist approach (Jones 1996: 48).

At the same time, Clause IV had a deep symbolic resonance within Labour – not just on the left but also within the trade union movement – and unified many of the different strands of the party in pursuit of a wider vision. Even if many in Labour no longer believed in public ownership of the means of production, Clause IV had a deep significance, as exemplified by Harold Wilson's analogy in his opposition to the change: 'we were being asked to take Genesis out of the Bible; you don't have to be a fundamentalist in your religious approach to say that Genesis is part of the Bible' (Jones 1996: 61–62; Jones 1997). This need for Labour leadership's sensitivity to party sentiment was now an integral part of it.

A central part of Gaitskell's argument on changing Clause IV was that it would benefit Labour's standing in the country as a whole; in this sense, Gaitskell was more sensitive to political strategy than previous Labour leaders (Heppell and McMeeking, cited in Crines and Hayton 2015: 36). Indeed, one of his most famous speeches – his critique of the Common Market at the Labour Party Conference in 1962 – was perhaps the product of a political strategy to in fact unite the party. The 'thousand years of history' speech shocked his colleagues by his associating himself with a position normally seen as on the left of the party (Heppell and McMeeking, cited in Crines and Hayton 2015: 38). But the speech was in many ways typical of Gaitskell's character – a relentless appeal to statistics, a consistent, unflagging interest in building a convincing argument, and a repeated emphasis of 'rely[ing] on the facts' and ensuring the arguments were 'evenly balanced'. But there was also a populist slant to his speech too, mirroring some of the arguments used by Eurosceptics today:

> 'We must go in,' they say, 'not because the power of logic, of fact and conclusion suggest that it is to our advantage; we must go in because the people who really understand it, the top people, all want it.' They contradict themselves. If their minds are so arid that they can think of no other arguments, they are a long way down in the intellectual class. But what an odious piece of hypocritical, supercilious, arrogant rubbish is this! And how typical of the kind of Tory propaganda we may expect upon the subject – the appeal to snobbery: 'the big people know best; you had better follow them!' It is all on a par with the argument of inevitability. ('You cannot escape: you must be with it. You must belong, no matter to what you belong.') What a pitiful level of argument we have reached! (Gaitskell 1962)

If he had used more of the lyricism of his 'civilization' and 'fight again' speeches elsewhere he might have had more luck with Clause IV, at least.

HAROLD WILSON 1963–1976

Harold Wilson was politically one of Labour's most successful leaders, winning four General Elections (in the sense that he became Prime Minister, even if Labour did not necessarily win a majority of seats or even most of the votes), balancing the party's left and right factions and, for a while at least, enthusing Labour with a powerful political energy and direction (Bale, cited in Jeffreys 1999). Yet, while Attlee was a successful Prime Minister but poor Opposition leader, Wilson revelled in Opposition but struggled in government (Fielding 2013). He was, over time, seen as an untrustworthy figure (Hill, cited in Crines and Hayton 2015: 58) who stood on the left in the 1963 leadership contest (and challenged Gaitskell from the left in 1960) but stuck to the Labour right-wing's traditional positions in government. George Brown, one of his competitors in the 1963 contest, observed that 'If we are to die in the last ditch Harold won't be there. He will have scrambled out' (Pugh 2010: 324).

Wilson was accused by critics of being over-optimistic, lacking clear political principles, and failing to deliver his promises when in power (Hill, cited in Crines and Hayton 2015). Denis Healey's analysis is typical of his detractors: 'He had no sense of direction, and rarely looked more than a few months ahead. His short-term opportunism, allied with a capacity for self-delusion which made Walter Mitty appear unimaginative, often plunged the government into chaos. Worse still, when things went wrong he imagined everyone was conspiring against him...' (Jeffreys 1993: 80). Wilson's paranoia developed in government as his early promise began to be overwhelmed by events seemingly out of his control. In the late 1960s, he insinuated to colleagues that the Chancellor was plotting to take his place (Jeffreys 1993: 72) and he had a difficult relationship with the media after a dispute about D-notices (issues related to newspapers breaching national security) in 1968 (Bale, cited in Jeffreys 1999: 123). Wilson also feared that he was being spied on by the secret services, and some have claimed that there was indeed a plot to overthrow Wilson and undertake a military coup (though there is no consensus as to the degree of reality of the plot) (Wheeler 2006). He also ran an inner circle, a 'kitchen cabinet' of key political advisers, headed by the influential Marcia Williams (Bale, cited in Jeffreys 1999: 123; Pugh 2010: 324–325). What was clear was that a growing sense of persecution (perhaps another consequence of leadership, and one bequeathed to the party) became a significant factor in Wilson's premiership and his leadership style.

Wilson succeeded in capturing both left and right as party leader through his canny use of his humble background, his promotion of both equality of opportunity and economic planning, and his unwillingness to fundamentally change the status quo within the party, either by upsetting the traditional hold on Shadow Cabinet positions on the party's right or by, as Gaitskell had, deliberately provoking the party's left (Bale, cited in Jeffreys 1999: 222). Wilson developed a distinctive character with his trademark pipe, exaggerated Yorkshire accent, and love of tinned food and HP sauce (Hill, cited in Crines and Hayton 2015: 46) that marked him out as both 'ordinary' and classless, symbolic of the meritocratic impulses of his leadership (he had taught at Oxford in the 1930s – where incidentally his Yorkshire accent was decidedly less marked). Wilson was able also to balance – one could say catch the wave of – Labour's romantic and rationalist traditions by combining a preference for technocracy and economic planning with a reputation for a thoroughly wide-eyed idealism (Bale, cited in Jeffreys 1999: 122–123).

Wilson's essentially *ambiguous* character placated party divisions for much of his time as leader (Bale, cited in Jeffreys 1999: 122). Richard Crossman's diary noted: 'What are Harold's long-term economic objectives for this country? Does he want to go into Europe or doesn't he? I don't think he knows himself ... His aim is to stay in office' (Jeffreys 1993: 72, quoting Crossman's diaries). This opportunism had the benefit of allowing Wilson to maintain party unity. For some though, he never really 'lance[d] the boil', as witnessed by the return of internal party dispute in the years after his departure from office (Bale, cited in Jeffreys 1999: 128). This is a constant within the party (in which case the 'boil' analogy is perhaps inappropriate), but how it is handled is crucial. In the 1970s, Wilson went along with the left-wing shift in Labour politics rather than fight it – as doubtless his predecessor would have done – thereby, perhaps, laying the groundwork for the internal battles ahead (Jeffreys 1993: 86). Miliband would face the same accusation in the aftermath of the 2015 election. The evidence suggests though that at heart Wilson was on the party's right-wing – as part of the Nuffield Election study, Wilson said his 'main aim was economic growth and a restructuring of industry', which were 'much more important than abstract values of equality' (Bale, cited in Jeffreys 1999: 124).

Wilson was a very good speaker and in his 10-year battle with Edward Heath comfortably outmatched him at PMQs (as well as Macmillan in fact – e.g., the way he rhetorically claimed virtue for Labour and charged the Conservatives – and Macmillan – with 'indolent nonchalance' in their dealing with the Profumo scandal (Hill, cited in Crines and Hayton 2015: 47–49)). His most famous speech was the 1963 'White Heat of Technology' speech to the Labour Party Conference. The speech is a crucial part of

Labour history and is important still for a number of reasons. First, it exemplified how Wilson successfully captured the zeitgeist of the 1960s by positioning the party as a force for progress and modernization (Hill, cited in Crines and Hayton 2015: 52). Second, it successfully married socialist principles and ideas with future policy challenges (Hill, cited in Crines and Hayton 2015: 53). Third, it challenged the party ('no room for Luddites in the Socialist party') without dividing it, galvanizing Labour on to a victory in 1964. The speech helped to give the party a new direction after the interminable disputes over Clause IV and unilateral disarmament of the Gaitskell era, focusing on the new challenges and opportunities of technology, rather than the traditional left–right divide (Hill, cited in Crines and Hayton 2015: 54–55). Fourth, it depicted the Conservatives as out of date and reliant on an 'old boy-network approach' (Wilson 1963; Hill, cited in Crines and Hayton 2015: 54). This strategy ran through the 1964 campaign (Jenkins 1964). Fifth, it appealed to a group of 'intermediate voters' (skilled working class/lower middle class on rising incomes) that Labour needed to reach out to in order to adjust to Britain's changing economy and reverse Labour's electoral decline (Fielding 2013). In this sense Wilson, like Blair, was able to define Labour's path and marry a personal narrative – in his case as a lower middle class man from Yorkshire who worked his way up (with considerable intellectual acumen, see Goodman 1995) – with his political vision of a socially mobile, prosperous Britain harnessing the scientific revolution with economic planning. The truth, however, was that in office Wilson did not live up to these ambitions. Jeffreys speaks of the 'bitter disillusionment' of the Wilson governments, where little was seen to be achieved overall, beyond educational reforms, small redistributions of wealth and significant progress on social and moral issues, notably with respect to homosexuality, equal pay, abortion, and racial discrimination, and the abolition of capital punishment (Jeffreys 1993: 60–61). We should also stress that a lot of these courageous reforms were often led by Home Secretary Roy Jenkins. In 1966 major cuts in public spending and wage freezes as part of the 'July measures' in response to the government's economic troubles (and Wilson's initial refusal to risk devaluation) set the government on a disillusioned and disillusioning path to decline (Jeffreys 1993: 68). After a promising first 2 years in power, Wilson's government began to go off the rails after the July measures were announced, despite the heady rhetoric of Wilson's early period as leader. And in 1967, after eventually being forced to devalue, there was one piece of rhetoric that in part proved his undoing – his TV address after Britain's devaluation where he tried to reassure a very sceptical public that devaluation did 'not mean, of course that the pound here in Britain, in your pocket or purse or in your bank, has been devalued' (Hill, cited in Crines and Hayton 2015: 58, quoted in Sandbrook 2010). This attempt to 'spin' the bad economic news, when the government had desperately tried to avoid devaluation in the previous months, helped to secure his reputation as a wily if not devious political operator.

Wilson also had a very difficult relationship with the trade unions during his time as Prime Minister. One of his great challenges was the 1966 Seamen's strike. The strikers demanded a wage rise, going against the government's pay policy. Wilson insinuated that the strikers were Communists by referring to them as 'politically motivated men'. The phrasing jarred with other Labour politicians (why should unions not be politically motivated, they wondered) and harmed his standing with the unions (Hill, cited in Crines and Hayton 2015: 51). The real blow, however, to Labour–union relations emerged with the publication of *In Place of Strife*, a White Paper by the historic left-winger Barbara Castle on a new settlement for the trade unions. *In Place of Strife* alienated many in the Labour movement with its call for secret ballots, official strikes, and mandatory 'cooling off periods'. Wilson was forced to back down after considerable opposition emerged in the Cabinet, including from Callaghan, who appeared to pose a leadership threat to Wilson (Jeffreys 1993: 73–75). All of these developments shaped the party's and wider public's view of Labour leadership.

Morale within the Labour Party fell further as the government's 'hard slog' Budgets continued during 1967, 1968, and 1969. Further damage to morale was done after the government tightened border controls as Kenyan Asians were made to leave Kenya and left stateless in 1968. Within the party this was seen as the kind of thing only a Conservative government would do. The decline in local activism took its toll in a series of damaging local election results in the late 1960s and a fall in party membership (Jeffreys 1993: 71–80). In 1970, despite polling suggesting that Labour would overcome its challenges to secure a third victory against an unpopular Ted Heath, low turnout and a significant decline in support for Labour among manual workers put paid to such hopes (Pugh 2010: 345). Labour's defeat was clearly a personal blow to Wilson. Speaking to (a young) David Dimbleby as the results coming in made clear that a Conservative victory was inevitable, he said the defeat was a 'disappointment', bristled when asked about his personal feelings, and sternly rejected the question of a leadership challenge (BBC 1970). Wilson was clearly diminished by the defeat and failed to deliver new energy into his now permanently squabbling party (Jeffreys 1993: 84). The left began to gain momentum within Labour – led by Tony Benn, who had undergone a kind of Damascene conversion from centrism after his role in the first Wilson government (Jeffreys 1993: 85). In (as ever) an attempt to maintain party unity, Wilson was forced to compromise with the left – adopting, for instance, a more critical position on the EEC (Bale, cited in Jeffreys 1999: 126–127). When Heath called an election in 1974, Labour were far from well placed to capitalize upon what had been a disastrous Heath government but, amid general disengagement and a surge in Liberal support, Wilson scraped back into Number 10, despite Labour winning a lower share of the vote (though slightly more seats) than the Conservatives (Jeffreys 1993: 86–87). Wilson settled the immediate chaos by stabilizing the economy and doing a deal with the striking miners, hoping to repeat his 1966 victory with a follow-up election in October. This barely worked, however, as Labour only scraped a majority of three.

Wilson spent his final years in office struggling with a deeply challenging economic context and a tiny political majority. Still, his skills as a tactician were put to good use – not least in the 1975 referendum on Britain's membership of the EEC, where he allowed his ministers to campaign on either side, thereby ensuring party unity while securing a handsome victory (Jeffreys 1993: 88–90; Pugh 2010: 352). His resignation in 1976 came as a surprise for many, and there was a range of unsubstantiated rumours as to why he had chosen to stand down, but he had always planned to retire at 60 and, after four electoral successes and a good European referendum result, it is not so surprising that he took the decision he did (Jeffreys 1993: 93; Bale, cited in Jeffreys 1999: 127). He may also have had concerns about his health (Goodman 1995). Wilson dominated Labour politics for well over a decade. His leadership brought new qualities to the post. He demonstrated that managing the 'wings' of the party was one of the central tasks of Labour leadership. Leaders and would-be leaders (like Tony Benn), moreover, could also employ the rhetoric of different parts of the party to political effect. All the aspects of Labour's many narratives were now being put to full rhetorical use by a range of figures. Wilson's leadership brought to the forefront the rhetorical conditions of achieving government as well as the sometimes deleterious political effects of such lyricism in the aftermath of victory. By the end of his career, however, Wilson had also reinforced the notion within the left that defects in the leader's *character* were at the heart of the government's failure to deliver on promises.

JIM CALLAGHAN 1976–1980

Jim Callaghan has typically been seen as an exemplary 'Old Labour' politician with a trade union background, a socially conservative outlook, a political style reliant on consensus with Labour's different factions, and a corresponding 'corporatist' approach (Morgan, cited in Jeffreys 1999: 133, 145, 148–149). He was a pragmatic 'safety first' politician, more cautious than Wilson but similarly lacking in a clear ideology (Jeffreys 1993: 93–94). Callaghan faced challenges during his tenure as Prime Minister (Morgan, cited in Jeffreys 1999: 146), and analysis needs to bear in mind the significant political and economic limitations facing Labour in government in this period. Although conciliatory, Callaghan was willing to challenge his party, for example his 1976 Conference speech containing the anti-Keynesian '[we] used to think that you could spend your way out of a recession ... I tell you in all candour that that option no longer exists' (Meredith, cited in Crines and Hayton 2015: 76). Callaghan was therefore able to challenge party consensus through an appeal to economic realism, and even drew on Labour thinkers like Tawney to argue for major policy reform (e.g., his 1976 Ruskin speech on education) (Meredith, cited in Crines and Hayton 2015: 84–86). Even the pragmatists now drew upon the party's philosophers as a rhetorical resource.

Callaghan's style of rhetoric often relied on a kind of quiet, unpretentious *ethos* – in particular an appeal to his 'homely' values, his experience in government, his consensual style, and his trade union background. He offered a 'common sense' approach to political communication (Meredith, cited in Crines and Hayton 2015: 86), rooted in a political conservatism (small 'c') but also sensitive to change – and because of his respect across the party, he felt capable of leading Labour onwards (Meredith, cited in Crines and Hayton 2015: 83). In his final Conference speech as Prime Minister, Callaghan combined an emphasis on 'traditional [Labour] values' with hope for the future, decrying the Conservatives as 'as out of place as a penny-farthing on a motorway' (Callaghan 1978). This was, however, only months before the Conservatives came to power and won four consecutive General Elections, and dramatically changed the nature of political leadership and political communication in the UK.

Callaghan was effective at using humour to emphasize his down-to-earth 'ordinariness' and mollify his party at times where divisions were manifest. In 1978, defending his wage restraint policy while recognizing his colleagues' concerns, Callaghan struck a penitent tone with a light-hearted joke:

> I must say I felt at some stages yesterday like the old Scotsman who died and
> went up to heaven and as he got to the pearly gates he was met by St Peter.
> He thought he had been pretty good in life and St Peter reeled off a whole
> set of sins and said: 'You are condemned to outer darkness.' And the old
> Scotsman said: 'I didna ken that I had sinned.' St Peter replied: 'Well you
> ken the noo.' (*Laughter*). Well, all right, I ken the noo. (Callaghan 1978)

At times his homely appeal backfired. At the 1978 TUC conference
Callaghan communicated his decision not to call an election by way of a
music hall song:

> There was I waiting at the Church, waiting at the Church, waiting at the
> Church, when I found he'd left me in the lurch, Lor' how it did upset me.
> All at once he sent me round a note, here's the very note, this is what he
> wrote, 'can't get away to marry you today, my wife won't let me!' (Meredith,
> cited in Crines and Hayton 2015)

This strange choice of song, implicitly drawing a parallel between the
Labour Party and a philandering husband and fiancé – elaborating an analogy that did not really fit – confused his audience and the wider public, and
irritated his colleagues in government (Morgan, cited in Jeffreys 1999: 147).

The lack of rhetorical effectiveness here presaged the unawareness of
the oncoming storm that would give power to the right for two decades.
There was, however, one more, this time monumental communication
error to come: at the onset of the Winter of Discontent, Callaghan's comments that 'I don't think other people in the world would share the view
[that] there is mounting chaos' as he arrived back tanned from a conference in Guadeloupe were re-transmitted by *The Sun* with the headline
'Crisis? What Crisis?' (BBC 2000; Morgan, cited in Jeffreys 1999: 147).
As the country ran into chaos (captured by acres of uncollected rat-infested
rubbish on the streets), a vote of no confidence brought the government
down and elections were called (the irony here was that regarding the
overall improving economic situation, Callaghan was probably right).
Callaghan, now fully aware that he was caught amid a 'sea change' in
British politics, expected defeat (*The Economist* 2005) despite his personal
ratings being stronger than those of Margaret Thatcher. He stayed on
as leader after the 1979 defeat to oversee changes to the leadership election itself. Callaghan's final days as leader were marred by infighting and
recrimination (Jeffreys 1993: 102–104; Morgan, cited in Jeffreys 1999:
148). In his last speech as leader, recognizing the poor light in which

he was now seen by many within Labour, he urged the party: 'For pity's sake, stop arguing' (Callaghan 1980). It was not to be. In fact, the internecine fighting was just beginning, and became highly personalized and deeply damaging. A final comment on his persona is apposite here. At the end of his premiership his well-fashioned undramatic style began to look like inattention to problems; hence the effectiveness of *The Sun*'s 'crisis' quotation (or rather mis-quotation). This kind of style can be extremely successful in a range of ways, but carries with it disadvantages, in particular the notion of inaction if the political environment changes.

MICHAEL FOOT 1980–1983

Michael Foot's period as Labour Party leader (lasting two and a half years) has become a central piece of Labour Party mythology, providing a point of reference for later contenders to set themselves against, much as – paradoxically – the MacDonald betrayal had for Labour 50 years earlier (the one setting too much store by leadership, the other not enough) (Shaw, cited in Jeffreys 1999: 151). After a deeply challenging time in government – marked by economic crisis and capped by the Winter of Discontent, a parliamentary vote of no confidence and an election defeat that brought Margaret Thatcher to power – Labour in Opposition began to tear itself apart despite Callaghan's staying on to steady the party transition (Shaw, cited in Jeffreys 1999: 153). After Callaghan stepped down in 1980, Foot decided to stand for the Labour leadership. Like his pre-war predecessors, Foot was – like Corbyn 35 years later – a reluctant leader, with little interest in power. But his friends in the party – who feared that the favourite for leader, the right-wing Denis Healey, would prove too divisive – orchestrated a campaign to persuade him to run. He was seen, paradoxically, as a unity candidate – on the left of the party, but a key figure in the former government – who could heal the growing left–right divide, which it has to be said he did in part through the respect he generated across the party as regards his personal integrity and intelligence. There was some suggestion that backing Foot may have been in part the product of an attempt to sabotage the party by some on the right, who were already thinking of leaving (one MP who voted for Foot said he did so 'because I thought he would make the worst leader for Labour') (Shaw, cited in Jeffreys 1999: 154–155).

Foot was certainly an unusual choice of leader. Known as a superb orator and intellectual (and having a huge library (BBC 1997)), he was elected to Parliament in 1945 (though lost his seat in 1955) and became known as a left-wing firebrand, with his spirited attacks on the Kemsley press and on the government's foreign policy (Shaw, cited in Jeffreys 1999: 152; Stewart, cited in Crines and Hayton 2015: 93, 95). A recurring theme of his speeches before the war was his opposition to appeasement (e.g., his book *Guilty Men* written in 1940 with two other journalists), and many of his later speeches harked back to the failures of the Chamberlain government in the 1930s (Stewart, cited in Crines and Hayton 2015: 100); so he mixed various strands within the party and transcended the left's unequivocal pacifism. Foot took Nye Bevan's seat in 1960 and continued to challenge the Labour leadership on issues such as unilateral nuclear disarmament, EEC membership, and industrial relations. At Party Conferences in 1966/1968, Foot positioned himself as the 'authentic' voice of socialism, challenging the Wilson government's record (Stewart, cited in Crines and Hayton 2015: 97).

Remarkably, in the 1970s Foot changed tack, entering the Labour government of 1974–1979 and becoming Employment Secretary from 1974 to 1976. But he was still and remained, in the words of a *Times* journalist, 'the living embodiment of Labour's conscience' (Crines 2011: 71). In government he developed the 'Social Contract' (a somewhat ambitious Rousseauist term) which sought to reformulate the relationship between the state and the trade unions through voluntary agreements in the context of rising inflation and major trade union disputes (Crines 2011: 71; Jeffreys 1993: 88). A number of these measures were attacked: the 'closed shop' was condemned by newspapers as an attack on press freedom, leading to Foot making a number of enemies in the press (which did not help when he became leader – perhaps mirroring some of Miliband's own later media difficulties); and Foot faced challenges on his wage proposals from others in the Labour Party – at one point he threatened to resign if a statutory pay policy was introduced as part of the package (Crines 2011: 73–77). Despite this, Foot was seen as a loyal member of the Cabinet, and when Wilson resigned in 1976 ran as the main left candidate, coming second in the leadership race (Crines 2011: 78). He mixed, and set a precedent for, a kind of leftist radicalism and party (and government) loyalism. He also reaffirmed the left's claim to be the 'conscience' of the party; an issue the centre and right of the party always had rhetorical difficulties with, which would have rhetorical consequences after the May 2015 defeat.

Despite his prior reputation for intelligence and integrity and his experience in government, as leader Foot struggled enormously. His greatest challenge was, in fact, to reconcile his two main qualities, party radicalism and party loyalty, reconciling his former role as tribune with managing the party at a time there were major splits appearing (Shaw, cited in Jeffreys

1999: 156–157): the defection of the 'Gang of Four' to create the SDP on the right, and the Bennite faction (which at this time controlled the NEC) and the Militant Tendency on the left (Shaw, cited in Jeffreys 1999: 167); and there was over and above these a myriad of other 'soft' left, centre, and right groupings. The party seemed to be splitting asunder under his too tolerant leadership. I said above his greatest challenge was reconciling his own qualities; in fact he was also a victim of Labour's historical ignorance of the springs and modalities of leadership itself. How could the 'living embodiment of Labour's conscience' bash the party into new and re-electable shape? Foot may have been seen by some as a unity candidate but his election as leader helped to precipitate the SDP split (Shaw, cited in Jeffreys 1999: 158). On the left, Foot's natural instincts were towards reconciliation and liberalism – he saw it as wrong to prevent people in the party from challenging the leadership, not least because he had done it himself so much in his earlier years (Shaw, cited in Jeffreys 1999: 156–157). But this left him open to charges of weakness – with Tony Benn in particular running for the deputy leadership and then, after losing, radicalizing his rhetoric further, by, for example, calling for the renationalization of oil without compensation (Shaw, cited in Jeffreys 1999: 159–161), and gathering around him a new and highly vocal radical left within the party. In 2015, Corbyn was not a 'unity' candidate as Foot had been in 1980, but the range of issues facing him as regards leadership and dissent was identical.

Foot's time as leader, in fact, became more and more desperate, with a surge in support in the polls for the SDP and further internal arguments emerging in Labour over how to respond to both Peter Tatchell and the radicalizing movement around him, and Militant on the left. The Militant Tendency in particular caused a major headache for Foot. The threat was that Trotskyist figures were trying to undermine then control the Labour Party from within via 'entryism'. This challenged Foot's commitment to a liberal, open party. More importantly it began to make him appear indecisive rather than just democratic, and set the conditions for the press onslaught against him. Eventually, Foot was compelled to address the problem of Militant and called for an inquiry. The final report of the inquiry, rather than banning Militant outright, suggested a 'Register' of non-affiliated groups within the party and stated that Militant 'would not be eligible to be included on the proposed Register' (Shaw, cited in Jeffreys 1999: 163). But the situation was very unclear; Militant threatened legal action, and Foot only expelled a small number of individuals, further conveying his reputation as weak, indecisive, and old-fashioned in the public mind. He was attacked on the left as a sell-out to his old cause – not of

Trotskyism of course but of a kind of 'let 100 flowers bloom' approach to
the left; besides, the differences between say Foot, Peter Tatchell, Derek
Hatton, Mick McGahey, Dave Nellist, Eric Heffer, or Linda Bellos were
lost on the average *Daily Mail* reader, so that Foot just seemed in the public mind as being overwhelmed by the 'loony left'. And he was attacked
on the right of the party for not being tough enough with radicals (Shaw
cited in Jeffreys 1999: 164). It is quite clear, however, that most of the
others in the party did not know what to do either.

Foot's leadership image in the media was also important in his period as
leader. While he was a commanding presence at Party Conference and in
public demonstrations, he struggled to adapt to the changing demands of the
media and the personalization of politics, and he was a weak performer on
television. His nephew, the socialist Paul Foot, aptly described his television
appearances as constantly being in 'parentheses', with his meandering, witty
style and his efforts to please the different wings of his party, going against
the media's preference for soundbites (BBC 1997; Stewart, cited in Crines
and Hayton 2015: 104) (he would probably have thrived on the BBC's
Brains Trust with Julian Huxley and Malcolm Muggeridge in the 1950s,
as indeed he did on platforms with Paul Soper). Austin Mitchell MP said of
Foot: 'He was hopeless in the personal interview style of the 1980s, peering
short-sightedly around, with a tendency to interrupt which alienated viewers, coupled with a willingness to follow lines set by the interviewer instead
of seizing the initiative, obscuring issues instead of speaking simply' (Shaw,
cited in Jeffreys 1999: 166–167). He was very quickly brutally caricatured by
the press as a clueless, weak, eccentric, and old-fashioned leader with no sense
of style, and – anticipating Miliband and the Aardman animated character
Wallace – was compared to the TV scarecrow character Worzel Gummidge.
One of his most infamous moments was his wearing of a 'donkey jacket' at
the Cenotaph in 1981 for Remembrance Sunday (although in fact it was
an overcoat from Harrods – a tiny echo of the left's many dilemmas in this
area: why did they not say?). The media hounded him for being disrespectful
(BBC 1997). This and Foot's leadership was one of the first indications of
the dramatic political consequence of 'trivia' in the modern period, a kind
of prelude (and here inversion) of 'celebrity politics'. And a strange kind of
celebrity politics in that his real adversary and nemesis of the Hampstead
intellectual was the dutiful, properly dressed at the Cenotaph, lower-middle
class, patriotic, monarchist Margaret Thatcher. My suspicion is that Elizabeth
Windsor would have much preferred a long afternoon's conversation about
constitutions and English history with Footy, than 5 minutes with Margaret
Thatcher. Nevertheless, beyond the media caricature, the Foot vs Thatcher

leadership styles raise wider cultural questions about the role and status of intellectuals in UK public perceptions. In France, it would have been Thatcher's style that would have been lampooned and Foot's intellectualism respected. As it was, refracted through the media, he was depicted as an Aldermaston Ban-the-Bomber being dragged unwillingly to commemorate the Empire's war dead. Did none of his entourage think of countering these attacks with his patriotic, non-pacifist, anti-appeasement credentials? Foot's fate must have been instrumental in his successor's realization that the PR effort in the Labour Party was now an 'imperative imperative'.

Foot's legacy (of sorts) was of course the modernization of the party under Neil Kinnock (one of Foot's central supporters), John Smith, and then much more radically, Tony Blair (Shaw, cited in Jeffreys 1999: 165–168). Often described as one of Labour's last 'romantic' leaders, Foot was a party member described by Callaghan as 'totally and unambiguously loyal' (Shaw, cited in Jeffreys 1999: 158) who rejoiced at New Labour's victory in 1997 and on a personal level at least was sympathetic to Tony Blair – saying that 'My view is that anybody who joined the Labour Party at the time I was leader can't be accused of being an opportunist' (Freedland 1998; BBC 1997). Foot reinforced within Labour's mythology the idea of integrity and party loyalty as essential leadership qualities while at the same time reinforcing the idea that such qualities were necessary yet not sufficient, or were even antithetical to success.

NEIL KINNOCK 1983–1992

Neil Kinnock's leadership legacy is a mixed one: his double electoral loss at the hands of Margaret Thatcher and John Major is the prism through which his leadership is judged, yet his considerable modernization efforts throughout the 1980s helped pave the way for Labour's return to power in 1997. When Kinnock became leader in 1983 the party really was a wreck, faced with its worst electoral result since 1918 (in terms of share of the vote) and torn apart by bitter infighting. Kinnock (eventually) successfully cast out the Militant Tendency – making it, I should stress, a highly personalized undertaking. He reformulated the party's more extreme policies, and kept it a serious contender for power amid the rise of the SDP–Liberal Alliance (Westlake, cited in Jeffreys 1999).

Kinnock was from a Welsh mining family, and was one of the Labour Party's most unequivocally working class leaders (Westlake, cited in Jeffreys 1999: 173–174). Initially on the left of the party, he was seen as the

natural successor to Michael Foot after Labour's 1983 election failure – full
of energy (he was 41) and oratorical skill. In his youth he was inspired by left-
wingers like Nye Bevan; but Kinnock became a pragmatist and modernizer
as leader – eventually challenging the left of the party on unilateralism,
Europe, nationalization, the closed shop and, of course, Militant (Westlake,
cited in Jeffreys 1999: 175–176). Kinnock's leadership did, however, get
off to a bad start: he was faced with a war between Margaret Thatcher and
the National Union of Mineworkers (no strike and its clashes had ever been
televised like this, and it lasted for a heartrending year from March 1984
to March 1985). Kinnock later said he 'was absolutely helpless' – strongly
sympathetic to the aims of the miners, but at the same time disagreeing with
their strategy and aware of the need for Labour to appeal to the country as a
whole. While he privately urged the miners' leader, Arthur Scargill, to ballot
NUM members, he did not say so publicly; yet he still gave the impression
that even if Scargill had he still would not have fully endorsed the miners.
The result was that while the interminable strike lasted he was perceived
as weak on the right and traitorous (and weak) on the left. It was a devas-
tating year for the mining communities, and Kinnock was himself from a
South Wales mining family. Coverage of the effects of the strike upon the
divided communities and families in real adversity and yet defeated dignity
was media gold. For the Labour Party it was a media disaster. According to
Kinnock himself, his indecision was his most regrettable mistake (Westlake,
cited in Jeffreys 1999: 179; Shipton 2014) and, personally, it must have
been agony. It is clear that this perception of Labour leadership weakness –
Foot then Kinnock – had become a fundamental resource in the rhetoric of
Labour's internal and external opponents.

Kinnock, however, excelled at public oratory – particularly at 'platform'
speaking (I put the inverted commas as there were now also television 'platform' events like the broadcast Party Conferences) – combining a distinc-
tively Welsh style of rhetoric and delivery that was full of passion, poetry,
and spontaneity. He was said to often 'arrive at a meeting and, not even
bothering with a few words on a scrap of paper … just start talking' (Drower
1984; Moon, cited in Crines and Hayton 2015). In a 1995 BBC documen-
tary, Kinnock, reflecting on his abilities, said that 'one of the main reasons I
became elected leader of the Labour Party, lies in the field of being a mobi-
lizer, an advocate, an articulator, an enthuser … in order for a body to have
life, it needs a heart and a stomach, and a backbone, as well as a brain' (Moon,
cited in Crines and Hayton 2015; BBC 1995). Kinnock offered a visceral,
emotional oratory that Moon described using the Welsh term 'hwyl' – a

musical, almost religious style of preaching that captured and spirited away its audience (Moon, cited in Crines and Hayton 2015: 128–129). The most famous example of Kinnock's 'hwyl' in action was from his 1983 Bridgend speech, ahead of the General Election and his period as Labour leader:

If Margaret Thatcher wins on Thursday,

I warn you not to be ordinary.

I warn you not to be young.

I warn you not to fall ill.

I warn you not to grow old.

(Kinnock 1983)

The repeated warnings, the spare language, the cadenced phrases, the measured pauses, the shifts in pitch – all combined in Kinnock's speech to express a haunting vision of Conservative rule (Moon, cited in Crines and Hayton 2015: 131). But she won.

Kinnock's powerful oratory was bolstered within the Labour movement by his authentic working class upbringing (the *ethos* to his *pathos*). Throughout his leadership, Kinnock outlined his vision of the party referencing his roots in poor mining communities, as well as depicting Thatcher as extreme and divisive. This meant that when Kinnock was required to challenge party orthodoxy he was able to rely on his background as a robust shield to criticisms of betrayal and hypocrisy (Moon, cited in Crines and Hayton 2015: 132–135), a fundamental leadership character trait. One of his most famous speeches was at the 1985 Party Conference where he made an impassioned call for a form of socialism that blended 'idealism' with 'realism' and delivered a stinging rebuke to Militant-led Liverpool council:

I'll tell you what happens with impossible promises. You start with far-fetched resolutions. They are then pickled into a rigid dogma, a code, and you go through the years sticking to that, out-dated, mis-placed, irrelevant to the real needs, and you end up in the grotesque chaos of a Labour council – *a Labour council* – hiring taxis to scuttle round a city handing out redundancy notices to its own workers. (*Applause*) I am telling you, no matter how entertaining, how fulfilling to short-term egos – (*Continuing applause, commotion*) – I tell you, and you listen – I'm telling you, you can't play politics with people's jobs and with people's services or with their homes. (Kinnock 1985)

Given the previous challenges Foot had faced with the Militant
Tendency and the deep rifts within the party, Kinnock faced an unen-
viable task in taking on Militant. But in this speech Kinnock sustained
his pragmatic message with a striking emotional address. His anger and
outrage – his emphasis and repetition of 'Labour council' to indicate his
disgust at the hypocrisy of Militant leaders, the evocative language of
'scuttle[ing]' politicians and 'grotesque' behaviour, and the commanding
no-nonsense line 'I tell you, and you listen' – provided an effective safe-
guard in what was undoubtedly very difficult political territory. On top
of this, Kinnock made his case for reform through an appeal to his own
humble roots and to his deep personal connection with the Labour Party
(Moon, cited in Crines and Hayton 2015: 133–135); from our perspective this is a startling example of the use of a ritual leadership moment and
the 'personalized political', the use of 'self' to doctrinal purpose:

> I say to you in complete honesty, because this is the movement that I belong
> to, that I owe this party everything I have got – not the job, not being leader
> of the Labour Party, but every life chance that I have had since the time I
> was a child: (*Applause*) the life chance of a comfortable home, with working
> parents, people who had jobs; the life chance of moving out of a pest and
> damp-infested set of rooms into a decent home, built by a Labour council
> under a Labour Government; the life chance of an education that went on
> for as long as I wanted to take it. (Kinnock 1985)

The contrast here with Blair could not be starker. Kinnock irrefutably
belonged to the movement and was at pains to take the whole party with
him on his modernizing journey, making clear that he would not jettison
the values and principles of Labour in his bid for electability, but that it
was his duty to persuade voters of the right course rather than 'dogmatise
or browbeat'. Blair, on the other hand, was seen as an outsider (ideologically 'alien' as described by Rentoul, cited in Jeffreys 1999) who dragged
a desperate party towards his vision after four electoral defeats. Kinnock
is an illustrative and unusual example of one part of the left of the party
using its leadership narrative and claims to authenticity to defeat another
part of the left, in particular by shaming it and depicting it as inauthentic.
This use of high rhetoric, however, to overcome Militant had a second-
ary effect of making Kinnock himself seem like a 'firebrand' to the wider
public; and – always a 'communications' nightmare – highlighted for the
wider public Militant's influence within the party.

One of the sad ironies of Kinnock's leadership was that the very qualities that enthused and carried respect within the party proved problematic for Labour's ability to connect with the wider electorate (Moon, cited in Crines and Hayton 2015: 135). Kinnock was undoubtedly a great speaker but, despite his efforts at appealing to a consensual politics, his fiery speeches seemed to turn off the voters that Labour needed to reach out to. Moreover, according to some, his working class Welsh roots, while endearing to the party, brought out a strain of anti-Welsh sentiment among the English which, bolstered by the tabloid press ('Welsh Windbag' etc.), hampered Labour's presentation (Moon, cited in Crines and Hayton 2015: 138). Kinnock's advisers told him that he needed to show gravitas and over time he began to 'wrap himself up in grey flannel suits and grey woollen phrases', despite Labour's pollster warning that parts of the public preferred the more jovial Kinnock (Beckett 2014). As with Foot, attempts to improve Kinnock's image seemed only to compound the problem. We have here a real dilemma in terms of left leadership persona, but also a challenge to Labour's top minds which they did not really address.

Kinnock is remembered for his electoral failures. The first defeat in 1987 was not the problem: Labour's campaign was perceived as professionally run and Kinnock recognized that given the huge defeat in 1983 he would have to play a 'two-innings match' to eventually achieve a Labour government (Westlake, cited in Jeffreys 1999: 176; Kinnock 2000). But the second defeat in 1992 was a real shock. The parallels with 2015 are clear. First, the polls in both elections predicted a Labour victory/hung Parliament which compounded the sense of failure all the more when it came. Second, Kinnock, like Miliband, expected at best a minority Labour government which raised the question of how to govern effectively. In his case, Kinnock reached out to the Liberal Democrats by inviting them to join a working party on electoral reform. This strategy backfired, alarming anti-Labour Liberal Democrats and angering anti-Liberal Democrat Labourites (Westlake, cited in Jeffreys 1999: 184–185). Third, Kinnock, like Miliband, struggled with questions of economic credibility. Kinnock (and Shadow Chancellor John Smith) proposed a 'Shadow Budget' that was then ruthlessly exploited by the Conservatives raising the alarm on Labour's 'tax bombshell' (Westlake, cited in Jeffreys 1999: 185). (Miliband's 'triple lock' in the 2015 Labour Manifesto had no such obvious political consequences, but it came to public attention very late and appeared to do little to address public concerns about Labour's spending.) Fourth, the media attacked Kinnock, like Miliband, mercilessly – *The Sun* famously splashing on Election Day the headline 'If

Kinnock wins today will the last person to leave Britain please turn out the lights' (*The Sun* 1992). While the impact the media actually had on the party's prospects is contested, particularly given it was a short campaign, it is hard to deny that this treatment had impact on the national political debate (Westlake, cited in Jeffreys 1999: 186) and on public perceptions of the Labour leader.

One of the enduring myths of Kinnock's leadership and the 1992 campaign was the electoral impact of the April Sheffield rally. The rally was a political event on a grand scale, attracting more than 10,000 Labour activists. It was like a French or American campaign rally, the like of which UK parties had no experience of. But while those who were there remarked on the strength of Kinnock's speech and the positive atmosphere in the crowd, on television the rally translated disastrously – appearing odd, triumphalist, and out of touch. In particular, Kinnock's repeated cry to the crowd 'We're alright' (or perhaps 'Well alright'), which was widely broadcast, was seen as a fundamental error by the Labour leader, appearing hubristic and unserious (Westlake, cited in Jeffreys 1999: 181). Why was this one phrase fixated on so vehemently? According to Moon, it was a 'breach' of the 'restraint' Kinnock had shown as leader under the guidance of advisors such as Peter Mandelson (Moon, cited in Crines and Hayton 2015: 137; Mandelson 2010). Kinnock subsequently explained that 'This roar hit me and for a couple of seconds I responded to it; and all of the years in which I'd attempted to build a fairly reserved, starchy persona – in a few seconds they slipped away' (Leapman 1995). While much of the blame laid upon Sheffield was hyperbolic (and typically post-election hindsight), the experience of the rally and its aftermath had a deep impact on Labour, and one that still plays its role in the party. During the 2015 campaign, Labour's much-mocked decision to engrave its pledges into stone was described by some as Miliband's 'Sheffield rally' moment (Crace 2015). What we should take away from both these trivial moments is once again in the contemporary period how untrivial the political effects of the trivial can be.

Despite not winning a General Election, Kinnock's achievements within the Labour Party were consequential – at a time where its very existence was threatened with infighting, splits, and electoral irrelevance; he pulled it back from the brink and set the stage for the New Labour years (Westlake, cited in Jeffreys 1999: 187). Nevertheless, Kinnock still struggled to connect with the public. This was perhaps most straightforwardly captured by Kinnock's (repeated) analyses of Labour's electoral failures. For example, in the wake of the 1987 result, he claimed that the British public 'voted for division' and had a 'surrender mentality' and blamed the 'portrayals of large chunks of the British press' (BBC 1987), this suggesting a somewhat dismissive stance towards the voters' choices, marking a striking difference in tone with the rhetoric of the New Labour era. It is without doubt that some of the British press had and has a quite scandalous right-wing bias, much more vicious than the left's or than the rightist press elsewhere. That, however, is just one of the conditions of performance for a left leader in the contemporary period. Kinnock's leadership raises major questions of the Labour Party's relations with the world beyond the party.

JOHN SMITH 1992–1994

John Smith's leadership of Labour was short, but his sudden death and 'arrested' leadership has played an important role in party memory (McSmith, cited in Jeffreys 1999: 193). He is perhaps the most loved leader by party activists in recent history, described by some – particularly on the left of the party (ironic, given his former reputation as a right-winger before New Labour) – as 'the greatest Prime Minister we never had' (Johnson 1995). It is worth stressing here that this notion of the 'lost' leader (Henderson, Morrison, Healey, Benn, Williams, Jenkins, David Miliband, *inter alia*) has always informed Labour thinking and mythology. This is a much less pronounced feature in Conservative mythology. There are some lost leaders (Rab Butler, Iain Macleod, perhaps Reginald Maudling, David Davis, for some), but mainly it is a question of 'great' and 'bad' leaders (the latter usually having to walk the plank).

Born in a Conservative area of western Scotland to a Labour family, Smith entered Parliament in 1970 while continuing to practise as a lawyer, becoming a QC in 1984. He was a formidable parliamentarian and gained a strong reputation in Parliament for his hard work in committees and later his abilities as a speaker. He was also seen as a pragmatist and on the right of the party, deciding with other rebels to break the Labour whip and vote in favour of the UK's place in the Common Market in 1971 (McSmith, cited in Jeffreys 1999: 194–196). In 1987, Smith took the post of Shadow Chancellor where he developed policy on Exchange Rate Mechanism membership, the minimum wage, and tax and spending. The latter proved to be a likely factor in Labour's defeat in 1992 with Smith proposing an increase in the top rate of income tax from 40 to 50p and changes to National Insurance, an overall 'direct tax' rise of 19p in 1989, locking in a controversial policy well before the election, and then refusing to compromise when other Labour voices were urging caution. Nevertheless, after the 1992 defeat and Kinnock's resignation, Smith fought off left-wing challenger Bryan Gould to become leader. For some, Smith was the 'one more heave' candidate. Irrespective of the right/left divide, modernizers such as Blair and Brown found him too cautious. During his short period of leadership he did, however, successfully replace the block vote with one-member-one-vote for General Election candidates by (barely) winning a vote at Party Conference – helping to send a positive message about Labour's willingness to confront vested interests within the party (McSmith, cited in Jeffreys 1999: 199–206).

Unlike Kinnock who sometimes changed his view on key issues, Smith was seen as a politician of utter integrity (intransigence), and as someone who disliked spin – advisers such as Mandelson who encouraged a more 'flexible' approach fell out of favour during his leadership (McSmith, cited in Jeffreys 1999: 204–205). He was an excellent rhetorician in the House of Commons, regularly using cruel wit and humour to undermine his opponents. Smith approached debate in the House of Commons in a lawyerly fashion, primarily relying on *logos* in his rhetoric – there are clear parallels with Gaitskell who Smith admired (and who in fact was impressed by Smith's oratorical abilities as a student during a visit to Glasgow in 1962 (McSmith, cited in Jeffreys 1999: 194)). Smith made little use of emotion (other than humour) and preferred instead to dissect his opponents' arguments. But this made him a mediocre speaker outside Parliament (Pettitt, cited in Crines and Hayton 2015: 151–152), raising again the growing divide between parliamentary rhetoric and media style, an issue that had informed Labour leadership for a century.

Smith adopted a more conciliatory tone than other Labour leaders (Gaitskell, Kinnock, Blair), preferring to eke out compromises than face down factions (and the infighting of the 1980s had subsided when Smith took on the leadership (Pettitt, cited in Crines and Hayton 2015: 142)). But Smith had a strained relationship with Kinnock – inadvertently showing up Kinnock with a superior parliamentary performance during the Westland affair (Pettitt, cited in Crines and Hayton 2015) – with whisperings that Smith would make an effective replacement for Kinnock *ahead* of the 1992 election (McSmith, cited in Jeffreys 1999: 201). But the general respect for Smith, which increased after his untimely death, became paradigmatic in the party; he soon became considered an effective and principled leader, and therefore a reference point for leadership style.

TONY BLAIR 1994–2007

Tony Blair is one of only three Labour leaders (along with Attlee and Wilson) to win a majority at a General Election and the only leader to win three consecutive elections. Blair's 'leadership legacy', however, is a mixed one – respected by some in the Labour Party for his successes but seen by others as fundamentally untrustworthy, even reviled, an 'ideologically-alien body-snatcher' wilfully ignorant and dismissive of the party's roots and values (Rentoul, cited in Jeffreys 1999: 208–209). In the country as a whole, his reputation was greatly diminished over his role in the Iraq war and, in fact, his reported lucrative post-prime ministerial career (which he always maintained was wildly exaggerated).

On Blair's formative political experience John Rentoul and Martin Pugh represent the two opposite poles of thought. Rentoul takes at face value Blair's claim that 'I wasn't born Labour, I became Labour'. According to Rentoul, (cited in Jeffreys 1999: 211), Blair's socialism was in part a product of his Christianity, which he picked up from his mother and developed at university. His beliefs were in line with some of the Christian socialist thinking of the early Labour leaders (even noting at one point that 'Jesus was a modernizer' – God help us). Moreover, while Blair did not participate in student politics and was never seriously involved in trade union work as a barrister, when he did join Labour after university he became a 'Labour loyalist' and his early views in the 1980s were mainstream Labour thinking (for instance, advocating public owner-ship in a 1982 speech – 'the resources required to reconstruct manufac-turing industry call for enormous state guidance and intervention'). But the 1983 election signalled a significant shift in direction. Rentoul argues that Blair was part of a strand of Labour thinking that was on the left pre-1983 (contrasting with the traditionalist Callaghan Labour right), on the soft left in the 1980s, before becoming 'modernizers' in the 1990s. Blair's shift then was dominated by a realization that in order for Labour to win it needed to change fundamentally (Rentoul, cited in Jeffreys 1999: 209–213). Pugh's account contrasts with this: he argues that, far from being influenced by his church-going mother, it was Blair's right-wing father that proved key to Blair's political early years – endowing him with an understanding of Middle England Conservatism (Pugh 2010: 389–390). For Pugh though, Blair was more or less an empty shell – he joined the Labour Party as a careerist (partly under the influence of his wife, Cherie Booth) and showed little interest in the history and internal mechanics of the party. With few ideological roots, Blair was easily influenced and impressed by political figures who he perceived to be 'winners': from Bill Clinton to Margaret Thatcher (Pugh 2010: 389–393). There is truth in both accounts, though Rentoul's seems more convincing given the copious evidence of Blair's early beliefs (and indeed as Michael Foot remarked it is hard to accuse Blair of being a careerist given that he joined while Foot was leader!). We can also say that, given the post-Callaghan decade and the myriad evolutions in British society, Blair really did represent, by 1997, where a majority of the UK 'was' in terms of beliefs and dispositions. For us, what is interesting from a leadership perspective is that both views inform perceptions of Blair. But crucial to both of course was Blair's role in transforming the party under his leadership. Indeed, his speeches presented a picture not just of a reluctant face-lift for pragmatic gain but of a deep ideological and emotional journey (a 'coming of age' story) for New Labour, a journey that, for Blair, Blair himself was destined to take his party on (Blair 2011).

In his early speeches as leader, Blair made use of his impressive oratorical skills to persuade the party of this modernizing course. Of course, after four election defeats, the party was primed for radical change – but Blair's compelling, *pathos*-heavy, quasi-religious rhetoric sealed the deal as it were. His 1996 Conference speech – the last before the 1997 General Election – illustrated his rhetorical undertaking and its connection to party narrative. Again and again, Blair coaxed his audience towards the New Labour vision of modernization, pragmatism, and centrism with a series of appeals to Labour's history and traditions. He opened with the final public words of John Smith before his death – 'A chance to serve, that is all we ask', melding the pragmatism of New Labour's commitment to becoming a party of government with a reassurance that, despite Blair's changes, he was honouring the former cherished leader's memory. He also echoed Wilson's 'white heat' speech by grounding his speech with a reference to 'an era of extraordinary, revolutionary change at work, at home, through technology, through the million marvels of modern science' (using the coming turn of the millennium to symbolize the changing Britain he wanted to lead). He spoke of the need to address Conservative-leaning aspirational voters with references to Labour's seminal 1945 and 1964 victories:

> I know in my own constituency, the miners in 1945 who voted Labour did so so that their sons would not have to go down the pit and work in the conditions that they had. (*Applause*) And in 1964 their children voted Labour because they saw the next generation's chance to go to university and do better than their parents had done.

And Blair instilled a moral duty in Labour for electoral success through pragmatism with an emotional appeal based on the desires of an elderly Labour member (classic Aristotle: *ethos*, *pathos*, and *logos*):

> And when a 76 year-old widow from Liverpool, a party member since before I was born, sends me a Christmas card that says 'Tony, please, for me, win,' then I tell you we have a duty to win, a duty for her and millions like her.

These personalizing parables of Labour morality had always existed, but took accelerated rhetorical significance in the era of celebrity politics. Most interestingly, the speech was an example of Blair marrying his personal qualities as leader with both the party's and the country's need to/ desire for change. Blair made clear that Labour must change in order to win again; but he used the same language to describe not just Labour but Britain as a whole, finishing his speech with the line 'Let us lead it to our new age of achievement and build for us, for our children, their children, a Britain – a Britain united to win in the 21st century.' Britain 'winning' was, of course, about economic not electoral success, but it is striking how Blair's language effectively identified Labour with Britain – also mirrored in his claim that being 'For all the people or for a few' was the dividing line between Labour and the Conservatives (Blair 1996); there are parallels between Blair's speech here and some of Miliband's pre-2015 election speeches – in particular the similar refrains 'for the many, not the few' and 'Britain can be better than this' (Miliband's campaign slogan).

In parenthesis, Blair's conception of leadership was distinctive for Labour – in his view, leadership was to be 'seized', not passed down over generations with 'Buggins' turn' (Blair 2011: 52). This had dramatic consequences for Labour's view and experience of leadership. Blair wanted Smith to challenge Kinnock for the leadership before 1992; after the election, he urged Brown to stand against Smith. His crucial decision to put himself forward for the leadership after Smith's death – when Brown was expected to be the next leader – sowed the seeds for the decade-long Blair–Brown rivalry, but was born of a deep inner self-belief (Blair 2011: 59–74). There is a striking parallel between Blair's move against Brown and Miliband's own decision to stand against his brother. Blair's determination, moreover, to win was matched by a fear of losing, and this is always understated as a determining factor in leadership studies; despite the polls showing an extraordinary Labour lead, the experience of 1992 clearly influenced Blair's mind-set. When victory did come in 1997, the speech marked the *emotional* climax of the New Labour strategy – 'We always said that if we had the courage to change that we could do it, and we did it.' Yet Blair was clear to reassure voters that no concealed left-wing platform would emerge once Labour was in government; he argued that they were elected as New Labour and would govern as New Labour (Blair 1997). We can see here a distinctive but effective rhetorical appropriation of emotion by the centre/centre-right ground.

Blair's early years as leader were dominated by the discourse of modernization and progress, as epitomized in his 1999 Conference speech on the 'Forces of conservatism' (BBC 1999). Blair himself represented the change he wanted to bring to Britain through his 'youth', openness, impressive television manner, and apparent ordinariness. But Blair also employed the rhetoric of 'unity' and 'one nation' – remarking, for instance, in his 1997 victory speech: 'And tonight, the people of Britain are uniting behind New Labour. They are uniting around basic British values, uniting to put the divisions of the past behind us, uniting to face the challenges of the future, uniting at long last as one nation.' Indeed, looking at his early Conference speeches, Blair referred to 'one nation' once in 1994, twice in 1997, three times in 1998, and once in 1999; after 1999 he stopped using it until 2004, where he boldly stated that 'It is New Labour that now wears the one nation mantle.' 'One nation' was not a key theme of Blair's leadership but was certainly a recurring motif from his early years. The Miliband leadership could have derived great advantage by rhetorically incorporating Blair's lyricism.

Blair's oratorical abilities were matched by adept presentational skills on both television and radio, something which had eluded many past Labour leaders. As Prime Minister, he adopted a 'presidential' style that sometimes alienated party members and members of his own Cabinet. As a result of Labour's infighting in the 1980s, Blair and his advisers were eager to have full control over the party and were distrustful of trade union leaders and other party figures who did not sign up to the New Labour vision – going so far as to prevent Ken Livingstone from running as Labour's candidate for London Mayor (Pugh 2010: 399–406), a foolish move which, given New Labour's rhetorical adeptness, they could easily have 'reconciled' and 'appropriated'. After the Labour landslide in 1997, Mandelson reportedly worried to colleagues about the newly elected Labour members, concerned that, because many had not been expected to be elected, they were unknowns and so posed a risk for Labour (Channel 4 2007a, b). Blair's style of government – with its control freakery and emphasis on a closed circle of advisers, the 24-hour media cycle, and media management over policy substance – faced regular criticism both from within and outside the party and created a real fracture between the party and the rank and file. More importantly, the idea of leadership betrayal/distance was again reasserted after the Iraq war, and this arguably as vehemently as in 1931.

While many (both within Labour and on the outside) perceived the New Labour project as a question of tactical 'triangulation' between left and right, Blair truly saw it as a distinctive 'Third Way' ideology. Blair believed that Kinnock, while a modernizer of sorts, took the wrong approach in trying to persuade the party to compromise with the electorate, as if Labour and the public were in disagreement and they needed to split the difference. For Blair, 'the voters are right and we should change not because we have to, but because we want to' (Blair 2011: 49). New Labour was, therefore, born not just of electoral desperation but of a fundamental ideological belief that the outdated dogma of Old Labour should be rejected; that public services needed reform; that welfare should be designed to support people into work; that Labour should celebrate wealth and business; that Britain's foreign policy should be outward looking; and that a number of Thatcher's liberalizing reforms in the 1980s were right (Blair 2011: chapter 3). This and its post-2010 aftermath would come back to dominate the debate in the 2010–2015 period, especially Miliband's search for an alternative, equally successful rhetorical register.

At New Labour's core was Blair's embrace of ambition and success, which marked him out as fundamentally different from his colleagues, including Brown: 'Basically, I understood aspiration. I like people who want to succeed, and admire people who do …. Did I want a nice home? Yes' [a good response]. 'Did I prefer a five-star hotel to a two-star? Yes' [a bad response]. (Blair 2011: 115). For the most part, Blair's instincts were (economically and socially) liberal, though on crime he had an authoritarian streak (developed during his time as Shadow Home Secretary) and was highly aware of how out of touch Labour was with the public on the issue: 'Except on law and order, I am by instinct a liberal' (Blair 2011: 266). This is a little-known but strong feature of social democracy which could be exploited much more effectively by the left; one thinks of Jules Moch or Pierre Joxe in the French context. Despite his middle class upbringing, Blair saw himself as having a greater affinity with Labour's working class (small c) conservative tradition than with, say, its Fabian tradition. This was reflected in his belief in the importance of community (and his corresponding commitment to law and order issues, particularly anti-social behaviour) and his attraction to his Sedgefield constituency

(Channel 4 2007a, b). Blair's politics were also shaped by his Christianity: 'in a sense' religion came before politics (Blair 2011: 79). Blair, then, seemed to hold deeply moral views (most arguably not of the traditional Labour variety, or rather the now 'received' Labour variety). This was to have momentous consequences later in his premiership.

Early in Blair's tenure, his qualities as a leader who could voice the hopes, anxieties, and sorrows of Britain were exemplified by his speech after the death of Princess Diana. His famous line 'she was the people's princess' was taken as a touching tribute at a moment of national mourning (Channel 4 2007a, b), and this several days before the Queen's tribute.

Blair's 10-year period as Prime Minister, however, was dogged by his difficult relationship with his Chancellor, Gordon Brown. In terms of our analysis, we should note that such muted antagonism had never happened before to this degree. Brown had always expected that he would take over as leader (indeed Blair saw himself as number two to Brown until he made his pitch for the leadership (Channel 4 2007a, b)). Once Labour took office, Brown increasingly began to undermine Blair by running a separate political operation from the Treasury and preventing Blair from making key decisions (e.g., over Britain's entry into the Eurozone). Unwilling to confront Brown, Blair sustained an uneasy relationship with his Chancellor, who increasingly made it clear that he wanted Blair dislodged. The parts of this that filtered out to the public laid the groundwork for changes in attitudes to Blair. In part as a result of his challenges with Brown on the domestic front, Blair became increasingly interested in foreign affairs (Channel 4 2007a). His early interventions in Kosovo and Sierra Leone bolstered his resolve on the international stage – Blair advocated a ground invasion in Kosovo to stop Milošević, a position that was later vindicated and that helped to convince Blair of the virtue and necessity of the doctrine of humanitarian interventionism (Channel 4 2007a; Blair 2011: chapter 8). As Blair's years in office continued, this strong foreign policy focus proved to be his political undoing – the aftermath of the 2001 terrorist attacks in New York led to a partnership between Blair and US President George Bush that involved conflict in Afghanistan and then Iraq. For Blair, 9/11 was a crucial turning point in his premiership – one that defined his political outlook and view of the world, and in many ways he became a different kind of Prime Minister. His decision to join with the US in invading Iraq lost him core support within the party and distanced him from former friends and colleagues, but the impression given was that he believed it was his moral duty to support the US, regardless of domestic opinion.

Ironically, in Blair's early years he was criticized for his political pragmatism and apparent ideological relativism and for his willingness to do what it took to get elected. In the aftermath of the invasion of Iraq it appeared rather that ideological stubbornness and moral righteousness were his primary weaknesses (Channel 4 2007a, b). Blair was seen on the left as a traitor (in some cases a war criminal), much as MacDonald was before him (though of course for very different reasons – indeed, MacDonald lost favour for his opposition to World War I). Blair's 2005 election victory was a hollow one, with a much weaker share of the vote and a reduced majority – mainly down to the fact that the Conservatives were still in political disarray under Michael Howard. As Blair's popularity fell, the Labour Party began to turn against him, and after an attempted coup in 2006 he was forced to confirm that he would leave before the 2007 Party Conference (Blair 2011: 619).

In his final Conference speech as Prime Minister in 2006, Blair urged his party to maintain New Labour, to reject 'comfort zone' politics, and to go on to win a fourth election victory. As ever trying to persuade his party, he drew on Labour's values to affirm the need for modernization ('We won not because we surrendered our values, but because we finally had the courage to be true to them') and ironically pointed out that many 'Old Labour' policies were now in fact more relevant to the challenges of globalization than they had been in 1997, joking 'have I become Old Labour?' Clearly scarred by the turn in public opinion since Iraq, he urged: 'The British people will, sometimes, forgive a wrong decision. They won't forgive not deciding' (Blair 2006). Unfortunately, his successor would not follow this piece of advice. The mood of party disapproval surrounding Blair's resignation would have major long-term effects. Blair was now unpopular in the party because of Iraq, not because of New Labour or the Third Way. Post-2010 it was the unpopularity that enabled the elaboration of One Nation to be a wholesale rhetorical rejection of New Labour, with all the consequences this would have and which we shall examine in the following chapters. It is also worth noting that it was by this time no longer the clashes with Gordon Brown but the Iraq issue that was pushing Blair towards the door, transforming his persona – given the high hopes of the early 1990s – into that of the ultimate demonstration of the corrupting power of leadership. It was as if an era was over. Into this twilight stepped his rival.

GORDON BROWN 2007–2010

Gordon Brown cuts a forlorn figure in Labour's roll-call of leaders and Prime Ministers, lifting UK leadership itself – or seeing it descend – to the level of the Shakespearean. A political rising star in the late 1980s and 1990s, an economic talent and a political heavyweight, Brown was on the road to the Labour leadership as John Smith took over the party in 1992. But Blair outmanoeuvred him to take the leadership after John Smith's sudden death in 1994, with an apparent deal that Brown would have unprecedented powers to lead economic policy as Chancellor and that Blair would step down and Brown would take over at some point in the future (perhaps after two terms, according to some) (Wheeler 2007). Sadly, Brown's strong reputation for economic competence and political genius began to diminish after 10 years in government; and the 3 years as Prime Minister would seriously damage his reputation, a development that tells us much about leadership performance.

Brown's 10-year tenure as Chancellor established him as one of the leading politicians of the age. After initially making some major policy announcements – in particular, granting independence to the Bank of England – Brown developed a reputation for securing economic stability after the 'boom and bust' of the Conservative years. Known as the 'Iron Chancellor' (Atkins, cited in Crines and Hayton 2015: 174), Brown kept a tight rein on spending for the first 2 years in office (Brivati 2007), before increasing investment in public services in later years (partly in an attempt to guarantee support within the party for his future leadership). His communication style relied on explaining economic policy and the use of *logos* (as a legitimation of *ethos*) and rational argument to justify decision-making. As Blair's unpopularity grew and Brown became more frustrated with Blair's unwillingness to specify when he would step down as Prime Minister, he started to broaden the content of his speeches and implicitly challenge Blair (for instance, his 2003 Conference speech finished with the line 'This Labour Party – best when we are boldest, best when we are united, best when we are Labour', was seen as a pitch for the leadership and an attack on Blair's own phrase 'best when at our boldest') (Atkins, cited in Crines and Hayton 2015: 174–177). At the same time, in private he schemed against him – deliberately delaying revealing his Budgets until the last moment and blocking Blair's decision to join the Euro (Wheeler 2007). Brown was trapped between his desire for the top job and his unwillingness to destabilize the party by dethroning its leader. Eventually, as Blair became increasingly disliked within the party over Iraq, and relations between the two (and especially their entourages) reached a low point, the Prime Minister was forced to clarify when he would resign after a plot against him in 2006, and – with no other politician daring to stand against him for the leadership (other than left-winger John McDonnell, who could not secure enough nominations for a challenge (BBC 2007)) – Brown finally was appointed to the job he craved (Wheeler 2007).

Brown took over at Number 10 promising to head up a government 'of all the talents' after accusations that he ruled with a 'Stalinist' iron fist at the Treasury (Wheeler 2007; Seldon and Lodge 2011). He lived up to this at first by promoting a number of Blairites (including Jacqui Smith as Home Secretary) and running a more open, consensual Cabinet than Blair (Channel 4 2008). Brown, however, faced a number of alarming challenges in his first few months in the job – an attempted terrorist attack, flooding, another occurrence of Foot and Mouth disease, and a run on Northern Rock, all 'real' politics, as opposed to party infighting. His adept handling of these crises won him plaudits and he secured a 'Brown bounce' in the polls – seen as a potential father figure who would transcend party politics to lead the nation (Channel 4 2008). It was not to last.

This initial popularity was short-lived, and even contributed to the depth of 'the fall'. Brown was urged by some to capitalize on the lead in the polls by calling an early election. After weeks of flirting with the possibility, Brown eventually decided against the idea (worrying in particular about the combative Conservative response at their Party Conference). In one swoop his authority was undermined, his reputation for decisiveness diminished, and his political strategy revealed as both devious and incompetent – he was, in some sections of the media, reduced to a laughing stock with, for example, Liberal Democrat Vince Cable describing him as transforming himself from Stalin to Mr Bean in a matter of weeks (Channel 4 2008; Atkins, cited in Crines and Hayton 2015: 182). Like Callaghan before him, the question of when to call an election proved to be the beginning of a period of dramatic decline. Years of one image (competent) were overtaken almost overnight by another (useless). This is an extremely good illustration of how one single act or non-act can transform leadership status.

Brown then faced a string of policy and communications disasters which fatally wounded his premiership: the loss of Her Majesty's Revenue and Customs (HMRC) data, the axing of the 10p tax rate (which Brown had introduced in 1999 as Chancellor but which returned as a major controversy), the MPs' expenses scandal, and the resignation of spin doctor

Damian McBride (Channel 4 2008; Watt and Wintour 2009; BBC 2009). Finally, the financial crisis in 2008 undermined his reputation for economic stability (although he was seen by many as providing sound leadership, particularly on the world stage, during the crisis itself) (Atkins, cited in Crines and Hayton 2015; 182). But this was a battle of rhetorics where Brown should have been demonstrating that Brown the Iron Chancellor was now the Iron Prime Minister. At the same time, Brown was criticized heavily for his poor communication style and his inability to connect or empathize with the public (Atkins, cited in Crines and Hayton 2015: 182). He tended to rely on a direct, heavy-handed approach to speech-making that involved (like Gaitskell) reeling out statistics – which compared unfavourably to Blair's dexterous, persuasive style (Theakston 2011). Brown sought to emphasize political differences with the ideologically nimble Blair with references to his 'moral compass', but the phrase was mocked as a new-found reliance on spin and superficial, amateurish media management (Theakston 2011; *The Guardian* 2009).

Brown also began to appear to lack a strategic vision. Having yearned, schemed to reach power, he seemed not to have many ideas for what to do with it (Atkins, cited in Crines and Hayton 2015: 181). He was, as we have seen with other Labour leaders, a micromanager, a poor multi-tasker, and combined indecision with rigidity (Theakston 2011: 15, 25–26). This catalogue of traits was very quickly picked up by support staff and then the wider public. While initially skilled at building a coterie of 'Brownite' loyalists, he became known for an unstable management style – including fits of temper and sulking – and lost the support of colleagues, resulting in a series of attempted coups to replace him as leader (Hughes 2010; Theakston 2011: 13, 19–20, 29). This had an untold effect upon the party's projection of unity; the same dilemma of a publicly displayed disunity was echoed in the aftermath of the 2010 and 2015 defeats.

In the 2010 General Election, Brown's attempt (Brown 2010) to portray his leadership as offering stability at a time of economic turmoil was undermined by his poor communication skills (including his infamous awkward smiles) and perhaps too by the fact that voters were tired of 13 years of Labour government, particularly one that had ended presiding over such volatile economic conditions (Atkins, cited in Crines and Hayton 2015: 183–184). Brown's failures were further compounded by the excruciating 'Gillian Duffy moment' in the election campaign, in which Brown was caught dismissing a Labour supporter's concerns about immigration as 'bigoted' and was forced to apologize, somewhat abjectly. According to media accounts, the episode highlighted that Labour was out of touch with its voters, particularly on the subject of immigration (Porter and Prince 2010). My view is that his reaction to the Duffy episode was the worst of all reactions, akin to Miliband's 'respect' for 'White Van Man' in 2014 – Labour would have done better to make a non-apologetic response. The election campaign ended in one of Labour's worst ever defeats and Brown was forced to resign after he failed to agree a potential coalition deal with the Liberal Democrats (Adonis 2013; Atkins, cited in Crines and Hayton 2015).

Drawing upon the above commentary, I would like now to look briefly at some of the key themes regarding leadership that emerge from the party's history and which have become part of the 'leadership paradigm', and which we need to take into account when appraising leadership popularity. Themes involve reluctant leadership, 'fatal flaws' of character, notions of 'responsibility' in government, hostility to leadership, a sense of being out of touch, centre/periphery tensions, Cabinet issues, communications, and leadership's relation to Conference.

NOT WANTING THE LEADERSHIP

A recurring feature of Labour leaders is a lack of interest in the top job itself, particularly in the early years of the party. Hardie had little interest in the leadership, seeing himself as more of a maverick politician; MacDonald often complained about the position; Henderson was far from willing to take over in 1931; Lansbury did not see himself in the role, but after the 1931 split and electoral wipe-out became the only obvious candidate. Later in Labour history, Foot had little desire to be leader but colleagues asked him to stand against Healey in an attempt to restore party unity. Of course, this theme is not a consistent one: many of the battles for the leadership have been distinctly ambitious and acrimonious. But it does raise the question of why so many leaders were reluctant to take the reins. For some (Hardie, Foot, Corbyn), it was in part because they were unwilling to sacrifice their outsider status – being Labour was about being radical, but leading Labour meant becoming part of the establishment; and in part because they did not really appreciate what it involved. For others (Henderson), it was in part a reluctance to take over at a time of internal conflict, where the leadership would inevitably become a lightning rod for recriminations and accusations of betrayal. But 'reluctant leadership' became part of the texture of Labour discourse.

'FATAL FLAWS' AND 'DOWNFALL'

Each of Labour's leaders has been imperilled – and often destroyed – by a so-called 'fatal flaw', even the Labour titans, MacDonald, Attlee, Wilson, and Blair. The 'fatal flaw' became a component of Labour's mythology (that is, the 'flaw' may be not be genuine but is widely perceived to be so) and reverberated down the generations – so that future leaders are shaped by the perceived errors of their predecessors. This is reminiscent of myths that inform our notion of tragedy like Hamlet (procrastination), Brutus (righteousness) and Othello (jealousy). Crudely put, the flaws can be described as follows: MacDonald was castigated for his ego; Henderson for his conservatism; Lansbury for his naïve idealism; Attlee for his timidity; Gaitskell for his belligerence; Wilson for his craftiness; Callaghan for his sanguinity; Foot for his intellectualism; Kinnock for his inconsistency; Smith for his cautiousness; Blair for his narcissism; and Brown for his obsessive nature and indecision. There is perhaps a pattern to the flaws – veering between, on the one hand, a tendency to not rock the boat, an inherent Labour conservatism (in the case of Henderson, Attlee, Wilson (in office), Callaghan, Kinnock, Smith, Brown), and on the other hand radicalism and/or over-ambition, whether on the left or the right (in the case of MacDonald, Gaitskell, Wilson (in opposition), Foot, Blair, Brown and Corbyn). Intriguingly, it is difficult to know which category to place Miliband in. I need to stress again here that these character traits were ascribed to the leader's persona. They may or may not have been true but were *perceived* as being so, and it is this that influences perceptions of leadership itself.

Some of these characteristics stood out strongly in Labour's history and shaped perceptions of future leaders' behaviours – notably MacDonald's betrayal (see below) which shaped the party's leadership for years to come and played a key role in the party's choice in 1935 of Attlee over Morrison, who was seen as too assertive a politician (Pugh 2010: 241; see also Heppell and McMeeking (cited in Crines and Hayton 2015: 44) on the impact of Gaitskell's choice of *logos* over *ethos* in his rhetoric). Wilson's political ambiguity arguably contributed to a left-wing backlash in the 1970s and early 80s; and Blair, whose radical departure from Labour traditions and presidential leadership style (Foley 2000; Sopel 1995) shaped Miliband's subsequent leadership style in the party. Character and leadership persona therefore are formative in party evolution.

Alongside these 'fatal flaws' (ambition, indecision, vanity, and the like) is the Labour tradition or myth of the political downfall – particular moments that set in motion and lead to defeat. The most celebrated moments are: Ramsay MacDonald's 'betrayal' in 1931 when he formed a National Government to deal with the economic crisis (feeling that only he could do so); Ernest Bevin's brutal critique of Lansbury's pacifism at the Labour conference in 1935 which led to the latter's resignation; Wilson's devaluation speech in 1967 which precipitated a period of long decline for his leadership; Callaghan's music hall performance in 1978 at the TUC conference where he failed to call an election, which precipitated his fall and the party's exit from power for nearly two decades; the 1992 Sheffield Rally which may have cost Neil Kinnock the election; Blair's decision to support the US in invading Iraq after 9/11; and Brown's indecision over whether to call a General Election in 2007, fundamentally weakening his political hand. Miliband's 'fatal flaws' became part of the narrative very quickly after the 2015 defeat: inexperience; lack of bold imagination; hesitation over strategic choices. The point we need to remember here is that these notions of tragic flaws and fundamental wrong choices made (and therefore 'wrong roads travelled') have become part of the 'texture' of the party narrative regarding leadership.

RESPONSIBILITY WHEN IN POWER

Like any party with a tradition of radicalism, Labour has always been confronted with an opposite political pressure to show responsibility in government. And the Labour Party from its early days was a party of discretion, duty, and allegiance to cultural norms, norms that were deeply held within much of the working class: monarchism, respect for Parliament, as well as colonialism and patriarchy. Typically the right of the party was preoccupied with a need to show that Labour was credible, responsible, and capable of being a 'natural party of government'. For MacDonald and Henderson, responsibility was paramount, necessitating Snowden's attachment to (crippling) economic orthodoxy in the first two Labour governments. Attlee, who at first respected MacDonald's approach, believed he went too far in sticking closely to Conservative policy, even before MacDonald's 'betrayal' (Jago 2014). In response to the timidity of the MacDonald era, the Attlee government was clearly far more ambitious in the scale and depth of its mission; yet it too, as the new 'natural party of Government' (Patrick Gordon Walker MP wrote in his diary at the time that he believed 'we're going to be in for 20 years of power ahead of us' (Pugh 2010: 290)) stuck to economic convention by trying to postpone devaluation and attempting little constitutional experimentation (Pugh 2010: 288–294). Similarly, the Wilson government, despite high hopes, also stuck to convention by trying to delay devaluation, and took harsh short-term economic measures to address the balance of payments deficit, claiming 'No responsible Government could have acted otherwise' (Wilson 1968). The New Labour years of course were also dominated by the notion of restoring economic credibility and providing responsible government to reassure swing voters – Brown famously promised 'prudence with a purpose' (Elliott and White 1998). 'Responsibility' thereby became a rhetorical expectation, and accusations of its opposite a major rhetorical device for and against leadership.

CIRCUMSCRIBING THE LEADER'S POWER

Labour leaders have always had to engage with other sources of power in the Labour Party, from the NEC to the trade unions, although the relationship between these bodies has changed substantially over time. As a party of the centre left, as we have seen, Labour has always felt uncomfortable with the idea of the leader having too much power, in case leadership descended into authoritarianism and (by definition) then took the wrong road. At the same time, Labour's Prime Ministers – notably MacDonald, Attlee and Blair – showed a tendency for distancing themselves from the party once taking office. Each of these features fuelled the party's hostility to leadership, and the sense that almost by definition leadership *means* betrayal of principles. So the scepticism about leadership has philosophical and logical, but also 'traditional' and mythological reasons for its attitude to and misunderstandings of leadership.

MacDonald very early on developed a personalized style of leadership that ignored many of the party rules – for instance, choosing his Cabinet independently of the National Executive in his first administration (Jago 2014). The troubling years of MacDonald's rule – and its shocking denouement in 1931 – created a deep-seated fear of presidentialism and authoritarianism within the Labour ranks. In the 1930s in response, the General Council took virtual control of the party, with trade unionist Ernest Bevin playing a central role (Weiler 1993: 70). Later, Gaitskell's revisionist efforts repeatedly clashed with the wider party – with his attempts to reform Clause IV encountering widespread hostility among trade unionists, forcing the plans to be watered down (Jones 1996: 54–55). In the 1970s, the NEC swung leftwards (in part as a result of reaction to the *In Place of Strife* White Paper); and the *Labour Programme 1973*, agreed by Party Conference, pushed Labour to the left despite Wilson's misgivings about some of the proposals, not all of which made it into the 1974 Manifesto (Thorpe 2008: 188–190). The central issue for our argument here is that leadership itself becomes an element in and even a danger to party trust and cohesiveness. Miliband would pick up on this but to debateable effect and success, particularly given the growing opaqueness of One Nation, so that by 2013, the right in the party considered him too leftist and the trade unions too rightist, and this in large part because his narrative had become incoherent.

After Labour's defeat in 1979, the left – frustrated by the Wilson–Callaghan governments and energized by the claims to leadership of Tony Benn – began to further circumscribe the leadership and the PLP in the name of party democracy, securing changes to party policy, re-selection rules, and the way the leadership contest itself was conducted (Jeffreys 1993: 108–110). After the 1983 defeat, Kinnock attempted to take back control of the party through a series of organizational reforms that centralized power – from setting up a Campaign Strategy Committee to decide on campaigns and the media (which helped to marginalize the NEC) to transferring power on Labour selections from Constituency Labour Parties (CLPs) to party headquarters (Allan 1993). Smith continued with the party reforms by finally managing to pass One Member One Vote (OMOV) for candidate selection at the Party Conference in 1993 (Pugh 2010: 386). Blair made further changes to the party, putting greater control over policy into the hands of the leadership (Buller and Toby 2011). He put more power in the hands of members in order to prevent left-wing activists blocking reforms – such as his decision to ballot members on the change to Clause IV (Seyd 1999). This meant that there was less confrontation between the NEC and the leadership in the New Labour years, and the Labour Party Conference – such a source of conflict and often discomfort for Labour in the past – became a far tamer affair (Assinder 2007). The overall effect was to allow party leaderships to develop a kind of leadership 'elegance' unencumbered by calls to order, the counter to this being that calls to order of the leadership by, say, union leaders would appear more startling than before. The effect of these developments, coinciding with the rise of the 'celebrity culture' (see Chapter 4), was (a) to bring party leaders to the very forefront of media attention and (b) to create a well of feeling (or at least a rhetorical resource) throughout all the component parts of the party that the centre (leadership) was draining the periphery of its powers and vitality, and using the wider membership to do so – one of the greatest ironies of these developments being the Corbyn 'insurgency' of 2015.

Being 'In or Out of Touch'

Perhaps Labour's greatest challenge throughout its history has been its mission to 'speak for Britain' and not merely a part of it. Throughout its history it has been the institution most representative of the values and norms of the 'people of Britain'; at clear moments – most strikingly post-1945, but also the mid-1960s (where England's football victory in 1966 was well timed with Labour's) and the late 1990s – it often succeeded in being in tune with, almost embodying, national sentiment. However, it often fell short, being drawn back to more partisan concerns and a more 'purist' narrative. This connection/disconnection has been a feature of the party and its leadership from the beginning; it raises the question of course 'in touch with what?' the grassroots or the nation, and in what ways these are or are not the same, and if so (or not) how party discourse should deal with this. The leader has also played a major role in embodying, or not, a national moment. Attlee did not embody the 1945 spirit (Labour won despite not because of his leadership (Pugh 2010: 289–290)), but Wilson's provincial, lower middle class background captured the meritocratic spirit of the age, as did Blair's modern style in the 1990s. It has to be noted, however, that with an infinitely more difficult claim to embracing the whole nation, the Conservative Party has been significantly more politically successful at it over the last century or so. If this is so, when the Labour Party claims to represent the vast majority of the nation, it is demonstrably not. The role of narrative and leadership for both parties is central to this twentieth and twenty-first century 'settlement'.

Some Labour leaders – both in manner and ideology – have often been strangely out of touch (Denver and Garnett 2012). Lansbury's pacifism was clearly discursively inadequate to a left electorate as fascism and fear of it grew through the 1930s; Callaghan's conservatism was somewhat old-fashioned in the 1970s (and was overtaken by a 'radical conservatism' in Thatcher who – ironically and tellingly – was even more old fashioned); Foot's eccentric style and left-wing beliefs (particularly on unilateral disarmament) felt out of place in the Cold War 1980s (in spite of Greenham Common), particularly as Thatcherism began to take its grip and international relations were often expressed in highly personalized 'summitry'. Even Premier Brown, with his awkward communication style, was seen as a leader from a different age: 'it is clear that Brown would have been more comfortable in an age when Prime Ministers didn't make embarrassing forays onto YouTube, but were judged on their speeches and treated with deference on the rare occasions they permitted themselves to be interviewed' (Massie 2009).

LOCALISM

The Blue Labour narrative of the 2010s illustrated Labour's confused relation with localism and tried to revive its pre-World War II commitment to local associations, mutualism, and movement politics (Beech and Page 2014). Pugh's account of Labour's early years indicates the importance of local efforts in developing the party infrastructure, building ties with working class communities, and edging closer to power. Initial attempts to win seats relied on choosing messages and approaches that were appropriate in local political contexts (often in the context of the party's crucial relationship to the Liberals) – for instance by allying with workingmen's clubs in order to find a way into working class communities (Pugh 2010: 74) – though it has to be said these efforts were complicated by Nonconformist views on temperance and respectability that distanced party members (including Hardie) from potential working class voters. It also has been almost written out of history that the Liberals themselves were often very good at this local aspect of politics and at creating local loyalties. Party leaders recognized the importance of municipal elections in testing the party's ability to govern. In the 1920s, for instance, the leading organizer and party figure, Herbert Morrison, Secretary of the London Labour Party (and leader of the LCC 1934–1940), developed a thriving civic infrastructure for Labour members, including ward parties, dances, choirs, fairs, festivals, sports and drama associations, and a legal advice bureau. The trade union movement was a bedrock for local CLPs, providing both members and subsidies (Pugh 2010: 134–144). Indeed, the first set of Labour leaders were well versed in these local efforts – from Lansbury's experience with Poplarism to Attlee's local campaigning in Stepney and Henderson's promotion of door-to-door canvassing (Pugh 2010: 134, 144). The Blue Labour advocates of the 2010s would see these as the golden years before 1945, until 'statism' imposed itself, and this to the extent that, rhetorically, 1945 was often seen as the deviation, the wrong road chosen, with all the rhetorical implications this had. In parenthesis, it is worth noting that this dualism never went away, and in the mid-2010s the really successful leaders were not the national ones but the local ones, such as Labour council leaders and mayors in Manchester, Newcastle, Leeds, Birmingham, Sheffield, Leicester, Hackney, and Newham (*The Guardian*, 26 August 2015).

Post-1945 Labour became dominated by a philosophy of state centralizing: 'although four in ten Labour members had local government experience they allowed the [Attlee] government to remove control over hospitals, gas and electricity from elected councils, and require all their loans to be approved by the Treasury' (Pugh 2010: 289). Indeed, Tristram Hunt argued that the state-centred approach became rooted much earlier, in 1918 when the party signed up to Clause IV. Wilson's vision of state central planning further distanced Labour from its earlier local roots (although he did support devolution). And while the New Labour years were committed to some decentralizing reforms – such as elected mayors, Scottish and Welsh devolution and, of course, the Good Friday Agreement – the infighting and 'loony Labour' council fiascos of the 1980s made Labour leaders suspicious of giving power to local authorities. The rhetoric – Blair's claim that 'the era of big, centralizing government is over' – was not really true, as was evidenced by the introduction of a series of prime ministerial units to direct and control policies from Downing Street (Smith et al. 2013). Both doctrinally and rhetorically this centre/periphery tension would become and remain one of the dominant strains within Labour discourse, particularly after the 2010 and 2015 defeats.

Leading the Cabinet/Shadow Cabinet

Labour leaders have taken markedly different approaches to managing their Cabinets or Shadow Cabinets. On the one hand, there have been the consensual, open leaders – epitomized by Attlee's management of his Cabinet, searching for compromise between his heavyweight ministers (while at times taking risks and playing the leader, for instance deciding Britain should build an atomic bomb without the whole Cabinet knowing) (Pearce, cited in Jeffreys 1999: 91–93); as well as Callaghan's calm yet commanding premiership (Morgan, cited in Jeffreys 1999: 145). On the other hand, there have been the closed, controlling types – most obviously MacDonald, who patronized his Cabinet, failed to manage or delegate, and overloaded himself by taking the role of Foreign Secretary as well as Prime Minister in his first government (Wrigley, cited in Jeffreys 1999: 30); Wilson, with his isolated 'kitchen cabinet' and conspiracy theorizing; and Blair, whose 'sofa government', and his highly active and effective use of his Director of Communications, Alastair Campbell and others, met accusations of control freakery (Oborne and Walters 2004; Campbell 2008).

At the same time, leaders have often had tortuous relationships with other senior figures (typically deputies or Chancellors/Shadow Chancellors) that have cut across the open/closed style of Cabinets complicating leadership still further. MacDonald's crucial relationship with Henderson crumbled during the second Labour government as MacDonald grew suspicious of Henderson and they parted over the 1931 crisis; Attlee and Morrison were enemies, and Attlee reportedly stayed on as leader until 1955 to deliberately prevent Morrison from succeeding him (Pugh 2010: 309); Wilson and Callaghan's relationship was a difficult one, particularly after Callaghan opposed Wilson and Castle's *In Place of Strife* reforms (McKie 2005); and Blair and Brown's relationship while close at first deteriorated into a kind of muted power struggle and undignified tussle, as Brown increasingly urged Blair to step down so that he could replace him. Crucially, the nature of the relationships between the 'two at the top' share core similarities: typically a begrudging recognition of respect; competition of an 'alpha-male' kind, and a sense of threat; and a slight, though usually not pronounced, ideological divide. The crucial point here is that all these clashes have always been overtly personalized. Miliband's image in the 2010–2015 period suffered from the *absence* of these elements; although he had a 'team', because of the nature and unexpectedness of his election, he was an isolated figure. He had no 'career rival', apart from a kind of ghostly presence of his absent brother. This suggests that perhaps an adversarial duo may in fact be beneficial to a leader. Miliband's possible notional adversary, Ed Balls, could not fill this role for a range of reasons which in fact had significant effects upon Miliband's own leadership. Ed Balls went through to round three of the 2010 leadership context, but even then gained only 16 % of the vote – the two brothers took the rest of the vote, with in fact 'nothing' between them. In that round, David was ahead of Ed by 1½%. After his election, Miliband snubbed Balls in October 2010 by appointing Alan Johnson as Shadow Chancellor. When Balls did become Shadow Chancellor three months later, the party memory of the scale of the Blair/Brown antagonism precluded *any* rivalry. They simply ignored each other, which was, if not even worse, then a bizarre display of the leadership duo. However – and this seriously undermined Miliband's image and style – Balls' attitude constricted the scope and effect of Miliband's One Nation rhetoric. Ed Balls' own economic agenda almost silenced Miliband's economic narrative and Balls' 'unvoiced voice' became a kind of 'No we're not' to a raft of initiatives with economic implications from Shadow Ministers and from Miliband himself. And, crucially, as we will show, Balls did not embrace the One Nation narrative at all, severely limiting its rhetorical resonance. It was questionable too, even at the time, whether either Miliband or Balls either respected or feared the other; and given that Miliband had not been supported by most MPs in 2010 his 'legitimacy' as leader was fragile. I shall return to this in the Conclusion.

Changing Communication Techniques

Apart from three notable exceptions, Labour leaders have tended to struggle to adapt to new developments in communication, and the party has always, always, always had a troubled relationship with the media. We can divide the party's leaders into two groups: those who successfully harnessed the changing media's power to communicate with the wider public (Lansbury initially (a founder of the *Daily Herald*), Wilson, and Blair) and those who were suspicious of it, often seeking refuge in more traditional communication methods (Attlee, Foot, Brown). Labour's leadership 'communication' became an issue and has remained so since the 1920s (Toye 2011). Early Labour relied heavily on platform speaking, which would soon have limited reach (Pugh 2010: 143–144), and the sound quality of MacDonald's speeches compared poorly to Baldwin's 'fireside manner' via the wireless, although MacDonald did 'catch up' with modern methods (Morgan 2006: 102). (For a video clip of MacDonald see MacDonald 1931.) Labour also faced heavy opposition from the Conservative-leaning media. This was exemplified most famously in the Zinoviev letter affair, which helped Labour to lose the 1924 election by alarming voters that Labour might have Communist tendencies – this was badly handled by MacDonald, who hesitated before responding to the claims. Beatrice Webb described MacDonald's response as 'shifty and bungling management' (Wrigley, cited in Jeffreys 1999: 31). And this bias has remained ever since, apart from the New Labour period. In the 1930s, BBC newsreels were pro-National Government. This was countered somewhat by the left-leaning *Daily Mirror*, whose support helped Labour reach out to a large swathe of working class voters (Pugh 2010: 241–243). But Attlee hated the media (Pearce, cited in Jeffreys 1999: 94), and was an awkward interviewee. In one television interview in 1950, Attlee was asked if he had anything he wished to say on the eve of the election campaign. Attlee replied 'No' and after an awkward pause that was the end of the interview! Labour lost (quoted in Brivati 1997:189; originally in Blumer et al. (1996)). Gaitskell was more ambitious, 'pioneering the use of party political broadcasts' (Stuart 2013), but he struggled against Macmillan who outshone him 'as a lighthouse does a glow-worm' (Heppell and McMeeking, cited in Crines and Hayton 2015: 45; quoting *The Sunday Express*, 10 September 1958). Wilson, on the other hand, was one of the first politicians to truly master the art of television performances, and proved excellent too with an autocue (*The Guardian* 2000). Callaghan was also a decent media performer, but was outclassed by the Thatcher machine and perhaps the changing times (Brivati 1997: 189). Both Foot and Kinnock struggled with the media; even though they were revered as platform speakers, they were torn apart in the press, in particular through their caricatural depiction in cartoons (as was Miliband). Blair became a true master of the television performance and media management, in particular the 'soundbite', though his successor Brown struggled on camera (saying 'struggled' is generous). (He was famously criticized by the MP and former minister Hazel Blears for his use of YouTube to communicate to the public (Brown 2009; Helm and Hinsliff 2009)). We shall come on to Miliband's relationship with the media in Chapter 4.

LEADERSHIP AND CONFERENCE

The importance of the annual Party Conference has been transformed dramatically over Labour's history (we could say it became less dramatic). In earlier generations, Conference was a site of bitter political infighting – where Bevin tore apart Lansbury in 1935, Gaitskell made his 'fight and fight and fight again' speech in 1960, and where Kinnock took on Militant in 1985 (Minkin 1980). But after the modernization of the party organization in the 1980s and 1990s, Conference became a space for the leader to set out his vision without any risk of heckling or challenge (Pettitt 2012). While in the past conferences were memorable, more often than not for policy arguments and doctrinal debate as well as rows, in later years they stood out for their set piece speeches such as Blair's 'forces of Conservatism' speech in 1999 (Assinder 2007), or Brown's 'no time for a novice' speech in 2008 (plus of course Miliband's 'One Nation Labour' speech in 2012). Corbyn's leadership challenged the prevailing *doxa*.

CONCLUSION

I want to summarize the discussion by looking, essentially, at how Labour leaders have affected leadership, how it has been 'practised', how it has been perceived, and what the consequences have been. What I want to demonstrate is that, to paraphrase Durkheim on contract, all that is in leadership is not leadership-specific; that there is a whole series of barely perceived but major effects informing Labour leadership that have accumulated as it were over the century and which 'shape' and form the parameters of leadership itself, well beyond the defined 'powers' of party or prime ministerial leadership; that Labour leadership is not just an 'office' and a 'function' but is also a dynamic *process* shaped by the comportment (and achievements, mistakes, and failings) of the office-holders, and the ways in which it has been exercised, has entered the 'imaginaire' of the party, and affects it profoundly.

I can make three points. First, the behaviour, success, mistakes, and misperceptions of all the leaders have created the idea (in spite of the left's rudimentary sense of leadership itself) that there are 'good', 'great', 'poor', and 'nefarious' leaders. In this the Labour Party echoes mythologies about leaders and leadership which inform our society and culture more generally. And like Shakespearian characters they rise and fall on Fortune's Wheel, but do so also because of their own flaws or qualities. If we look at the way in which, say, MacDonald, Gaitskell, Wilson, Foot, Kinnock, Blair, and Miliband are represented in the party imagination, there is, as if underlying 'normal' attitudes to leftist political leadership, a fashioning mythology related to archaic 'great men' theories. Even Jeremy Corbyn's insistence during the 2015 leadership election that his campaign was 'not about personalities' betrayed a deep, almost ancestral fear of tyranny as well as a disdain for contemporary concepts around 'celebrity culture'. And as celebrity politics increases, anti-celebrity politics becomes a growing rhetorical resource.

Second, this question of the relationship of the party to the wider culture has always had a major influence upon leadership (Heffernan 2005). MacDonald's sense of 'government responsibility' (which in his case restricted his action) has always been a major caution, even an impediment for Labour leadership, catching it in the dual dilemma of the party's shifting relationship to its electorate (itself shifting), and to both 'establishment' and culturally strong notions of patriotism and duty. Regarding the establishment's cultural sway, a fascinating piece of research would be how every leader from Hardie to Corbyn dressed, why they dressed so, and what the political consequences were. It lies outside the parameters of this study, but it would be fruitful to reflect upon the social and cultural as well as the political and economic conditions underpinning/facilitating the two boldest and most consequential administrations, Attlee's and Blair's; and relatedly why – in spite of a highly active left in the party and a discourse that is often radical lyrically – 'radical left' leadership has never gained traction beyond the party, even in government; hence much of the frustration of many MPs with Corbyn's victory in 2015. How ironic it is that the leader who presided over the party's most radical administration was Clement Attlee. (Reader, for those of you who – like me – did not know, the serving of port goes clockwise so our right hand is free to draw our sabres should the need arise. You could not make this up.)

Third, and this is a related point, one of the 'constraints' on leadership *style* (as well as upon policies and actions) is, as I have stated, the idea of 'responsibility'; another of great import is the idea of 'proximity', being 'in touch' – with the membership, the electorate and the times. This of course has often not been the case, and we have seen that being out of touch has often been seen as a cause of leader/party misfortune: MacDonald, Lansbury, Attlee at times, Callaghan (1978–1979), Foot always, and Team Miliband (being unable to find someone on the minimum wage to interview (*The Independent*, 4 August 2015)). All these are seen as having very negative consequences. Blair, both as party leader and as Prime Minister, was by far the most successful at being in touch with the wider public (Finlayson 2002) and 'the times' (although 'Cool Britannia' was of doubtful virtue). And the question of PR and 'communications' has, arguably since Wilson, come to dominate the projection of the leader beyond the party; and since Kinnock, the use of Conference to project the notion of the party united behind its leader, and a coherent leadership 'team'. What our analysis demonstrates in Chapters 3, 4, and 5 is how little this is really understood by the party.

This question of 'proximity' and being in touch has an echo inside the party related to the tension since the party's beginning up until today of the centre/periphery issue, the party leadership versus the 'grassroots'. Over the last few years this has taken the form of the 'Westminster Bubble' versus the party in the country and the latter's greater proximity to the 'real' and the 'truth' (perhaps not in Liverpool under Derek Hatton's (deputy) leadership or in Scotland...). This has been compounded by the fact that so many MPs are often Oxbridge graduates with a policy advisor or similar background, and so are vulnerable to the charge of never having worked in the 'real world' (wherever that is). The embourgeoisement of the party's elite has actually been going on since the 1930s, but has become a major rhetorical resource *against* the leadership, who – particularly in Ed Miliband's case as we shall demonstrate – found difficulty in turning this to any rhetorical advantage. Jeremy Corbyn's 2015 leadership campaign was organized around the notion, the rhetoric, and the powerful mythology of giving the party back to its membership.

CHAPTER 3

The Arc of Rhetoric and the Leader as Author

In May 2010 the Labour Party suffered a historic defeat at the General Election; historic in that the party's share of the poll (29%) was its lowest since 1918, historic in that the fall from power occurred after thirteen continuous years in government.[1] This dual quality of Labour's defeat would have effects on the fortunes and development of the party in the years after 2010 in two crucial respects. First, because the Labour government/leadership of Gordon Brown was seen as one of the major causes of the defeat there was no question that Brown, as had traditionally been the case in British politics in the nineteenth and twentieth centuries – from Gladstone and Disraeli to Wilson and Heath – might move to the Opposition benches as leader. Brown's fall from power was like a fall from grace. This in itself is an indication of how leadership has become a central focus: in politics now as in business, as in football management (perhaps less so in banking...) defeat does not allow the leader to fall back and regroup; falling on their sword is perceived as the only option. This is a little-commented illustration of how the leader has come to 'embody' the party, for better and worse.

The election of a new leader saw a process of Labour Party hustings throughout the summer of 2010 and campaigning and media coverage up until the election of the party's leader on 25 September 2010. The outcome was unexpected. These two factors, the 'fall' of Brown, in an almost

---

[1] An earlier shorter version of this chapter was published in Gaffney and Lahel (2013).

© The Author(s) 2017
J. Gaffney, *Leadership and the Labour Party*, Palgrave Studies
in Political Leadership, DOI 10.1057/978-1-137-50498-2_3

Shakespeare tragedy way, and the unexpected election of Ed Miliband, the younger brother of the long-assumed heir to Brown, David Miliband, constituted two formative conditions of the party's post-2010 development. Another formative effect of such a comprehensive defeat was that a space was opened up for a new narrative appropriate to the scale of the defeat, to the party's search for a new voice, and to the new leadership. The way that 'narrative space' was filled would have dramatic consequences later on.

Just as the leader could not simply move across horizontally, as it were, undramatically to the Opposition benches, because of the depth of the vertical fall, so could the language of the party not simply move across. This was, in part, functional: new leaders need new language in order to be what they are, new. More importantly, however, in this case, was that down with the Brown ship seemed to go the whole of the New Labour narrative, its vision, along with the discursive effects of some of its consequences: the Iraq war catastrophe, the fall-out from the financial crisis of 2008 (its non-anticipation of, its even being an accessory to, its – according to the constant referring by the now Chancellor George Osborne – not having 'mended the roof while the sun was shining'). We should add that by 2010, electorally as well as discursively, New Labour had no rallying quality, no traction either inside the party or with the wider public; but 'Old Labour' too was precluded. A new narrative alongside the new leadership was therefore an imperative. This perfectly natural development in political party renewal had, however, a highly problematic series of issues affecting it. We can identify the two central ones here; the first relates to party narrative, the second to party leadership.

How to Tell a Story

As regards a party narrative, the problem was also an opportunity. Because of the scale of the defeat, the length of tenure of office, and the Genesis-like 'fall' of Gordon Brown, the process of reconstruction would need to be extensive. The problem was which narrative to build, because narratives are related to ideology, culture, people, and memory. It would also have to dominate alternatives and be 'appropriate' to leadership. Ed Miliband had a certain amount of leeway to develop his own vision and narrative, and his own personal relationship with the narrative or narratives that would emerge; but again the question was which, and what the consequences of choice would be for his leadership image and for the party.

Party narrative's relationship to leadership raises the question of authorship. This issue has always presented challenges for left ideologies (socialist, social democrat, and republican), and the Labour Party is no exception; this is because these ideologies posit an impersonalism: the historical legitimacy of the 'movement's' discourse and ideology bears down upon any personalist claims. A complicating factor, of course, is that in the contemporary period, the focus upon leadership has become central to politics in the UK, especially since the dramatic personalization of politics by Margaret Thatcher from the 1970s onwards. The left generally copes with the issue of leadership and authorship by ensuring that the leader 'gives voice' (quite literally) to versions of the party's narrative, while allowing for the 'character' of the leader to inform the party's narrative through 'performance' (see Chapter 4). Ideologically, however, the issue is never squarely addressed. This in turn raises the question of what should be the relationship between narrative and leadership. It has always been the case that leaders have 'styles' which have greater or fewer consequential effects: Attlee's shy manner and dress code, Gaitskell's erudition, Wilson's idiosyncratic speech and so on. Blair managed this 'interpolation of self' extremely successfully, Brown much less so. And this was Miliband's challenge after 2010. One way of responding to this performative exigency, both for the leadership and the party, was to draw upon aspects of the party's personalized historical rhetoric (Gaffney 2016). Both party and leader can – and do – 'personalize' by drawing upon the 'ancestral gods'[2] such as Keir Hardie, R.H.Tawney, Jennie Lee, Richard Crossman, or Tony Crosland. One disadvantage of this referencing is that it directs attention away from the leader to the ancestor (say from Neil Kinnock to Nye Bevan); another is that it has divisive potential in that these figures often personify competing ideologies or cultures within the party; a third, that referring to them celebrates the past rather than what is to come. Party narratives in all political parties have either to dominate or reconcile, or do the former in the guise of the latter. Contemporary leadership seeks to rally all party opinion behind it. How the party and the leadership would deal with these challenges and constraints would be crucial; and how they then performed narratives 'outwards' towards the public would be even more so.

Two final points on the post-2010 Labour Party narrative/s. First, social-democratic parties have a strongly practical rhetoric as well as a more lyrical one (they need sound policies because they exercise government).

[2] Conversation with John Newbigen, former speechwriter for Neil Kinnock, May 14, 2013.

In the aftermath of 2010, however, the party needed to explore and emphasize the lyrical, not only for practical reasons (5 years till the next General Election) but for symbolic ones: it needed to find and develop a new narrative/ideology in order to (a) bind the party together (and rhetorically the Labour Party is highly 'emotional', sentimental even) and give it new life, and (b) give itself and the new leadership a rhetoric that would engage with the public, redefine Labour's values (or rhetorically present a redefinition), and help enhance the new leadership's image. Second, within the political discourse of the left there are a limited number of places the party narrative can go. Several researchers have shown the uses of the past in Labour discourse (e.g., Blair's references to the past for the purposes of modernization).[3] For a post-2010 Labour narrative, therefore, the three essential Aristotelian elements pertain: how the elements of the narrative are arranged, that is, the architecture of the narrative (in part, its *logos*); the lyricism and emotional register of the party's discourse (*pathos*); and how authorship and performance (*ethos*) of the narrative is organised *vis-à-vis* party 'memory' – for it must be dual, both party and leadership must share authorial voice, given our point above about the narrative conditions of 'giving voice'.

Let me identify and analyse the Labour Party's emerging narratives from 2010 (and the antecedents they implied): The Policy Review, Blue Labour, One Nation Labour, other 'narratives', voices, and intellectual input, Rutherford, Cruddas, Stears and others; and Miliband's own; and the emerging 'voice' from all of these and its interactions with activists/members, and other contributing thinkers (e.g., Sandel, Graf, Blond (Blond 2010)), and its coalescence into a narrative designed to fashion policy, mobilize the party and the public, and enhance leadership. I will use a corpus of the main texts.[4] Their provenance and development and

---

[3] I owe this insight to Mark Wickham-Jones (2013). See also Robinson (2013) and Wickham-Jones (2013a).

[4] For clarity I shall list the texts here. The references for our corpus, in chronological order, are: *Labour's future* (2010). See Rutherford and Lockey (2010) in Bibliography; BBC Radio 4 Analysis (March 21, 2011). *'Blue Labour'*, transcript. Available at http://news.bbc.co.uk/nol/shared/spl/hi/programmes/analysis/transcripts/21_03_11.txt; Glasman (2011); Labour Party (2011a); Glasman et al. (2011); Philpot (2011); Cruddas (2012b); Miliband (2012); Cooke, G., & Muir, R. (eds). (2012). *The Relational State*, IPPR; Miliband (2013a, b); *One Nation Labour – Debating the Future*. LabourList.org; Cruddas, J. (2013c). *Speech to IPPR on 'The condition of Britain'*. Available at http://www.ippr.org/press-releases/111/10331/jon-cruddas-mp-speech-on-the-condition-of-britain. An account of the origins, ideas, and personal relationships underpinning Blue Labour can be found in Davis (2011).

the way that they fed into one another from 2010 onwards were central to the elaboration of the One Nation narrative that, it was intended, would be carried forward towards the 2015 General Election by both the party and the leadership, and then into the election as a rhetoric of triumph. We know this did not happen, for reasons that will be explored in Chapters 5 and 6.

Generally, political narratives have two aspects with separate though related functions. That is to say, there are two aspects to the same discourse: (a) what is proposed, and (b) what is mediated/implied/pointed to. For the purposes of analysis, one can imagine these as 'practical' and 'symbolic'. I am concerned principally here with the latter. And we can see that the tension in the narrative/s that occupy discursive space from 2010 is between these two aspects. What I shall demonstrate is how the latter imposed itself in the period 2010–2013, and what the function of this was in terms of the party and the party leadership. A further finding is that, contrary to received opinion that sees the symbolic as the necessary accompaniment to or emotional legitimation of the 'real', here is an illustration of how the 'practical' itself was rhetorically used to legitimate the symbolic politics of the One Nation narrative in the post-2010 period, as the more lyrical/symbolic imposed itself and altered the nature of the Labour Party, certainly for the first 3 years. After its elements came together and it was 'launched', it then began to falter.

STORY AND PLOT

In Labour Party discourse in the recent period – as is now the case generally in discussions that range from scientific theory to chat shows – the expressions 'narrative' and 'story' abound. In fact, they are used somewhat loosely. In order to grasp the significance of One Nation Labour, let us define our terms and turn to narrative theory (where, it has to be said, the terms are also sometimes used somewhat loosely). I shall use (and doubtless abuse) some of the ideas from narrative theory in order to identify and analyse Labour's post-2010 narrative. I draw my model from the Russian Formalists (Lemon and Rees 1965; McQuillan 2000; Propp 1968), and make the distinction in narrative between story and plot; that is to say that to be a good story, the story told must have or 'tell' a plot. Plot often means different things in narratology, but for the purposes of analysis here we shall take plot to mean, not only the structure of the story, but also the structure the story tells. Successful stories reflect an underlying organization of ideas. In the fairy or folk tale, fable, romance, adventure story, and so on, a series of underlying requirements inform the story. The doctrinal discourse of a political party is no different. A narrative has a story and a plot, and these are not the same thing. The former is what happens (the Greeks built a wooden horse and entered Troy and recaptured Helen/the Labour Party reached power under the leadership of Ramsay MacDonald in 1924), the latter, its significance (if you use stealth and cunning and your enemy is foolish you will triumph/arrogant leadership will lead a great movement astray). We shall look at the emerging narrative in the Labour Party as if it were a story (with a plot), will examine the morphology of the story (its shape), and its function in terms of the party and leadership. In my accounting for the development of the Policy Review and all the other elements of the narrative, and the elaboration of One Nation, we shall focus on a range of texts. But the essential element to note is that the development of the Review, of Blue Labour, and then the elaboration of One Nation saw the party's discursive space, its ideology, revitalized with a new and consequential narrative that, paradoxically, through a return to its 'roots' would alter the party's identity and inflect considerably the party's leadership by offering Miliband a new leadership 'voice'.

At the beginning of 2009, Gordon Brown was the subject of a leadership crisis in which six Cabinet members resigned/were sacked (Home Secretary, Jacqui Smith; Communities Secretary, Hazel Blears; Work and Pensions Secretary, James Purnell; Defence Secretary, John Hutton; Minister for Housing, Margaret Beckett; and Europe Minister, Caroline Flint). Of the high profile resignations, James Purnell's was the most politically damaging for the status and authority of Brown. The former Blairite initiated a personal attack upon Brown's leadership and called for him to stand down as Prime Minister. In July 2009, Purnell launched Open Left, a 3 year project with the cross-party think tank Demos. The premise of Open Left was to 'rediscover the Left's idealism, pluralism and appetite for radical ideas' (Demos 2010). So the 'plot' there would be the idea of 'loss' or 'having lost the way'. The project organized seminars and published the outcomes of these seminars in e-books, for example, *We mean power: ideas for the future of the left* (Demos 2010). In May 2010, Open Left and the journal *Soundings* co-organized a seminar on the future of the Labour Party. The outcomes of the seminar were published as an e-book, *Labour's Future* in July 2010. The aim of the contributing academics, advisors, and journalists was to identify the Labour Party's relationship to the state, the economy, and to democracy. Two contributors, Jonathan Rutherford and Marc Stears, became central once Miliband was elected as party leader (Rutherford contributed to the Blue Labour narrative and a range of other publications, and Stears became Miliband's advisor, media aide, and speechwriter). The ideas underpinning *Labour's Future* (democratizing the party, localism, reciprocity, the relationship between the individual and the state, reforming the state and the market, and the idea of a new 'covenant' with the people) became the fundamental elements of the emerging narrative.

Labour's Future, edited by Jonathan Rutherford and Alan Lockey, was a prelude to the post-2010 narrative. It set the scene for what followed and was like a founding moment. In an interview with Alan Finlayson, Rutherford later elaborated this coming together of a select group. It led to two publications that were significant for the development of a post-2010 Labour Party narrative:

> I was closely involved in Compass and Neal Lawson introduced me to Jon Cruddas about 5 years ago and Jon and I started working together. I met Maurice [Glasman] a year ago. We held a day seminar with about 50 people and produced an e-book called *Labour's Future*. Maurice met with Marc (Stears) and Stuart White in Oxford and then the four of us met and we planned a series of seminars to continue the dialogue around building a coalition. About thirty people were involved and we produced an e-book *The Labour Tradition and the Politics of Paradox* out of the papers and some of the responses. (Rutherford 2011; we shall examine the second publication Rutherford referred to below.)

Labour's Future, therefore, *predates* Ed Miliband's election as party leader, coming at the time of the defeat of Labour at the General Election (and is significant too in that its origins and the small group of people meeting predate the election defeat itself). Its essential motif was that the party had 'lost its way' in a folk-tale like way. It also pointed Cassandra-like to an approaching calamity (the 2010 defeat), and the need to 'go back'. In the preface, Rutherford and Lockey (2010) stated that it was recognized and generally accepted by the contributors that *inter alia* 'Labour has to evolve a more ethical and emotional language for its politics, reviving its traditions to become once again the party of association and mutualism, rather than of a centralizing and controlling state.' It involved many of those who would go on to develop the post-2010 narrative, and several close to Ed Miliband, as well as many New Labour people (most of these latter would gradually fade away (or 'convert') as the One Nation discourse asserted itself, not least, as we shall see, because as it did so, its rejection of New Labour would become stronger). Narratively, it began to move *down* to a level of activism that was dramatically devolved (reciprocity, localism), but also *back* in that it began a rehabilitation not of pre-Blair Labour, but of pre-Attlee Labour. For example, Stuart White's essay entitled 'The left and reciprocity' in *Labour's Future* stated that reciprocity was a 'core value in social-democratic philosophy' and traced it back to Leonard Hobhouse and later R.H.Tawney. Heather Wakefield's contribution in *Labour's Future* advocated localism that was about people and not the market. She cited New Labour's centralized managerialism and the introduction of markets in the public services as destroying any notion of local democratic control. For Wakefield, Labour needed to rethink localism as 'people's experience of the state is at least as local as it is national'. I want to stress here that there is a spatial movement down and a temporal movement back, that is to say, that to maintain legitimacy (and if New Labour is depicted as 'up' and 'now') there is only down and back to go. This would be part of One Nation's richness and constitute one of its weaknesses.

Let us briefly mention two other contributions in *Labour's Future* (Neal Lawson and Jonathan Rutherford). Lawson stressed a critical evaluation of the role of the state, one which superseded both the bureaucratic state model (1945) and the market state (1980–1997). Lawson imagined a state that was made 'responsible and accountable through democratic engagement, and through people having a voice rather than expressing themselves only through exit or loyalty'. Rutherford's contribution was both reflective and prospective. He considered the 2008 financial crisis in which New Labour was implicated, and stated that Labour Party renewal would occur only once the party had recognized the part it had played in the crisis (this would become highly problematic later on). He then identified two major revisions of Labour politics in the last 60 years, Anthony Crosland's *The Future of Socialism* and Third Way politics associated with Tony Blair (*inter alia*, Giddens 1994), and argued that both were based on the claim that capitalism was working. For Rutherford, in this third period of Labour revisionism, post-2010, neither capitalism nor social democracy were working. Rutherford proposed two Labour solutions. First, an economy distributed across the regions to rebuild the local and national economy and achieve a more egalitarian society. Second, the rebuilding of the relationship with not only the working classes but the estranged middle classes. He also (re)introduced the idea of a 'Covenant' in politics based upon an ethic of reciprocity, and an ethical economy. The essential point for us to retain is that *Labour's Future* was both a prelude and a rhetorical rival to the 2010 Labour Party Policy Review that would follow. The ideas expressed in the publication were widened in the Oxford London Seminars publication, *The Labour Tradition and the Politics of Paradox* (Glasman et al. 2011); we shall look at this publication once we have examined the first part of the Policy Review led by Liam Byrne and Peter Hain.

POLICY REVIEW

Upon Miliband's election, a new development of the narrative was set in train *by him*, namely, the Policy Review (November 2010). This was, as we stated earlier, a normal feature of any new leadership (Neil Kinnock had done the same thing when he was elected leader). Several wings or tendencies within the party were involved, but a feature of the Review was the notion of a return down to the grassroots of the party; to go out and seek the views and pulse of the movement as a whole (this is a staple in leftist mythology; in the 2015 deputy leadership campaign it was the central rhetorical feature of Stella Creasy's campaign, and it became the essential motif of Corbyn's leadership after he was elected leader). The Review was part of the elaboration of a narrative-as-process.

The question that the Policy Review set out to answer was 'How does Labour win once again the chance to serve our country?' There was much output by the Labour Party on this question, including consultation papers, speeches, and interviews by Liam Byrne, Peter Hain, and Jon Cruddas (Byrne and Hain led the first part of the Policy Review (2010–2012) until Byrne's stepping down in May 2012, and Cruddas from 2012), local and national policy seminars and events, emails and various policy related output by Miliband (forewords and introductions in official Policy Review consultation papers), policy events, and speeches. Its first textual expression was *New politics. Fresh ideas* (Labour Party 2010), published in November 2010. In the Introduction, Byrne emphasized dialogue, stating that 'now is the time to build a new relationship with the people we seek to serve'; in so doing, the party would listen, debate, and discuss policy. The consultation paper then outlined four policy questions:

- How do we grow our economy and ensure good jobs and a sustainable future?
- How do we strengthen our families, communities and relationships?
- How do we put power in people's hands, from our politics to our public services?
- How do we secure our country and contribute to a better world?

What followed on from these four questions was another set of generic questions about the Conservative–Lib Dem coalition government's current approach: long-term challenges for family, neighbourhood and country; what Labour's priorities for action should be; and how Labour might re-earn trust. The first document of the Policy Review began by emphasizing forthcoming dialogue and discussion within the party. I can make two points here that characterize the document. The first is that the wider discussion was constrained by the somewhat directive nature of the questions. Second, the document, even though it made the required symbolic gesture, as it were, to go back to the party's base to ask those questions, moved very quickly to the issue of policy elaboration (rhetorically it was going 'down' but not 'back').

The Policy Review's Counter Narrative: Blue Labour

Maurice Glasman – community organizer, contributor to Open Left discussions and publications, academic and then Labour peer – was the main proponent of Blue Labour, conceived in March 2009. It was given political expression and wide coverage in a Radio 4 *Analysis* Programme in March 2011, and in an article written by Glasman in *The Observer*, 24 April 2011 (see Glasman 2011) and in a book (Davis 2011). There was also a very good article on Blue Labour by Richard Jobson (2014; see also Jobson and Wickham-Jones 2010).

Blue Labour was (or would have itself) a social theory. This was quite a radical rhetorical departure. Glasman argued for an almost mythical 'return' to Labour's roots, to its origins and essential purpose: essentially, to a reciprocal, mutualist, local, community-based socialism or social democracy (although he preferred terms like association, solidarity, and congregation as more 'progressive' than community). The prescription was 'modern' (and it had 'modern' philosophical sources like Karl Polanyi (1886–1964)), its communitarianism was of a contemporary multicultural type and it took an actively prescriptive approach; but in the imagination what was rhetorically constructed was an early-twentieth-century Britain:

communities, faith, family, reciprocity, mutualism/cooperation, the 'outside' somewhat precluded (a strong national patriotic feeling informed everything, including a hesitancy about 'outsiders'). In contemporary terms, this meant circumventing the corrosive social and economic power of banking, and a strong disapproval of uncontrollable immigration (but with the interdependent cooperation of all faith groups). In many ways, Blue Labour pointed towards an Arcadian England, and we should point out here something rarely noticed in the study of political discourse, that it is often not the ideational that informs the policy-practical (which it does) but conversely, the practical (these big banks don't work, there were too many Polish immigrants for the welfare services to cope, mutual societies did work, reciprocity does overcome *anomie* and alienation) that legitimates the mythical or lyrical (story illustrating plot). Beyond the critique of Blue Labour's appealing to reactionary thought, a more acid criticism was its nostalgia and possible political irrelevance (could this England ever exist, if indeed it ever did? And it 'seemed like' England rather than the UK or other parts of the UK). Whatever the truth, such accusations (we shall return to the idea of 'narrative attack' in the Conclusion) made Blue Labour potentially both contentious and divisive. Nevertheless, its highly evocative, emotional, and ethical registers made it rhetorically very attractive, particularly if New Labour were to be shown as having been in thrall to false idols. This was not long in coming. Rhetorically, therefore, Glasman's discursive invention of Blue Labour was a response to, a deepening of Byrne's *New Politics. Fresh ideas* initiative, but in its conception, like *Labour's Future*, predated it.[5]

In November 2010, Peter Hain, Chair of the National Policy Forum, was tasked by Miliband 'to write a consultation paper taking stock of the situation and setting out some key questions on what we should do next as we embark on the long road back to regaining the trust of the British people'. In April 2011, *Refounding Labour: a Party for the New Generation* was published. This was the second Policy Review consultation paper, the consultation process ending on 24 June 2011. It sought responses to four 'big questions' (and 63 associated sub-questions) on: (1) An outward-looking party; (2) A voice for members; (3) Renewing our party; (4) Winning back power. The outcomes of this consultation were published in *Refounding Labour to Win: a Party for the*

---

[5] There is a Road to Damascus element to Blue Labour in that Glasman made it clear that his 'conversion' to the doctrine he himself elaborated had as its founding moment the care provision surrounding his dying mother.

New Generation (Labour Party 2011). The consultation claimed 3,255 individual submissions, 20,354 hits on Refounding Labour websites, 66 events across the country, 184 party submissions, and 36 submissions from groups or affiliates. *Refounding Labour to Win: a Party for the New Generation* outlined the way in which the party perceived the four 'big questions' and associated questions, and then proposed recommendations, for example, 'the age which you can join the party will be reduced to 14 years of age'.[6] An accompanying paper, *Refounding Labour to Win: Summary Report,* was published in July 2011. The report summarized Hain's initiative and set out six forthcoming issues: building a more open and welcoming party; connecting with communities; increasing member participation and involvement; party leader, leadership election, elected representatives, and candidates; equality; a strengthened policy-making process. What is clear from the first two outputs of the Policy Review, *New politics. Fresh ideas* and *Refounding Labour to Win: a Party for the New Generation,* is that both documents focused upon two areas: policy and organization. What neither focused on in any detail (although appealing to notions of 'return' to basics and the grassroots movement) was ideology.

In June 2011, *A Better Future for Britain* (Labour Party 2011) was published. This interim paper summarized Byrne's November 2010 initiative, *New politics. Fresh ideas.* Byrne's initiative had resulted in almost 4 million contacts with the public, 70 public events with Shadow Cabinet spokespeople, a People's Policy Forum led by Ed Miliband, 6,000 attendees at consultation evenings, 2,000 written responses and 16,000 online responses, and hundreds of thousands of mailings. *A Better Future for Britain* was presented as a listening exercise and contained 60 unmediated responses, each giving the impression that the party had listened and was renewing its appeal. The responses were personalized and signed as Melanie, Surrey or John, Burnley – creating the impression of imagined dialogue within the party. *A Better Future for Britain* concluded by outlining four policy themes: (1) Getting the deficit down; Rebuilding our Economy to help the 'Squeezed Middle'; (2) Renewing the Promise of Britain for the next Generation; (3) Renewing Responsibility, Strengthening Our Communities; and (4) Our Place in the World – and 19 expert working

---

[6] *Refounding Labour to Win* also suffered in terms of its rhetorical and ideational legitimacy because of accusations that the exercise had been run by a consulting agency. See Hodges (2011, 2011a).

groups, each chaired by a member of the Shadow Cabinet. The third major output of the Policy Review, *A Better Future for Britain*, stressed policy and introduced the idea of party dialogue; it was, nevertheless, the third major party document in a row that had paid scant attention to doctrinal or ideological renewal. All of the Policy Review's outputs gave the impression of enormous activity 'down' to the grassroots, and 'out' across the country. The Policy Review was strongly what it said it was on the tin. This meant that it was rhetorically and ideationally inadequate to 'story'. The responses to the Review's questions were predictable, and all involved organization and policy. It is clear that what was not being sufficiently elaborated and given time to 'emerge' was a new narrative, discursive space for a new set of feelings (and emotions which we shall examine below). Partly because of the personality issues involved (Byrne was not popular on the left of the party), at Miliband's request, Byrne stepped down from the Review in May 2012 immediately after the publication of its first major iteration.

THE OXFORD LONDON SEMINARS

A wider intellectual/philosophical enquiry was, however, taking place, as we have seen. Between October 2010 and April 2011, that is, immediately after Miliband was elected as party leader, academics and Labour MPs and advisors took part in The Oxford London Seminars series on the Labour tradition. The seminars debated Labour tradition and modernity, nation and class, labour and capital, community and the individual, society and the market, the state and mutualism, and contrasted belief and empiricism, romanticism and rationality, obligation and entitlement. The debates led to the publication of *The Labour Tradition and the Politics of Paradox* in July 2011, edited by Maurice Glasman, Jonathan Rutherford, Marc Stears, and Stuart White. The preface was written by Miliband and the book was organized into four sections on 'Labour as a radical tradition' by Glasman; 'Democracy, leadership and organizing' by Stears; 'The future is conservative' by Rutherford; and 'Responses to the series' by four leading Labour figures. Each of the chapters had a series of short responses from a range of contributors drawn from academia (Ben Jackson, Mike Kenny), think tanks (Duncan O'Leary, Graeme Cooke) and New Labour/Blairites (James Purnell, David Miliband, Hazel Blears), and some closer to the emerging narrative (Jon Cruddas, David Lammy). Some were critical, e.g., Philip Collins.

Three observations can be made on the significance of *The Labour Tradition and the Politics of Paradox* for the development of a Labour

Party narrative. The first is that in the preface, Ed Miliband endorsed the publication, referred to the 'political energy and intellectual confidence' of the contributors, and welcomed the 'openness to new ideas and new approaches'. Blue Labour was mentioned in passing as the starting point for discussions on party renewal (and one of the very rare occasions of naming of Blue Labour by Miliband). Miliband's endorsement of this publication and its contributors meant (a) the legitimation of an unofficial Policy Review and (b) an implicit criticism of, or recognition of the inadequacy of, the Byrne/Hain Policy Review initiatives.

The second observation is that the four editors stated in their introduction:

> we were NOT trying to define policy or determine what should be done. We wanted to ask some fundamental questions about the condition of the country and the predicament of Labour following its defeat in the May 2010 general election ... The task of the Oxford London seminars was to signal the beginning of a new revisionism following on from Anthony Crosland in the 1950s and the Third Way of the 1990s. (Glasman et al. 2011: 9–12)

The contributors discussed issues such as family cohesion, equality and relationships, empowerment, and democracy. Thus, *The Labour Tradition and the Politics of Paradox* saw a widening of the ideas that were discussed in *Labour's Future* (mutualism, cooperation, and localism), a greater emphasis upon philosophy and ideas than many party documents, and the now increasing presence and contribution of Blue Labour, the latter presenting itself as a kind of ideational transcendence of two earlier major moments – Crosland and Marquand et al. – of Labour's doctrinal evolution. The final observation, paradoxically, is that in Glasman's essay on 'Labour as a radical tradition', there is no mention of Blue Labour, but the ideas that constitute Blue Labour (co-operation, reciprocity, mutualism, common good) were becoming expressed and asserted as the basis of the emerging Labour Party narrative across the board.

The New(-ish) Labour pressure group, Progress (more a *cercle d'idées* than a pressure group) published *The Purple Book* (Philpot 2011) in September 2011. The authors, many of them Blairites, contributed essays on Labour Party policy development.[7] *The Purple Book* saw the congregation

---

[7] Philpot, R., *'What is the Purple Book?'*. Available at http://labourlist.org/2011/05/what-is-the-purple-book/

of a very broad church within the party, with contributions by figures such as Liam Byrne, Tessa Jowell, Caroline Flint, Jacqui Smith, Frank Field, Alan Milburn, and Peter Mandelson; there were numerous 'straight' policy essays, less focused on philosophy, as well as many contributions from the authors of the emerging dominant narrative. The central thrust of the book was the rethinking of the state. There was even one essay by Ivan Lewis on One Nation itself. Throughout the 'emerging narrative' in these various texts, however, the One Nation authors flooded the discursive space with the ancestral gods and their ideas (Robert Owen, John Ruskin, Keir Hardie, Temperance, Christian Socialism, 1920s localism, R.H.Tawney, and the Co-op), justified now as offering advice and example to the elaboration of new models for how to reorganize the economy and society – although not a word about the Woodcraft Folk... .

What we see in *The Purple Book* are two things. First, an emerging narrative that draws upon historic Labour Party figures and the ideas in the two unofficial Policy Review texts (*Labour's Future* and *The Labour Tradition and the Politics of Paradox*). Second, the presence of the Blairites in *The Purple Book* was the last time that they appeared in strength as part of the elaboration of a post-2010 narrative. It was my view then, as now, that this was a major bringing together but missed opportunity for an ideational and especially rhetorical reconciliation and, through reconciliation, transcendence of the two dominant *mythical* and *doctrinal* strains within Labourism, 'return' and 'modernization'. I feel that if this discursive blending had taken place the subsequent history and fortunes of the Labour Party might have been very different. Although, as we shall argue later in this chapter, certain of the rhetorical choices made *precluded* to a certain – although not insurmountable – degree such an, in my view, imperative reconciliation if Labour were to win in 2015. An anecdote: Peter Mandelson's contribution was illustrative of the dichotomy. He was sceptical about 'romantic ideas about working class people turning back the clock'. But romance in both its 'sentimental' and 'story-telling' senses was fundamental to Labour's imminent revisionism. The rhetorical and ideational challenge was to create a romanticism that would overcome such scepticism (an irony being that Mandelson was the grandson of one of the 'ancestral gods', Herbert Morrison).

As mentioned above, in May 2012, at Miliband's request, Byrne stood down from the Policy Review and was replaced by Jon Cruddas. The initial Policy Review had focused almost exclusively and immediately upon policy and organization (and gestured towards dialogue within the party) as opposed to ideology and narrative. It was precisely this shortcoming that led to the second elaboration of the Policy Review. It is in the light of this that we should see the significance of Jon Cruddas' appointment to head the Policy Review. He was a surprise appointment; arguably a Blairite at one time, but if so, a critical and disillusioned one, and perceived as doctrinally on the left of the party. Cruddas, like Glasman, also had 'street cred' in that his background was 'ordinary'; he was, in addition, extremely erudite and considered one of the party's intellectual thinkers and, it should be noted strongly, one of its more lyrical speakers.

Cruddas took over the Review and, in 2012–2013, transformed it into a review of thought rather than of policy. He took the Blue Labour discourse and folded it into his Review while expanding the doctrinal remit to include, much more decisively, for example, contemporary culture, establishing the identity of cities and building city cultures and 'economies that power regional economic development' (Cruddas 2012b, *New Statesman* interview) in preparation for the elaboration of the 'One Nation' theme. The Glasman-style references increased under his chairmanship; all the 'thought' that had gone before was extended emotionally to include a kind of Dickensian or Elizabeth Gaskell-style of emotional indignation at injustice, and their overcoming and the imagining of a pre-1940 harmonious country. The Review Part II, as it were, as well as key speeches and interviews given (see *inter alia* Cruddas 2012a, b) at various stages, began to lift the discourse of One Nation to rally proportions, as if the narrative were catching a tide – as if Labour were celebrating a kind of Britain depicted by Danny Boyle in the opening ceremony of the 2012 Olympics. Glasman had been controversial. Cruddas began to incorporate Blue Labour's ideas into the mainstream party narrative with great rhetorical skill (going 'down', 'back', and 'forward' before 'offering' the narrative to the leader).

In his first interview (*The Guardian* 16 June 2012) Cruddas stated that the party lacked an 'overarching story' since the last election. For Cruddas, the story should be about 'rebuilding Britain' and 'national renewal' (rhetorically the 'rebuilding' evoking infrastructure – urban renewal, housing, transport, welfare services – was also a metaphor for a more spiritual reconstruction, and was one of the slogans of the 2012 Party Conference). Cruddas compared the present (financial crisis, Eurozone crisis) with the challenge that the Labour Party faced in 1945 and stated 'the way I look at it would be that in 1945 Labour locked in the organized working classes into an overarching story of national renewal, and that is the equivalent task at hand today'. The symbolic role of 1945 would, however, shift decisively over the next year.

Cruddas' first action on the Policy Review was to replace the Byrne/ Hain initiatives, including the policy groups, with three areas for reflection: the economy, politics, and society. Cruddas' second interview was in the centre-left current affairs magazine, *New Statesman*, entitled 'Building the New Jerusalem'. The title itself evoked a new (and old) beginning built and shared by all. Throughout the interview, Cruddas made reference to the themes in *Labour's Future*, *The Labour Tradition and the Politics of Paradox*, and *The Purple Book*, for example, a moral economy, social value, shared responsibility, reciprocity, relationships, social renewal, co-operation, the common good, social liberty and a Labour covenant. For Cruddas, 'the task is to strengthen and improve the institutions of our common life to make sure we have an economy, a society and a political system that people feel part of' (Cruddas 2012b). We can see how Cruddas was drawing the emerging party narrative into the mainstream of exchange.

The replacement of Byrne with Cruddas was, therefore, not just a policy-related issue, but a moment in the post-2010 period where the party leadership clearly took the decision to develop an approach based upon ideas and their significance in political and social life. Throughout the interview, Cruddas reimagined a post-2015 British society, one that celebrated cities, had flourishing regional (and moral) economies, a British society that was connected – people who respected and trusted one another – and a society that valued equality and liberty. We see echoes of the Arcadian Britain that Glasman advocated in his initial descriptions of Blue Labour. It was, significantly, a concerted imagining of the future, but in large swathes *as the past*.

ONE NATION, TWO AUTHORS

In October 2012 at the Labour Party Conference in Manchester, Ed Miliband used 'One Nation Labour' as the formative theme of his keynote speech. I analyse in the next chapter in much greater detail Miliband's performance at Manchester 2012. Here, let us concentrate on the rhetoric of One Nation as regards Miliband and his 'capturing' of what we might call the 'story so far'.

Miliband introduced One Nation in this way:

Friends, I didn't become leader of the Labour Party to reinvent the world of Disraeli or Attlee. But I do believe in that spirit. That spirit of One Nation. One Nation: a country where everyone has a stake. One Nation: a country where prosperity is fairly shared. One Nation: where we have a shared destiny, a sense of shared endeavour and a common life that we lead together. That is my vision of One Nation. That is my vision of Britain. That is the Britain we must become. (Miliband 2012)

I can make two points here as regards his 'authorship' of One Nation. First, he developed the idea and its implications throughout the speech, always referring to what One Nation was for him and according to him, and these in a highly rhetorical manner. Second, his telling of the One Nation tale was not a simple reporting to the audience of what it was, either ideologically or in terms of policy (though both of these perspectives were present), but in terms of his own very personal and emotional story: his childhood, moral and emotional commitment, his personalized envisioning of a better world, his acute sense of injustice, references to his family, country, and so on (we shall come back to this). Miliband left the Conference with the press and the party acclaiming his performance and leadership; he also took with him as 'his' the now highly rhetorical narrative of One Nation.

The most significant development of the One Nation narrative was its becoming central to leadership at a particular and crucial moment of its development, in the course of 2012. At the Manchester conference, because of the leader's speech, One Nation became the official language of the party, and this because the leader aligned himself with it. Conversely, through appropriation, 'it' became 'his'; thus mediating if not resolving the question of authorship. And it became his not simply because he adopted it but because he did so in a highly personalized, interpretive, and emotional way. There were three ways in which, prior to Manchester 2012, Miliband became, in part, the author of the rhetoric.

First because, quite simply, it flourished under his leadership, displacing and pushing out other themes, gaining and occupying discursive space, becoming a thematic cluster, with its original 'authors' – Rutherford and Glasman, for example[8] – remaining central as the narrative was modified through time. Also, several people very close to Miliband became associated with the narrative, a few of them – Stears, for example – active from early on.

---

[8] Glasman himself moved in and out of favour given his many controversial interventions.

Second, he became personally associated by offering forewords and introductions to the narrative's developing iterations; a couple of illustrations show a developing personal enthusiasm. For example: 'I believe this document is a frank assessment of our party's present condition and its future prospects. But it is only the beginning. We must listen to our members and look outward to the people whose support we seek at election time ... our task is nothing less than the refoundation of the Labour Party: "The People's Party"' (see Miliband's Foreword, *Refounding Labour to Win: a Party for the New Generation*). And: 'You may not agree with all the views expressed in this book. Nor do I. But I believe strongly that a vibrant debate across the party, in all its colours, is a necessary condition of renewal and of returning to power' (Miliband, Foreword, *The Purple Book*). It is as if he and the narrative were drawn to one another as he developed rhetorical assertiveness and it gained discursive dominance.

Third was what we might call his 'executive involvement' as he gradually took control of the version of the narrative suited to his leadership and its rhetorical/thematic expression. He appointed Byrne to set up a review. He then sacked him (May 2012), replacing him, as we have seen, with Jon Cruddas, who then lifted the whole narrative to a dramatically higher level. And by choosing someone both independent and competent, Ed Miliband became even more positively associated with it, through its refraction through Cruddas.

The discursive aftermath of Manchester 2012 saw the dramatic valorization of One Nation, and its association with Miliband's thought and persona. A new phase of One Nation began after Manchester, culminating in a new party narrative, and a series of rhetorical initiatives which enhanced One Nation to the point of making it – and its now principal voice, the party leader – the voice of a transformational party behind a transformational leader. But it was not to last, and we shall come back to this in Chapter 5.

Miliband used the three Policy Review themes developed by Jon Cruddas as sub-narratives of One Nation Labour (One Nation economy, One Nation politics, and One Nation society. Cruddas also edited spin-offs on Society and the Economy[9]). The development of One Nation Labour by Ed Miliband after Manchester 2012 was constant (for a period of time). Let us look briefly at three speeches and one interview: the Fabian Society

[9] Cruddas, J. (2013a) Introduction, in *One Nation Society*, http://www.policyforum. labour.org.uk/uploads/editor/files/SOCIETY_one_nation.pdf

Annual Conference speech (January 2013); an interview with *The Times* (March 2013); the People's Policy Forum speech (March 2013); and the 'Progress' Annual Conference speech (May 2013).

In his Fabian Annual Conference speech, Miliband vividly described his vision of a post-2015 British society:

> The idea of a country which we rebuild together, where everyone plays their part ... we know this idea [One Nation] is a deep part of our national story because we have so many different ways of describing it, 'all hands to the pump', 'mucking in', 'pulling your weight', 'doing your bit'. Turning this spirit of collective endeavour of looking out for each other, from something we do in our daily lives, to the way our nation is run. That is what One Nation is about. (Miliband 2013)

The down-to-earth liveliness of Miliband's rhetoric here is reminiscent of a kind of rallying war-time spirit. And his use of stark opposites is a classic rhetorical device:

- Short-termism in the City/long-term wealth creation;
- All have the opportunity to play their part/not just a few;
- Chief Executive pay goes up and up and up/and everybody else's is stagnant;
- Responsibility should apply to those on social security/ responsibility matters at the top too;
- People should have more power and control over their lives/so that everyone feels able to play their part, not left on their own;
- We can build a united/not divided Britain.

In a series of interviews and speeches thereafter, One Nation still did not develop into specific policy proposals. There were increasing references by Miliband to the values of One Nation Labour. These included the role of individual responsibility, 'genuine fairness', and obligation ('we can achieve as a country if we come together'). Miliband used the example of the spirit of the London 2012 Olympic Games to evoke a One Nation collective spirit which involved members of society 'Pulling together. Coming together. Working together. For the good of ourselves, and the good of the country. That's what makes anything possible. That's how we can get our country moving again. And that's how we can meet our challenge to change Britain' (Miliband 2013a). Thus, for Miliband, 'One

Nation Labour is the modernizing force in the Labour Party and the country today ... Rights and responsibilities are at the core of what we believe for our society. Because One Nation is about everybody having opportunity and having responsibility to play their part' (Miliband 2013b).

I can make two points here. First, in describing his vision of a post-2015 British society, he incorporated the ideas in the publications already discussed: that is, *Labour's Future* (democratizing the party, localism, reciprocity, the relationship between the individual and the state, reforming the state and the market, and proposing a new covenant with the people); *The Labour Tradition and the Politics of Paradox* (widening the ideas in *Labour's Future*); and *The Purple Book* (decentralization, redistribution, social mobility, inequality, communities). My essential point is that Miliband legitimated the discourse of Blue Labour and others and folded them into One Nation. Second, One Nation Labour was a politics appropriate to a society where 'responsibilities' were as salient as 'rights'. The co-existence of rights and responsibilities promoted a One Nation just society based upon reciprocity, mutualism, and the common good – each and all constituent elements of Blue Labour, but also of Blue Labour's conservatism.

ONE NATION, ONE AUTHOR

After Miliband's 2012 Conference speech, One Nation became the Labour Party policy narrative (or pre-policy narrative). In January 2013, *One Nation Labour – Debating the Future* (Cruddas 2013a) was published by LabourList.org, an independent progressive e-network. Edited by Cruddas, it was the first textual expression of Part III of the Policy Review and development of One Nation as a post-2010 Labour Party narrative (for a diagrammatic representation of the overall narrative arc see Fig. 3.1). The contributors were drawn from academia, think tanks, and the like, and included Maurice Glasman, Sonia Sodha (Head of Policy and Strategy at the Social Research Unit), Graeme Cooke (Research Director at the Institute of Public Policy Research (IPPR) and former head of the Open Left project at Demos), and several Labour MPs. This group of Labour thinkers represented what we might call an orientation towards policy that was based upon the ideas, research and scholarship of One Nation. There were Cruddas' three Policy Review categories, all prefaced with a long section on One Nation itself. The contributors concentrated upon justifications of policy and how policies would work in practice: for example, the reinvention of trade unions and employee representation

OPEN LEFT PROJECT AT DEMOS (Purnell, Rutherford et al)

Labour's Future (07/2010).

2010 GENERAL ELECTION

Labour loses power.

Resignation of Gordon Brown.

Election of Ed Miliband.

POLICY REVIEW MARK I (11/2010-05/2012) (Byrne and Hain)

New politics. Fresh ideas (11/2010).

Refounding Labour to Win (04/2011).

A better future for Britain (06/2011).

REVISIONIST NARRATIVE (10/2010-10/2012) (Rutherford, Glasman, Stears, White)

The Labour tradition and the Politics of paradox (07/2011).

Blue Labour (conceived in 2009 but first politically expressed in 03/2011 in a Radio 4 Analysis programme and an article in *The Observer*).

(The *Purple Book*, policy essays, many by Blairites, although the last time that they appeared in strength).

POLICY REVIEW MARK II (05/2012-) (Cruddas)

Replacement of Byrne by Cruddas.

Cruddas interviewed in *The Observer* (06/2012) and *New Statesman* (09/2012).

ONE NATION LABOUR (Ed Miliband)

Ed Miliband keynote speech at Labour Party Conference (10/2012).

POLICY REVIEW MARK III (01/2013) (Cruddas, Rutherford, Glasman, Stears)

inter alia:

IPPR *The Relational State* (11/2012).

Ed Miliband, Fabian Society annual conference speech (01/2013).

One Nation Labour – debating the future (01/2013).

Radio 4 Analysis programme: 'Labour's New New Jerusalem' (05/2013).

Ed Miliband 'One Nation Social Security' speech (06/2013).

Jon Cruddas speech on 'One Nation Statecraft' (06/2013).

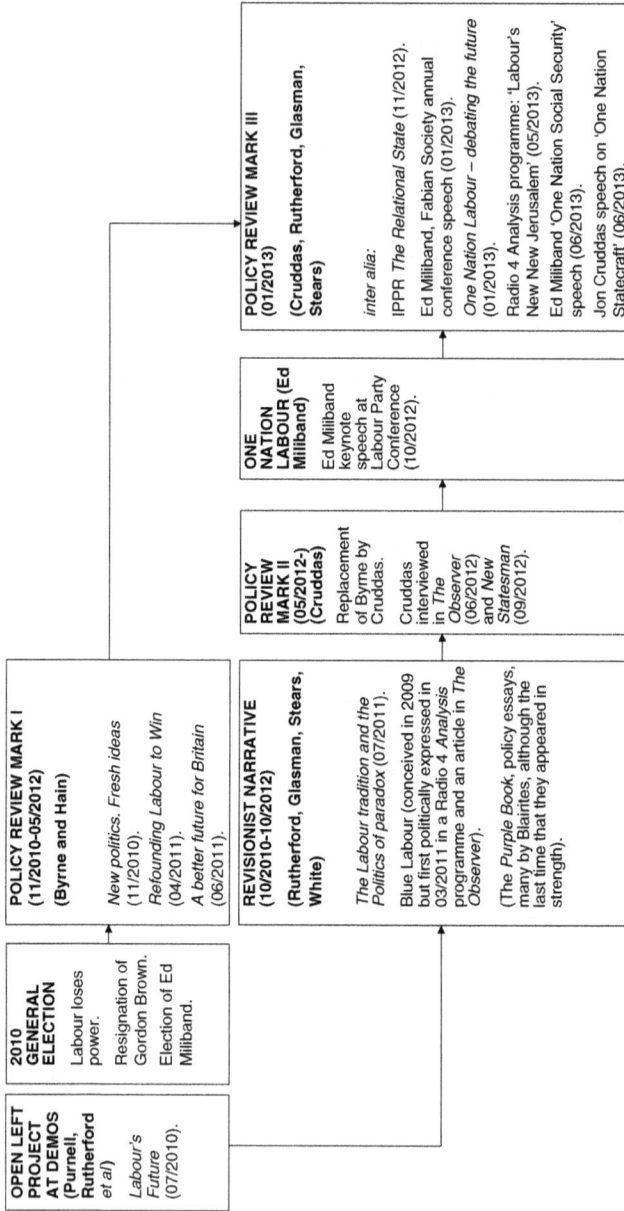

Fig. 3.1   Corpus of texts and timeline of the One Nation narrative (for the full corpus see footnote 4 on page 84)

on company boards; political parties and courts to generate account-ability; rethought corporate governance and the role of employee rep-resentatives. What we see in *One Nation Labour – Debating the Future* is not policy elaboration but the 're-imagining' of aspects of society and the polity. Under Cruddas' leadership, as we have seen, the Policy Review ceased to be a Policy Review and resembled a rhetorical and ideological exercise until 2013, but the 'actual imagining' of society, as it were, now saw policy implications emerging, all of which were based upon/would follow from the One Nation narrative. In the January 2013 publication and in two following speeches, One Nation discourse was given a further lift, essentially through the high rhetoric of Cruddas and the other contrib-utors, all of whom celebrated One Nation, but drew attention to Miliband himself as their inspiration. Here are two such endorsements, by Tristram Hunt and Maurice Glasman in *One Nation Labour – Debating the Future*:

> It is now just over three months since Ed Miliband made his One Nation conference speech. When a speech can be instantly recalled by a single phrase, it is usually a good indication of its effectiveness. And there can now be little doubt that it galvanised the party and stimulated thinking. (Hunt)

> In order to generate energy and to succeed in opposition it is necessary to have a narrative, a strategy and an organising concept that can give plausibil-ity and coherence to the swelter of initiatives, policies and programmes that swirl around the Westminster Village ... This is what Ed Miliband achieved at the last party conference with One Nation Labour. (Glasman)

References of this kind abound in the text, linking the text's authors to the leader through their inspiration by One Nation, as if Miliband was the *author* of the narrative.

In May 2013, the spring after the September conference, in a Radio 4 Analysis programme entitled 'Labour's New New Jerusalem', Maurice Glasman, Sir Robin Wales (Labour Mayor of Newham), Jeremy Cliffe (*The Economist*), Polly Toynbee (*The Guardian*, and here a critical voice), and Andrew Harrop (General Secretary of the Fabian Society – also critical) took part in a programme that explored the central state and Labour's approach to welfare. The programme began with an extract from Attlee's (1951) Party Conference speech in which he described 'building Jerusalem'. Jon Cruddas and Marc Stears were both quoted and their cri-tiques of that 'Jerusalem' cited. For Glasman, reconstituting relationships in the welfare system was an essential corrective to the dominance of the central state. He advocated a contributory welfare principle and the move from entitlement to responsibility. Sir Robin Wales advocated strongly against centralization and for localism, and provided an example of the 'Workplace' scheme in Newham – a scheme that operated as a semi-Job-centre, and which provided advice and personalized help (mock interviews, administrative support) for local people seeking employment. Robin Wales' contribution to the programme was to demonstrate the *practical* significance of Blue Labour's localism.

We should retain three essential points from the programme regarding the significance of 'Labour's New New Jerusalem' for the elaboration of One Nation Labour. The first point is that Glasman made no reference to Blue Labour in the programme. From a symbolic and practical perspective, this was significant, as after Miliband's 2012 Conference speech, Blue Labour drifted into One Nation. The main characteristic of Blue Labour – community and constituent values of co-operation, reciprocity and mutualism, patriotism and the common good, responsibility, and obligation – were all folded into the discourse of One Nation Labour. We see this in Glasman's contributions to the programme. The second point is that Wales' several interventions, in his description of the Workplace scheme in Newham, was describing One Nation *in practice*: that is, in one locality *now*, in all localities *tomorrow*. Third, there was boldness in the interventions of all the participants, a kind of assertiveness now *vis-à-vis* not just New Labour but the whole of the post-war settlement. One Nation was being presented as full of 'promise' for tomorrow. What we see in 'Labour's New New Jerusalem' is the party getting closer to policy, having ideologically and intellectually refounded itself for a post-2015 Britain.

In June 2013, Miliband delivered a speech entitled 'A One Nation Plan for Social Security Reform' at Newham Docks. In this alone, we see leadership endorsement of Wales and the ideas that he set out in 'Labour's New New Jerusalem'. The speech focused centrally upon social security expenditure. In the speech, Miliband outlined four forthcoming policies:

- Cut costs by helping the long-term unemployed back to work;
- Make sure jobs are well paid to reward work, so the state does not face rising subsidies for low pay;
- Get the cost of renting down by ensuring more homes are built – thereby reducing the welfare bill;

- Cap social security spending by focusing on the deep-rooted reasons benefit spending goes up.

However, there is one essential characteristic of the speech that is significant for my analysis, that is, Miliband's emphasis upon what he called the 'four building blocks' of a One Nation social security system (and their constituent values): work, rewarding work, investing for the future not paying for failure, and recognizing contribution. In his elaboration of the four building blocks of a One Nation social security system, we see references to values that Miliband had used in previous speeches and interviews. For example, the discussion on work was related to the founding principle of the Labour Party and then related to responsibility. Miliband then endorsed the Newham 'Workplace' initiative undertaken by Robin Wales and, in so doing, localism became part of the One Nation social security strategy. On rewarding work, Miliband referred to 'responsibility being borne by all' and evoked the value of fairness. On the final two 'building blocks' (investing for the future, not paying for failure and recognising contribution), responsibility, fairness, and equality were repeatedly evoked. In the speech, we see the beginnings of One Nation policies developing (see Miliband 2013c).

LET THE WORD GO FORTH

Four days after Miliband's speech on One Nation Social Security Reform, the head of the Policy Review, Jon Cruddas, delivered a speech at the Local Government Association on 'One Nation Statecraft' (Cruddas 2013d). The speech illustrated the way in which a post-2015 Labour Party would govern. There were, however, once again, no specific policies but strong allusions to policy; localism, investment for prevention, and collaboration were the three organising principles of One Nation Statecraft. However, it was Cruddas' references to values throughout the speech and references to memory and traditions in the conclusion that are of significance for our analysis. I can make two points here. First, in Cruddas' references to constituent One Nation values he endorsed the ideas in the unofficial Policy Review texts (*Labour's Future*, Maurice Glasman's descriptions of Blue Labour, and *The Labour Tradition and the Politics of Paradox*). Let us look at four brief examples to demonstrate our point here on intertextuality on the one hand (creating a matrix and occupying all the discursive space), and a growing shared 'emotion' on the other:

'Unofficial' Policy Review texts	Jon Cruddas 'One Nation Statecraft' speech
Distinctive Labour values are rooted in relationships, in practices that strengthen an ethical life. Practices like reciprocity, which gives substantive form to freedom and equality in an active relationship of give and take. Mutuality, where we share the benefits and burdens of association. And then if trust is established, solidarity, where we actively share our fate with other people. These are the forms of the labour movement, the mutual societies, the co-operatives and the unions. (Glasman, in Rutherford et al., *The Labour Tradition and the Politics of Paradox*, 2011, p. 14)	We will push power downwards and build a new kind of state which is based on our values of responsibility, reciprocity and relationships ...
... there is a need to define a new sense of national purpose that is associative, democratic and free, and which can be defined by the ideas of the common good and the good society. (*The Labour Tradition and the Politics of Paradox*, 2011, p. 12)	A state which works for the common good ...
One of the central challenges we face is revisiting our approach to the balance between state and market. Historically, debates within Labour have often been conducted on the basis of a choice between 'more state and less market' or 'more market and less state'. That approach needs revisiting. (*The Labour Tradition and the Politics of Paradox*, 2011, p. 6)	We need to put relationships centre stage in service design and reconfigure services around networks, households and co-creation rather than being delivered by centralised institutions ...
... Labour has to evolve a more ethical and emotional language for its politics, reviving its traditions to become once again the party of association and mutualism, rather than of a centralising and controlling state. (*Labour's Future*, 2010, Introduction, p. 6)	Let's remember our traditions ... our history lies in mutualism, cooperation and organising
Labour originally grew out of a vast movement of voluntary collectivism. We should remember the co-operatives, mutual associations, adult schools and reading circles that constitute a proud tradition of mutual improvement and civic activism. (*The Labour Tradition and the Politics of Paradox*, 2011, p. 7)	

Our second point is that the various policy/non-policy expressions of One Nation Labour that emerged in 2013 were all iterations of Rutherford, Glasman, and Stears and their contributions in *Labour's Future* and *The Labour Tradition and the Politics of Paradox*. Both texts and Blue Labour generally were formative of a post-2010 Labour Party narrative, One Nation;

and in Cruddas' speech, which was about the future (Britain post-2015), the past was again evoked. Nevertheless, we can see that a pattern was beginning to emerge: ideational origins, policy proposals, a future One Nation Britain.

From the beginning of the Policy Review, Miliband drew upon a series of high profile academics and political experts. They played a significant role in commenting, contributing, and inflecting the overall narrative. Chicago-based activist and campaigner for Barack Obama, Arnie Graf, provided expertise on organizational effectiveness. Professors Jacob Hacker, Michael Sandel, and Danielle Allen (predistribution, moral markets, and a connected society) provided ideological justifications for change. They (and others) were brought in by Miliband (often to much fanfare) to offer advice. They all, moreover, echoed in a range of different ways aspects of Blue Labour/One Nation, and so offered a new perspective on old ideas. They became rhetorically associated with the overall narrative, either by contributing directly to it (or less directly e.g., Blond) or directly legitimating Miliband's ideas (Sandel), or his choice for party organization and purpose (Graf).[10] After 2012–2013 there then developed a tendency for some of these people to distance themselves/be distanced, and others brought in, which countered slightly what was a developing, discursive at least, atmosphere of community and solidarity.

After Miliband's 2012 Conference speech and in the course of 2013, there was the gradual widening and historical deepening of the status of One Nation. Much debate and organized events centred upon One Nation Labour. Let me briefly reflect upon two events – the first a series of events (One Nation Modernization debates and One Nation Labour conference at QMC) in early 2013, and stress their contribution to the elaboration of One Nation as a Labour Party narrative.

Progress and Compass co-organized three debates on One Nation Labour Modernization. The debates were held in the House of Commons and took place from March to May 2013, each with a range of panellists and a Q&A session that followed. The debates echoed the three themes of the Policy Review: (1) 'How do we create a good society?', (2) 'New or Blue, Radical or Conservative?' and (3) 'What should a modern state and public services be like?' In the debates, the party narrative was being carried forward, gesturing towards policy through dialogue while creating the perception of a post-2010 Labour movement on the move ideologically.

The second event was a 1-day conference on 18 April 2013 on 'The Politics of One Nation Labour' at Queen Mary, University of London. The papers presented were titled 'Labour, England, and One Nation'

---

[10] Although Glasman et al. referred inordinately to the 'ancestral gods', Miliband rarely did, referring more easily to the contributing voices like Sandel.

(Kenny 2013); 'One Nation Labour and the Conservative Tradition' (Blond 2013); 'One Nation and Blue Labour' (Glasman 2013); 'The Historical Origins of One Nation Labour' (Wickham-Jones 2013); 'Men, Women and Gender Equality' (Annesley 2013); and 'One Nation and the Welfare State' (Bale 2013). From this range of contributions, we can see the role of academics and experts in developing – while commenting upon and critiquing – One Nation as a Labour narrative. Stewart Wood's opening reflections at the conference were particularly illustrative of the elaboration of One Nation as a Labour Party narrative. Wood used the occasion in a particular way by constructing a historical 'arc' of neo-liberalism, as it were, not from 1997 to 2010, but from 1979 to 2010, thus equating New Labour with Thatcherism and neo-liberal folly, whose Armageddon was the crisis of 2008 and its aftermath. His reflections upon Margaret Thatcher/Thatcherism had a practical function: by seeing Thatcherism as a dramatic break with the post-war settlement he set up an ideational arc from 1979 to 2010, making 2010 a point of renewal and departure.[11] Implicitly, One Nation could be elaborated as a response not simply to post-2008 chaos, nor even to 1997, but to an arc of history that lasted from 1979 until 2010. It, 2010, became, therefore, the foundation moment of a new departure. But it was not just a foundation moment for the party but also, of course, a foundation moment for the new leadership, post-2010, of Ed Miliband. And in the course of 2013, the 'arc's' rise would be pushed even further back, calling into question the party's biggest mythology, the Attlee government of 1945–1951. Wood's emphasis upon Thatcher was therefore the clue to One Nation: a pre-Thatcher narrative for a post-Cameron Britain, whose 'source' lay before Thatcher. There was also, anecdotally, and in spite of the ideological disagreement, a real valorization of Thatcher by Wood as a political figure who personally redefined her era; the implication being that Miliband would do the same.

Discursive momentum therefore gained throughout 2013 through the establishing of One Nation rhetoric against not just one rhetorical 'source', New Labour, but against the Attlee government (and post-Attlee political philosophers, as we have seen, like Crosland). By undercutting this other rhetorical and ideational 'alternative' to New Labour and focusing upon its having taken one side of the Labour Party ideology (reliance on the

---

[11] Vernon Bogdanor's analysis (e.g., 'One Nation' seminar 19 March 2013, House of Commons) is correct but incomplete: there were practical and strategic, but also symbolic and leadership-related reasons why the post-2010 Labour narrative did not/could not valorize New Labour.

state) against the other (reliance on community), by 2013 One Nation could draw all its philosophical legitimacy (and all its rhetorical imagery) from the years between the founding moment of the Labour Party (c. 1900) and 1939, and represent *everything* since as a deviation. We saw the evidence for this in Radio 4's 'Labour's New New Jerusalem'. One Nation Labour thus became the true heir of Labourism, and Ed Miliband the direct descendant of Ruskin, Hardie, Cole, and Tawney. My view is that this might have gained traction if the other conditions (clear philosophically inspired policy proposals) had pertained.

ANALYSIS: STORY AND PLOT

Let us now draw our reflections together to see the plot of this story. A first question or triple-question to ask is what did One Nation see itself as being, what was it trying to do, and what was it actually doing? A first clue is the false start we can see, rather the several false starts made by the actual review/elaboration of policy. The first decisive moment of change was Ed Miliband's setting up the Policy Review in the first place, the second his then replacing Byrne with Cruddas in May 2012. This latter 'moment' had multiple effects (all of them beneficial) upon the party's narrative and upon Miliband's (and Cruddas') place within it; but what it also did was to push policy away from the emerging Review narrative to allow the widespread and sustained entry of what we might call social fantasizing (this is not a criticism), forcing the activity of the party towards reflection and the elaboration of a story that had a particular function. The ostensible and widely assumed reason for this was the time frame: it was too early to elaborate policy. The actual effect, however, was to embark the party on a quest (I shall explain this below) that would incorporate Blue Labour and its associated ideas and discourses dramatically into the emerging narrative. In this way, there was a romanesque element to the elaboration of the One Nation narrative, that is to say, a re-enactment of the party's history, in order to identify its contemporary purpose and offer to party and leadership a discourse and a style for the pre-2015 electoral period.

What One Nation had to do was to create a narrative (i.e., tell a story and elaborate a plot) of renewal that was appropriate to the party conjuncture (2010–2015). It also had to ensure that it was seen as legitimate and effective within the party, and attractive outside it. We need, therefore, to ask not whether it was legitimate but how it made its claim to legitimacy, and how it made its claim to being the authoritative voice in and of the Labour Party. The second and (virtually) unspoken thing it had to do, as well as aligning with the party, was to align with the leadership (and the leadership with it). The leader had to take authorship of One Nation and this in a context of a leader whose claim between 2010 and 2012 was contested and whose authority was weak.

There is a contradiction here, and therefore in my own argument, that from 2012 there were two authors simultaneously, enhancing and valorizing one another in an ongoing dynamic, namely, the 'new' party and the new leader. But it had to be the 'right' narrative (and the right leader). Let us look now at, as it were, where the river rose, how it ran and where, how it established itself and was irrigated, what were its tributaries, and how it flowed forward, gathering momentum, and how and when the party and leadership took it over and would carry it to the sea (2015…). Let us focus upon One Nation as a discursive phenomenon, and use our model drawn from narrative theory to identify its morphology and significance. In the next chapter we shall use rhetoric and performance theory rather than narrative theory. We have identified a narrative that runs from 2009 onwards, and which contains both a story and a plot. In the story that I have recounted the plot is the following: the recognition by the insightful few of impending calamity/catastrophe, which then occurs (disequilibrium). In its aftermath, and the fall of the king (for having been attracted to false gods) there must be 'a return', a return to origins to find the true path (back, to go forward to the future). This involves false starts, deviations, loss, punishment, or rejection of those who led us astray, and the *promise* of justice and retribution, enrichment, reflection, and a harmonious society (and a new king). The new leader embraces the new imagined world, articulating it; he enhances it and it enhances him (although no single individual or entity (party) can personify the hero as well as the leader can). The projection into the future (the end of the story, the denouement of the plot) is the projected triumph of the hero (leader/party), and the 'realization' of the imagined social harmony, mutualism, reciprocity, kindness, modesty, integrity, and the just role of the sovereign (party/leader), the dissemination of virtue and the true sharing of power, prosperity, and happiness (equilibrium). We can represent this narrative diagrammatically (see Fig. 3.2).

One Nation became by 2013 an 'appropriate' narrative, in part because of the way it evolved and represented itself as having evolved – its 'story' of a narrative that emerged tentatively, in 2009 (Open Left project at Demos; Glasman's early reflections) and developed dialectically to become, by 2013, a rally discourse around an idea and a leader that posited the (re)adoption by the party of one strain of (forgotten? abandoned? rediscovered?) Labourism (local, reciprocal, libertarian *and* conservative/conserving of) over another (statist, over-wieldy, having taken the wrong road, and the failure of its

	07/2009	05/2010	09/2010	11/2010–05/2012	03/2011–	07/2011–09/2011	05/2012–	10/2012	11/2012–	05/2013	2013–2014	2015
S T O R Y	Open Left. Thinkers and activists, Rutherford et al. Planning the Oxford-London seminars.	General election. Labour loses power. Fall of Gordon Brown.	Ed Miliband elected as Labour Party Leader.	Policy Review Mark I. *New politics. Fresh ideas. Refounding Labour. A better future for Britain.*	BBC Radio 4 Analysis programme 'Blue Labour'.	*The Labour Tradition and the Politics of Paradox.* *The Purple Book.*	Policy Review Mark II. Gradual rejection of New Labour.	Labour Party Annual Conference. Ed Miliband's 'One Nation' speech and Q&A.	Policy Review Mark III. IPPR: *The Relational State.* *One Nation Labour* – debating the future.	BBC Radio 4 Analysis programme 'Labour's New New Jerusalem'. Rejection of 1945 settlement.	Policy elaboration. IPPR: *The Condition of Britain.* Policy Review moving to policies.	General Election. Labour government. Ed Miliband Prime Minister.
P L O T	Small band of 'seers' and 'knights'. Cassandras anticipating doom.	Calamity. Catastrophe. Disequilibrium. Disharmony.	New leader gives instruction. Lonely certainty. Quest for (new) truth.	To go back down to the base/people (new/false starts) (Hain, Byrne). To return with answers (incomplete). Thinkers continue to reflect.	To listen to another forgotten voice/truth to 'imagine a perfect past/future (Glasman).	Other thinkers. Gathering. Reflection. Enrichment. + Other voices (Graf, Sandel, Blond, Wood, etc.)	New knight/philosopher (Cruddas). Rejection of those who took the wrong path. Promise. Narrative evolving.	Leader captures the narrative, makes it his own, fills it with emotion and hope. Inspires his following. Tells his story. Acclamation. Leader as author/protagonist of narrative/plot.	All bear witness to the leader's inspiration. One Nation becomes the party's narrative. Cruddas' rhetoric. Call to arms. Rally forming. Inspiration.	Depiction of new world built from re-connecting to old mysteries, forgotten truths. The exemplary past (refound) offers hope for today and the future.	Sharpening of weapons, gathering for the great battle. Inspirational rhetoric to rally the followers and the troops.	Triumph. Harmony. Happiness. Equilibrium.

Fig. 3.2 'Story' and 'Plot' in the evolution of the One Nation narrative

neo-liberal successor). It also dominated by 2013 because it had imposed a plot upon that story: a small band of thinkers/activists who came together almost by chance and nurtured a new (old) perception of an original and forgotten social democracy or communitarianism, adapted now to contemporary purpose (hence its *practical* aspects), fashioned through effort and adversity (becoming, through the rejection of New Labour, the entry of Blue Labour, and the adoption of One Nation, a *transcendence*, via Cruddas) and offered to the new leader (positing a synchrony between its 'voice' and his). Having adopted/created it, he gathered the movement around him (because it carried a vision of harmony and social equilibrium in the pursuit of the Common Good) and led the party (movement, country) to deliverance (this, in the future). The language of One Nation was therefore (seen as) appropriate both to the party and to the leadership. Only in this way, could it be sustained.

A first rather stark question we can ask, from both a systemic and practical point of view is, was it enough? Did it work? What I mean by this is did it work both as a social model and as rhetoric? It was around the notion of practicality rather than philosophical integrity that much of the debate turned. The London mayoralties (Attlee, Lansbury, Morrison (LCC)) in the 1930s *worked* (before these were led astray, dazzled by the false promises of the centralized state), the German model (which echoed One Nation) was an exemplar; small regional banks *work*, One Nation worked in Newham, and so on throughout. I can stress again here that, from my perspective, and contrary to most approaches on the interaction between political philosophy and pragmatism, the *latter* justifies and illustrates the *former* as much as the other way round. While I have focused here on the mythical and symbolic aspects of One Nation and its antecedents, in fact it set out to be practical, to provide a contrast with the practical consequences of its imagined alternative, the neo-liberal deviation that had led to 2008. Again, we can see here too that references to the practical reinforced the symbolic, rather than, or as well as, the other way round. This is essential to grasping the study of political party discourse: these were arguments which debated truth and would consider themselves scientific; they remained, however, discourses about truth, and were supported by the rhetoric of truth rather than a lived reality. They were an 'imagined' Common Good, rather than a demonstrable reality. One could argue that it is always thus.

THE CRITICS

One Nation's claims to integrity, pragmatism, effectiveness, and promise attempted to hold rhetorical sway but were vulnerable to those defending (versions of) the discourses that One Nation dominated, and this for two essential reasons. Like many though not all political philosophies or approaches, One Nation posited a harmony. Patriotism does hold the nation together, and Small is Beautiful. The citizens of communities know and care for one another. Families are strong. People are decent. Children are respected and respectful. Faith groups bring moral fibre and moral support to civil society. Everyone contributes. Everything works. This was its strength and its weakness. Harmony was its central tenet and its Achilles' heel, as it was here that its critics concentrated: that it was twee, Arcadian, Merrie England and, as Riddell pointed out on nostalgia: 'The risk for Blue Labourites lies in a Neverland inhabited by superannuated pigeon-fanciers who like Woodbines and Watneys and don't think much of foreigners. Britain is not a museum of nostalgia but a forward-looking country that became so sickened by new Labour's techno-cant that it now risks overdosing on the past'.[12] Historically (from the 1930s onwards), moreover, it was the version of socialism that could *not* impose itself, that did not work once national power was won. One Nation's 'inclusiveness' also meant that, like a belief system that asks you to 'buy into it', it was vulnerable to narrative attack because it would have itself transcendent of disharmony; and at a strategic level it had against it potentially all those who drew their inspiration from any part of Labour history and mythology that ran from 1940 to 2010... One Nation was not 'one'. Or, if it were, it would need not only doctrinal but policy texture, and very soon.

Roy Hattersley's early criticisms of Blue Labour[13] were particularly problematic in part because he could also draw upon a very strong mythology – he represented the Labour Britain of free school dinners and the abolition of rickets, cod-liver oil and Haliborange tablets, state education, and the NHS, against the Arcadian calls of 'hearts at peace, under an English heaven'.

---

[12] Riddell (2011). See also, Aaronovitch, D. (2011). 'Dreaming of Merrie Englande won't help Ed'. *The Times*. Available at http://www.thetimes.co.uk/tto/opinion/columnists/davidaaronovitch/article2956965.ece; also Bogdanor (2012); Bragg (2011); McCluskey (2013); and Toynbee (2013) in BBC Radio 4 *Analysis, 'Labour's New New Jerusalem'*. Available at http://www.bbc.co.uk/programmes/b01sm2g0

[13] Hattersley, R. (2011) in *'Blue Labour'*, BBC Radio 4 *Analysis*, transcript. Available at http://news.bbc.co.uk/nol/shared/spl/hi/programmes/analysis/transcripts/21_03_11.txt

In May 2013, Peter Kellner of YouGov stated that Labour 'has got to get match fit, it has got to prepare' (Kellner 2013). On 27 May, Radio 4 broadcast 'Labour's New New Jerusalem' – a 30-minute analysis of One Nation.[14] As I have argued, the programme was striking because of the way its advocates were assertive of the dominance of their narrative within the party, and were at great pains to point out not only its merit, but its practical success. It used the very practical achievements of the Labour Mayor of Newham as evidence, as well as very direct attacks upon the post-1945 welfare state. As a discourse of harmony, however, it was vulnerable to the criticisms of Polly Toynbee, who featured prominently in the programme, and this for two reasons: first because of her status on the left as one of its major thinkers over the last 20 years; second, because her criticism centred upon One Nation's potential inadequacies *in practice*, and its underestimation of the 1945 government's achievements.

The second reason for the vulnerability (and at one level its only purpose and potential strength) of the One Nation narrative was that by 2012–2013, alongside its unitary, 'migratory' nature, it had become highly personalized. It became the rhetoric of Miliband in every forum he performed within. The element of harmony and equilibrium meant, therefore, that One Nation became vulnerable through personal attacks upon or undermining of his persona. It is true that at and after Manchester 2012, Miliband's leadership status was, through performance, enhanced significantly (as I shall argue in Chapter 4). Criticisms of him or of One Nation now would have a salience they had not had before. Blair's admonition of April 2013 not to push the party leftwards[15] was a direct personal assault upon Miliband's leadership; as was trade unionist and General Secretary of Unite, Len McCluskey's (in the other direction):

> We believe that Ed should try to create a radical alternative. My personal fear, and that of my union, is that if he goes to the electorate with an austerity-lite programme, then he will get defeated ... Ed Miliband must spend most of his waking hours grappling with what lies before him. If he is brave enough to go for something radical, he'll be the next Prime Minister. If he gets seduced by the Jim Murphys and the Douglas Alexanders, then the truth is that he'll be defeated and he'll be cast into the dustbin of history. (McCluskey 2013)

---

[14]BBC Radio 4 *Analysis*. (2013). *'Labour's New New Jerusalem'*, 27 May 2013, Available at http://www.bbc.co.uk/programmes/b01sm2g0

[15]Blair (2013). See also Rutherford (2013).

These warnings (Blair) and threats (McCluskey) were not really attacks upon policy but upon the status of the leader. Miliband was, therefore, both strengthened and made more vulnerable by the wide-ranging One Nation discourse offered to him. It brought to the foreground his claim to strong and doctrinally informed leadership, but it meant that he would be vulnerable to attacks upon it, and the attacks themselves would undermine it and him because One Nation was a rhetoric of deliverance: a rhetoric that would bring deliverance in mythical terms (the land we shall migrate to) and practical terms (a policy offer); all 'led' by the inspirational leader.

From a theoretical point of view, we should stress that the leadership's relationship to the developing narrative was not analysed within the party in any meaningful way, and yet it was arguably the single most important issue in the period 2013–2015.[16] This is a serious issue, and one that affects leftist political parties and movements universally, namely, that one of the issues given very little thoughtful attention by the party – leadership and its relation to doctrine, and later policy – is, performatively, one of the most important. It is significant that nearly every contributor in *One Nation Labour – Debating the Future* referred, in a range that ran from a symbolic nod to a virtual genuflection, to the idea of the Miliband of Manchester 2012 as the inspiration of their own One Nation commitment and undertaking in the subsequent period. Every one of them said *that* he was an inspiration; not one of them said *how* he was. At best, leadership is an unknown in leftist discourse and thought, is misunderstood and ill-thought out; at worst, it is an ideological blind spot, an 'unknown unknown', with serious consequences for the functioning of a leftist political party.

CONCLUSION

Two final remarks are appropriate, one theoretical, one practical. Theoretically, our study has pointed to the dualism – and therefore, at one level, simplicity – informing the One Nation narrative. That is to say, that in order to impose itself, it represented the Labour 'universe' as a duality. There is One Nation (1900–1939; 2010 and beyond) and there were the lost paths, namely, the post-war settlement (1945–1979) and neo-liberalism (1979–2010). Swathes of influence upon Labour were omitted: Liberal thought (J.S. Mill, Lloyd George, Keynes, Beveridge), Suffragism and the women's movement, The New Left (parts of early New Left were included), Michael Foot's radicalism, Militant, Tony Benn's (and Jeremy Corbyn's) influence,

[16] Marc Stears' essay in Glasman et al. (2011) on 'Democracy, leadership and organising' and the responses to the essay in the text were the only iteration of this issue.

the evolution of trade unionism, the SDP phenomenon, Livingstone's mayoralty, the manifest successes of New Labour, and so on. This exclusiveness may have been rhetorically necessary, but it is worth stressing its role and effects. One Nation indicated the crucial role of memory in political discourse and ideology, but it was also a rhetorical resource that may or may not have reflected accurately that which was remembered. A related point is the question of the place of Utopian thought in political discourse. Space does not allow us to go into the point here, but it is worth stressing that it is a rhetorical resource *everywhere* in political philosophy and discourse.

The practical and concluding point we can make regarding One Nation is that – to the growing consternation of many by 2013 – it may have been necessary, but it was a long process which needed seamless development after Manchester 2012. We can see from our examination of the events and the texts of the period 2010–2013, that the central authors of what became the One Nation narrative were adamant that the doctrinal development of an alternative narrative was a necessary ideational high road to take in order to prepare the party for the future and align the discourse with that of the new leadership. In the course of 2013–2014 this would transmute into the next discursive battle for policy proposals and a legislative programme for the 2015 General Election. We shall examine in Chapter 5 how it did not do this adequately; policy proposals on a grand scale which were linked ideationally *and* to the One Nation narrative were an imperative.

The scale of the 2010 General Election defeat meant that space was opened up for a new party narrative appropriate to, first, the scale of the defeat; second, the renewal of the party's purpose; and third, the exigencies of the party's new leadership. Using narrative theory helps demonstrate the development of the One Nation narrative as a creative discursive moment in the Labour Party's history and the party political role of such creativity more generally.

CHAPTER 4

Rhetoric and Performance: Miliband's Finest Hour (Sixty-Four Minutes and Forty-Seven Seconds, in fact)

Political 'performance' is central to understanding contemporary British political leadership, despite the absence of a presidential system of governance. This chapter examines Ed Miliband in the context of an emerging scholarship on rhetoric, persona, and celebrity and the effects of individual performance upon the political process. Specifically, it analyses his 'leadership performance' at the 2012 Labour Party Conference. My analysis identifies the ways in which, through performance of 'himself' and the beginnings of the deployment of an alternative party narrative centred upon 'One Nation', Ed Miliband began to revise his 'received persona' through a range of rhetorical and other techniques which 'choreographed' the Party Conference.[1] Let us now look in detail and in all its dimensions at this moment of performance. In fact, it was Ed Miliband's finest performance. I will review some of the emerging theory on celebrity politics and leadership rhetoric and how it has taken us beyond notions of charisma.

There have been a number of related studies since John Corner's identification of three modes of leadership performance (iconic, vocal, and kinetic) (Corner 2000); and John Street's 2004 article on celebrity politicians. At a developed theoretical level, this research has grown in reaction to – although it actually complements – both economic and sociological approaches to the study of politics; namely, that what political actors do in the political arena and *how* they persuade other actors and the wider public to agree or to act are crucial to how politics works, and are also severely under-researched

---

[1] This chapter is an elaboration of Gaffney and Lahel (2013).

© The Author(s) 2017
J. Gaffney, *Leadership and the Labour Party*, Palgrave Studies in Political Leadership, DOI 10.1057/978-1-137-50498-2_4

(*inter alia* Corner 2000; Corner and Pels 2003; Drake and Higgins 2012; Finlayson 2002, 2004, 2007; Martin 2015; Street 2004, 2012; Wheeler 2012. For a political psychology perspective see Garzia 2014).

I am going to focus upon Ed Miliband's performance during the 2012 Labour Party Conference in Manchester as a consequent moment in the on-going political process. My approach focuses upon agency (political leadership) in relational complexity to structure (political institutions). I shall preface my analysis with a theoretical discussion of the recent literature on leadership performance and related topics (mediated performance, persona, celebrity, image, style, and political rhetoric). I will draw a series of theoretical and methodological conclusions from these and set the scene (rather literally) for our analysis of Miliband's Conference performance. I shall identify what I call the 'received persona', that is, the public image or images of Miliband which constituted the context – and in this case part of the reactive *raison d'être* – of his performance. I shall then examine the range of other performances during Conference 2012 which constituted the overall performance.

THEORETICAL CONTEXT: RHETORIC, PERSONA, AND CELEBRITY

Alan Finlayson (2002) analysed the self-presentation of then UK Prime Minister Tony Blair through style, appearance, and language and the creation of an imagined intimacy between himself and the wider public. Finlayson analysed a range of party broadcasts (1994–2001) indicative of what he termed New Labour's populism, a populism both displayed and mobilized through the construction of the character, Tony Blair (to be clear, this is a different notion of populism to the one I discuss in Chapter 5). The political party and wider cultural framework of celebrity and personalization enabled the symbolism of leadership to inform political processes and outcomes more frequently, and more successfully, than had been hitherto the case. For example, images of Blair indulging in a shared national pastime like drinking tea (from a mug rather than a cup and saucer...) conveyed notions of something shared with his audience through connecting obliquely with its cultural meaning systems. Audience (here, everybody watching/listening) contributes to and sustains cultural practices; and leadership performance can create a shared and, paradoxically, privileged set of relationships. The performance of a culturally apt image and identification with followers was formative of Blair's 'one of us' image (Finlayson 2002) and 'regular guy' persona (see also Abrams 1997).

James Martin's research used a similar interpretivist methodology to Finlayson. For Martin (2015), a political speech is a dynamic medium for mobilizing ideas as a form of action. Martin set out a rhetorical approach to political strategy which analysed (a) the rhetorical context, (b) the rhetorical argument, and (c) rhetorical effects. As mentioned above, John Corner (2000) argued that what he called political personhood was mediated *iconically* (political publicity such as photo opportunities); *vocally* (recording technologies which have allowed an increasing informality of public address); and *kinetically* – the political self in action and interaction (e.g., the 'high politics' of the international conference, the 'low politics' of the visit to the factory). For television in particular this required choreographic attention, not least to avoid 'accidents' in performance (for example, a previous Labour leader, Neil Kinnock, stumbled and fell backwards during a photo opportunity on Brighton beach in 1983. The clip haunted his leadership term (1983–1992); Ed's 'bacon sandwich' clip in 2014 was equally destructive). Cumulatively, the iconic, vocal, and kinetic enhance the 'personal' operating within a political culture and institutions, each offering opportunities and constraints for the use of persona to have political effect. *Media and the Restyling of Politics* (Corner and Pels 2003) comprised a comprehensive range of essays on political marketing, celebrity culture, and the personalization of politics. Pels pointed to the emotional dimensions of the restyling of politics and referred to the crucial place of notions of 'authenticity' in citizen evaluations of televisual political figures.

The central argument by John Street (2004) was that the celebrity politician was not an exaggerated or exceptional form of political representation, but characteristic of the nature of political representation generally. His later article 'Do Celebrity Politics and Celebrity Politicians Matter?' (Street 2012) asked what it meant to take celebrity politics seriously. His view was that celebrity politics and its effects varied across polities. He proposed comparative analyses into the process through which 'celebrity' was produced in different political and media systems. His insights demonstrate a particular finding relevant to my analysis here, namely, that celebrity and political performance are in a changing and dynamic relationship to one another. Street's (2004, 2012) assessment of political celebrity is also relevant to my analysis in that, as I pointed out in Chapter 1, I seek to understand the cultural and institutional conditions of contemporary political celebrity as well as the process through which celebrity gains political expression. Wheeler (2012) built upon the work of Street (2004) and asked to what extent celebrity politicians' 'input' aggregated forms of 'agency' to effect political outcomes. He used Barack Obama's 2008 election campaign as a case study to discuss how Obama defined himself and his relationship to opinion and the voters, and utilized innovations in communication technologies to re-engage with the American electorate. I note in passing that new forms of technology have altered the relationship between politicians and audiences; for example, new forms of e-activism (Hodges 2011; see also Bennett 2014) (Twitter, blogging, Facebook) have created imagined proximity to leadership actors and altered the 'pace' and arguably the stability of the relationship. My analysis explores the role and performance of celebrity as a formative part of this new relationship.

Research by Drake and Higgins (2012) combined political language, mediated performance, and celebrity. They reconceptualized celebrity as a process or a 'frame', as opposed to a quality that individuals possess; a celebrity frame has both performative and interpretive rules through which particular media publics are configured and addressed. Their analysis of the UK Leaders' Debates during the 2010 General Election campaign was particularly insightful as regards the candidates' use of different performative strategies to create the impression of authenticity.

Taking into account this emerging literature, my approach here concentrates on leadership performance rhetorically, performatively, and iconically. The growing body of UK research is a critical response to the emergence of the political actor/leader as a 'celebrity', an echo of the dramatic rise of the celebrity culture generally. My approach also takes into account the fact that since the emergence of celebrity politics, political leaders have become – falteringly, in many cases – part of a star system (Dyer and McDonald 1998; Dyer 2003). In UK politics from Margaret Thatcher onwards, the exigencies of attention to and effects of image, look, style, rhetoric, character, and comportment fostered an entourage of advisors and speechwriters. Alongside this, as the media in all its forms became more formative and, paradoxically, more 'fracturing' of persona in the political sphere, the perceived need to 'market' leadership and control and fashion the media brought centre stage, or rather backstage, the generation of Gordon Reeces, Peter Mandelsons, Alastair Campbells, and their successors, who understood their craft with varying degrees of comprehension.

There are several audiences I shall refer to where appropriate: the audience physically present, the media, and the wider public. These interact with each other, and the demarcations between them are permeable.

Then there are other audiences: adversaries, both internal and external, the international audience (of media and overseas political parties and guests), the 'casual' audience watching the Party Conference on television (or hearing or reading about it), political observers and academics, lobbies of different kinds, the now all-pervasive tweeters, and so on. Every individual, in fact, is an audience. Over and above this, and perhaps more importantly in terms of performance and rhetorical analysis, audiences, although 'real', are also 'imagined'. For example, the 'British people' exist, but most importantly as an imagined community with a particular character. Even the actual Conference audience is imagined as the party itself, or as an idealized community beyond the party machinery. Having said this, my focus here is on the performance itself rather than on the relationship between performance and audience; that said, at a push I would say that the imagined audience (the electorate, for example) is more important than the 'actual' audience.

There are two major factors driving political leadership image. The first is what the leader wants to do and say, and how he or she wants to appear, or 'seem', informed by a team of advisors and a party offering a doctrine and tradition (a narrative) from which to draw: what the leader would have himself or herself to be. The second is what happens – as with any creative act – after the fashioned persona acts in the political arena. Here the media, adversaries, cartoonists (and satire generally), bloggers, commentators, and the wider public, all receive *and contribute to* the elaboration of the performance and thereby, over time, to the persona. In part, Matisse's 'Seated Woman, Back Turned to the Open Window' is a brilliant painting, *Brief Encounter* a brilliant film because of the people who see them – if Max Weber (see Chapter 1) had been bolder he might have been right....

I should stress that, certainly for the purposes of analysis, the performance I analyse is, as I said in my acknowledgements, that of the persona of the political leader rather than the actual person. The persona and the person may be near-synonymous (although strangely this is of limited interest): the performance is the projection of the leader-as-persona; the projected persona is the result of the performance. The leader is real yet also 'imagined', constructed in terms of and for the purposes of the leader's relationship to the audience. The image itself, however, is not only that which is projected by a performance, but is also – is preceded by – the 'received view' that an audience has of a leader. My analysis here demonstrates how performance can alter the hitherto perceived image of a leader, and in Miliband's case at the 2012 Labour Party Conference in Manchester, quite markedly.

To recapitulate: leaders interpolate ideas, gathering them together (drawing for example, from a doctrinal or ideational cluster such as socialism or populism), projecting them – through the performance of the political persona – into the public sphere (Finlayson 2002, 2014; Martin 2015). Because the medium is overwhelmingly the media, the projection is a refraction that informs and affects how leaders and their ideas appear (Corner 2000). The projection of the persona will have emotional effects ranging from hostility, through indifference, to agreement, enthusiasm, even devotion (Corner and Pels 2003; see also Atkinson 1984, 2004). The now normative relationship between projected leadership and celebrity (Street 2004, 2012) constantly creates new forms of leadership persona which offer the idea of change in the relationship between leader and followers as well as in the persona itself (Wheeler 2012). The relational performance of persona is best understood as taking place within a framework of conventions and processes that is formative of performance which itself is embedded in a cultural context (Drake and Higgins 2012). I can add to this my own emphasis, first on the performance itself as an act or action. A linguistic analogy: everything that preceded the act – context, ideas, culture, received persona, and so on – is diachronic, like *langue*; the political performance itself is synchronic, like a speech act (*parole*) that mediates and alters the conditions of performance. Second, the persona and audience(s) are real, but more than that, are 'imagined' (one might say literally, though that is surely a contradiction, in this case 'idealized') perhaps in a rather more autonomous way than communities are imagined by Anderson (1983) and Gaffney (2001). And it is here that the rhetorical scope is given to the imagining, constructing, reinforcing, changing, and intensifying of the relationship between leader and audience, and this through rhetoric.

Before proceeding to my analysis, let me make or restate two theoretical/ methodological points. First, the performance of a political leader is now a formative moment in the ongoing political process. I shall take political performance to include the public actions, utterances, interventions, speeches, and general comportment of political actors constitutive of political persona. Part of persona is what we can call the 'received persona', that is, the persona that pre-exists current performance. And, as I have said, the configuration of institutions (e.g., the Conference and its leadership speech) that leaders perform within provides scope to personalize the self to political consequence, with all the opportunities and risks involved. My definition of political performance is therefore twofold: (1) physical, including the comportment, gestures, image, and style of political actors; (2) verbal and discursive, including the physical, but stressing the role of language and rhetoric and its deployment to political effect.

Second, style and image are not strictly performance – performative acts – in the sense that, for example, rhetoric is; however, they accompany, contribute to, and emerge from political performance; essentially, the repetition of particular leadership traits and the suggestion of character traits constitute leadership style. Image is the acquired public perception of a political actor. Tony Blair's image was partly constructed by him (and 'Team Blair') through physical and discursive performances, but also through performance as communicated to and refracted by the media to the wider public, and related to by the wider public. And the endorsement of Tony Blair's 'straight sort of guy' image by the media (in that case, radio) helped him constitute his publicly perceived political persona. The caveat – and it is a major caveat – is that political actors are not fully in control of their image either as they perform or as it refracts through the media. In some circumstances – often cumulatively – image goes out of control. The premiership of Gordon Brown, from the autumn of 2007 until May 2010, illustrated the cumulative negative impact of media portrayal, and the difficult-to-control refraction of leadership performance in the public realm. The fragility of persona is now self-evident; persona is susceptible to interpretation, reinterpretation, and often damaging representation. Political persona is now also susceptible to the same exigencies as celebrity persona (some of which are more stringent, e.g., ethical issues): sudden reversals, loss of reputation, the need for constant media presence, and persona affirmation, the constant display of personal qualities and character traits, the need to respond to events of a dramatic or ethical nature, to name but a few. Leadership performance now dominates the public dimension of the political process.

Let us now focus on the Labour Party Conference 2012 as a moment of the interpolation of leadership. My analysis proceeds from three angles. First, I shall refer to Ed Miliband's 'received' persona as a condition of his performance during Conference 2012. Second, I shall analyse a range of performances during the Conference period. In conclusion, I shall identify the ways in which, through political performance of 'himself' as it were, and the creation of a potentially alternative party narrative, Ed Miliband began to revise his mediated image and political persona, arguably from that of a weak opposition leader to a credible potential Prime Minister.

'RECEIVED PERSONA': AND MILIBAND'S 2012 PERFORMANCE

I shall refer briefly to four examples constitutive of Miliband's 'received' image and persona prior to the Labour Party Conference: 'Red Ed'; the ramifications of the 2010 leadership contest; and the depiction of Ed Miliband as Wallace (from Wallace and Gromit) by David Cameron and the media, and the consequences of these upon his persona.

First, during the 2010 party leadership election, Ed Miliband was referred to as 'Red Ed' by the media, the term portraying him as representing the left of the party, a view reinforced by the backing of trade unions in his leadership campaign and election. The term offered Miliband a certain campaigning radical image as a leadership candidate, but threw his leadership image into disarray once he became leader, underlining as it did the idea that the party had elected the 'wrong', the more marginal candidate. Second, both Ed Miliband and his brother David entered the Labour Party leadership election of 2010. A widely held view throughout the Brown premiership, and prior to the internal contest, was that David Miliband was the likely, almost 'natural' heir to the Labour Party leadership. The contest therefore had an emotional edge in which Miliband Minor beat Miliband Major as if usurping a crown, fratricidally. And he won by only 1.3 %,[2] raising questions about his broader legitimacy as party leader. He was the first Labour leader to have won under the post-1980 Electoral College system without gaining a majority of party members (Freedland 2010). Negative media representations of Miliband emerged in the immediate aftermath of the leadership election and persisted right up until Conference 2012.[3] Cumulative negative characterizations all pointed to Miliband's 'inappropriateness' as leader: 'geek' (Kite 2010); 'the man who shafted his brother' (Mount in Cowley 2012); a policy-wonk or an

---

[2] Ed Miliband won by 1.3 % after second preference votes were taken into account. David Miliband secured 37.78 % of first preference votes, compared to 34.33 % for his brother. But Ed Miliband won with 50.7 % of votes to David Miliband's 49.3 %, after the second preference votes of Diane Abbott, Andy Burnham and Ed Balls were taken into account. See H. Mulholland (2010) 'Ed Miliband defeats older brother in race to be Labour leader', *The Guardian,* http://www.guardian.co.uk/politics/2010/sep/25/ed-miliband-labour-leader

[3] A semi-authorized biography/analysis by two leading Westminster journalists gave a detailed account of the feud between the brothers, especially from the general election of May 2010 up until the Labour leadership election in September. (The book, however, was not especially critical of Ed Miliband.) See M. Hasan, M. and J. Macintyre (2011) *Ed: The Milibands and the Making of a Labour Leader* (London: Biteback Publishing).

out-of-touch North-London intellectual; a weak leader who was unable to command political authority and was not strong on policy detail; 'Miliband minor' (Deedes 2012); and the more sympathetic but problematic 'Ed the outsider, the underdog' (Hasan 2012). Third, a damaging depiction came from Prime Minister David Cameron at the beginning of 2011 when he likened Ed to the plasticine cartoon character, Wallace, from Wallace and Gromit (PMQs 2011). Ed's passing resemblance to the hapless, twitty inventor whose ideas rarely go according to plan portrayed him as a leader utterly ill-equipped to command political authority and repair the Blair/ Brown, now David/Ed, cleavage within the party. Miliband conceded that he was 'somebody who looks a bit like Wallace from Wallace & Gromit. If spin doctors could design a politician, I suspect he wouldn't look like me' (Miliband, *The Telegraph*, 7 December 2011). Bringing humour to the depiction diffused the somewhat on-going negative discussion about his character and image, but underlined his depiction as the less glamorous younger brother.

In sum, Miliband's received persona post-2010 and ahead of Conference 2012 had been relentlessly negative, in spite of the growing unpopularity of the coalition government. A range of traits associated with betrayal, lack of leadership skills and contested legitimacy undermined his status in the party and in the mainstream media. The dramatic deterioration of other leaders (several post-Thatcher Conservative leaders, and most recently Premier Brown) created a sense that Miliband's leadership status might actually collapse very suddenly (and that there might be an early leadership challenge).

Immediately prior to Conference 2012, the media focused a great deal on Ed Miliband's character and image, some sympathetic (on the left), most not. Let me mention briefly Miliband's celebrity-style interview in *New Statesman*, two critical articles on Miliband's character by Alan Johnson and Rafael Behr who wrote about Ed Miliband's charisma problem, and a highly publicized poll which compared Ed unfavourably to David. All of these acted as a kind of immediate context to the Manchester conference.

Three weeks before the conference, Miliband was interviewed by the left-of-centre current affairs magazine *New Statesman*. The interview entitled 'He's not for Turning' was five pages long. It began by describing the interview setting, Miliband's garden. The interviewer, Jason Cowley, romanticized the setting: 'it is one of those rare, luminous September mornings, the light diffuse and all the more beautiful because you know the days are inexorably shortening. The garden is overgrown, the grass damp underfoot in the early-morning sunshine.' After the oddly pastoral scene was set, Cowley noted Tom Baldwin's presence as Miliband's media aide who 'pulls up chairs and brings us tea' (echoes of Blair's tea mug). Indeed, the article itself echoed the *Hello!* Magazine celebrity interview that has become so pervasive in British culture; the interview that followed was highly personalized.

Miliband's use of the first person pronoun 'I', was widespread in the interview, and constantly drew attention to himself, and the books he read on holiday, his family and children, his personal tasks ahead, self-imposed challenges, as well as reflections on policies, spending commitments, and so on. The personal and what we have called 'the personalized political' interweave throughout the article. In between Miliband's responses to questions and personal insights, Cowley, Baldwin, and Marc Stears (Oxford academic and Miliband's friend) were helping create a new kind of Miliband persona, in that they portrayed the team of advisors and listeners quietly gathered around the leader as he reflected upon the future.

In terms of the presentation of the interview, Miliband was photographed twice in his nice North London garden (once in black and white and once in colour). In the first photo, Miliband is sitting on a bench, leaning forwards, hands clasped, looking slightly away from the camera, and smiling; relaxed, reflective, and approachable. In the second image, he is standing amongst some overgrown shrubs; with a slight smile and relaxed composure (hands in pockets). Both images (as well as the magazine's cover featuring Miliband) moved us away from previous 'received' images of Miliband, and prefaced a concerted and new leadership performance.

The second example of pre-Conference media was Alan Johnson's article in *The Guardian* (like *New Statesman* also left-of-centre) on 26 September entitled 'Ed Miliband, show us you have what it takes to be Prime Minister' (subtitle: 'His Labour Party is resurgent. But in Manchester Miliband must do more to demonstrate that he is a leader') (Johnson 2012). Johnson summed up the article: 'Ed Miliband now has the chance to show that there is an alternative. But there is no use earning the right to be listened to if you have nothing to say'. The semi-critical article by Johnson, a now 'fatherly' credible (and plain-speaking) political figure within the party, was an expression of an internal view regarding policy inaction by Miliband; but Johnson's mixing of the personal and policy-related was significant in its implication that any successful way forward depended crucially upon Miliband's upcoming performance – and it is clear that Johnson was conflating the 'leading' and the 'saying', so that

Miliband's Conference speech was being signalled as crucial to his leadership image. Any lack of rhetorical *and* policy substance, therefore, would be associated with a lack of political agency, and vice versa.

Third, days before Conference 2012, Rafael Behr wrote an article in *New Statesman* entitled 'Project "Ed's Charisma" – the mission to help Miliband loosen up' (Behr 2012). The article was not especially critical of Miliband; it did, however, note his perceived lack of charisma as being problematic in imagining him as future Prime Minister. Behr's article cumulatively illustrated Miliband's negatively received image by the media, colleagues, rivals, and adversaries. The writing of Behr's article immediately before the Conference offered a context to Miliband's forthcoming performance. A 'bad' performance at Conference would confirm the existing view that Miliband did, in fact, have a personal appeal problem; conversely, a positively received performance would alter the hitherto-held view. Both articles, by insisting upon the issue of character, displaced attention even further away from party and towards the leader's upcoming 'performance'.

The fourth and ostensibly damaging example of pre-Conference media was the stress upon the unpopularity of Ed Miliband in relation to David, outlined in a Populus opinion poll commissioned by the Conservative Party on 28 September 2012, 2 days before the Party Conference. The headline 'Two in three Labour voters want to ditch leader Ed Miliband for his brother David' once again raised the question of Miliband Minor's legitimacy as party leader. The article stated: 'Just one in four voters believes Mr Miliband is the right man to revive economic prospects, that 67 per cent of all voters think his party "chose the wrong brother", and that 65 per cent of Labour voters say David Miliband would do a better job' (Groves and Shipman 2012). Discussion of the poll was the cover story in *The Independent* and all the media covered the leadership issue (constantly referring to the term 'charisma') right up until the Conference. Character and performance, then, would be central to the Conference.

CONFERENCE 2012

Let us examine the following performances: arrival at Conference (29 September). Conference Day 1 (30 September) – including an interview with Andrew Marr and a lecture by Professor Michael Sandel to help provide context. Conference Day 2 (1 October) – presence at Fringe Events. Conference Day 3 (2 October) – Keynote speech. Conference Day 4 (3 October) – Q&A Session (and we might add his *absence* on the final morning, Day 5).

ARRIVAL AT CONFERENCE, 29 SEPTEMBER

Ed Miliband arrived in Manchester with his family, by train, 1 day ahead of the Party Conference. Two images of Ed and his family were given wide coverage in the mainstream media. The first image conveyed the 'ordinariness' of a young family travelling on a train (in Standard Class). The children were sitting on the parents' laps with toys and story books scattered across the table. In the second, the Milibands were pictured walking along the platform at Manchester. Miliband had his eldest child upon his shoulders and Justine carried the youngest against her hip. The images of the Milibands travelling to Manchester, use of economy travel and interaction with his children, portrayed Ed Miliband as a 'today's' father and husband who took his parental duties in his stride. These 'natural' images were 'staged' (in the first photo, the toys on the table are clearly arranged for the camera (as is the family); in the second, the Milibands depart the train with no luggage, no coats, and are the only people walking along the platform). Nevertheless, each photo would come across as 'natural', a party leader who appeared like 'a regular guy' in the Blair mode, a 40-something father of a young family, and relaxed – this would become very important – unpretentious, and accessible.

On the day that Ed Miliband arrived in Manchester, he conducted an informal Q&A with people (i.e., non-delegates) at East Manchester Academy. The location for the Q&A was outside the secure conference area. This was a high-risk image strategy given that heckling was a real possibility. The strategy did, however, convey the impression that Miliband was open to free debate.

CONFERENCE DAY 1, 30 SEPTEMBER: INTERVIEW WITH ANDREW MARR

On Day 1, Ed Miliband was interviewed by Andrew Marr for the BBC's weekly politics show *The Andrew Marr Show*. The 20-minute interview covered a range of issues, from policy making, the public and private sectors and party funding, to Miliband's relationship with trade union leaders, the economy, unemployment, bankers' bonuses, the NHS, and Coalition politics. Miliband's responses to policy questions were short and abstract, i.e., references to predistribution, fairness or opportunity for all; but the role of personal character in the interview, specifically Marr's questioning Miliband's image, leadership appeal, and popularity (see extract from transcript below) was central:

ANDREW MARR:

[...] and your own personal ratings, they're still pretty terrible. I mean very, very large numbers of people still saying 'I don't see this man as a future Prime Minister'.

ED MILIBAND:

I think it's quite a compliment actually that the Tories produced a poll yesterday about me. I think it shows I've got them worried. [...]

ANDREW MARR:

But however you regard all this stuff, it is part of the job of a modern leader to project him or herself in a way that people find appealing.

ED MILIBAND:

Sure.

ANDREW MARR:

And you've struggled to do that so far. What more do you do? How can you approach this, because you know it's not trivial?

ED MILIBAND:

Well that's your characterisation. Here's what I think. I think ideas matter in politics and I'm not embarrassed about that, right?

ANDREW MARR:

So the wonky stuff is ... you know it's fine. Wonk, geek, no problem with that?

ED MILIBAND:

Absolu... Look. No, let me be clear about this. You know I gave a speech last year at the Labour Party conference. It was controversial. I talked about the predator companies, predatory behaviour. I don't regret that speech because it spoke to ... and over the last year people said actually maybe he was right about that. And so look, you know I'm very clear about this. I'm my own person ... (See Marr 2012 for full interview video and transcript).

We can see from this that the references to policy and other issues were simply preludes, accompaniments to the central issue that would dominate the Conference, the character of the leader. We can see that Miliband's defence against Marr's deprecating remarks was very weak, as if he knew that there was nothing he could do here, only suggest a conviction, suggestive of something to come.

On the same day as Miliband's interview with Andrew Marr, Harriet Harman, deputy leader of the Labour Party, conceded in an interview for the BBC's *Sunday Politics* show that not many people knew who the Leader of the Opposition was and that Ed Miliband had a lot of work to do (see Harman 2012). The negative remarks, highlighting Ed Miliband's unpopularity in the public realm, created the discursive conditions for a 'comeback', as it were. It is as if Miliband's subsequent performances were being given a shape or a framework. We shall return to this point in our conclusion of this chapter.

LECTURE BY PROFESSOR MICHAEL SANDEL

Sandel's was, of course, not Miliband's own performance, but was crucial to its understanding. Harvard Professor Michael Sandel delivered a lecture to Conference on the afternoon of Day 1. The 45-minute lecture to party members and delegates explained 'predistribution' as an economic goal, a policy term that Miliband gestured towards in his 2011 Conference speech entitled 'Producers versus Predators' on responsible capitalism, and referred explicitly to in his speech to the progressive London-based think tank, Policy Network, on 6 September 2012, in his highly personalised *New Statesman* interview, and in the Marr interview the same morning. Sandel's presence at Conference 2012 illustrated Miliband's relationship with academics and their use of academic phraseology; the lecture drew attention to Miliband's elite academic background, but oblique references to being intellectual or being connected to intellectuals are not necessarily damaging. The appearance of a major public intellectual (and Sandel's lectures on YouTube were enormously popular) at the 2012 Conference stressed the insightfulness of the leader in his earlier, unpopular, but – through Sandel's endorsement – accurate analyses, thus elevating Miliband's status to that of someone who had understood before 'we' had. Sandel concluded his lecture:

> Democracy does not require perfect equality. But it does require that citizens share a common life. What matters is that people of different social backgrounds, different walks of life, encounter one another, bump up against one another, in the course of everyday life. Because this is how we come to negotiate and abide our differences and this is how we come to care for the common good. (Sandel 2012)

The quotation prefigured Miliband's forthcoming policy focus upon community, citizenship, and society, the main features of his speech the following day. The role of Sandel's speech overall was to justify both *ex ante* and *post facto* Miliband's insightfulness.

Conference Day 2, 1 October: Miliband's Presence at Fringe Events

At a fringe event on the Monday evening on Day 2, the meeting of the 'Friends of Europe' group, Miliband briefly attended with his wife, Justine (who stood to the side of the small stage in the audience), and comedian Eddie Izzard (who spoke after him). Miliband said (and this only 24 hours into the conference) that this was the fullest Fringe meeting of the 30 he had attended. Miliband's attendance at Fringe events alone illustrated his 'presence' during Conference 2012, somewhat altering the leader's relationship to the conference. No previous party leaders had attended so many Fringe events (in fact, Fringe events are by nature non-leadership events). It is clear that Conference 2012 was being 'inhabited' by Ed Miliband in a symbolic, unmediated relationship between himself and the conference attendees. Miliband then left the stage, re-joined his wife and slowly made his way through the room to the exit, all the while talking to groups and individuals. There is a subtle blending here of, on the one hand, proximity and accessibility (taking time to come; taking a lot of time to slowly exit accompanied by his wife) while underlining his special leadership status.

Conference Day 3, 2 October: Keynote Speech[4]

In a 65-minute-long speech without an autocue, notes, or teleprompter, through performing 'himself' as it were, Miliband began truly to inflect his received persona. My analysis of the speech focuses upon how he 'creates' the One Nation narrative, becomes its author, and 'shares' it with the

[4] Immediately before the speech, the conference hall was shown a 5-minute long video of Ed Miliband. The video entitled 'A Better Future', a mini-bio, contained personal references to Miliband's childhood and education. Post-keynote speech, however, the video was not mentioned by the mainstream media; in fact, it was almost immediately forgotten, Miliband's performance eclipsing it.

audience. Furthermore, we can demonstrate the 'offer' of a new relationship between the (new personality of the) speaker, and both the actual and
the 'imagined' wider audience.

KEYNOTE SPEECH: OPENING MOMENTS

The conference hall in Manchester was full. 'Rebuilding Britain' was the
slogan that was projected onto the image of a Union Jack. As part of
the backdrop, the left and right of the stage had another image of the
Union Jack with the text 'Labour' – a suggestion that political agency (Ed
Miliband) was about to elaborate a *new* narrative that was unlike New or
Old Labour.

As Miliband walked out onto the low stage, he was greeted with a standing ovation. He immediately greeted a small section of the party faithful
positioned on stage (who reflected youth, gender balance, and diversity);
the meet-and-greet was then extended to the wider conference hall as he
walked around the front of the stage waving at the crowd whilst uttering
'thank you, thank you very much' several times. Acknowledgement of the
audience is crucial in terms of imagined dialogue between speaker and followers. Miliband's opening statement was:

> Thank you so much friends. It is great to be in Labour Manchester. And you
> know Manchester has special memories for me because two years ago I was
> elected the leader of this party. I'm older. I feel a lot older actually. I hope
> I'm a bit wiser. But I am prouder than ever to be the Leader of the Labour
> Party. (Miliband 2012)

The opening statement countered the post-2010 ideas about his status
and authority as leader of the Labour Party, by evoking the idea of the
leader returning to the original place, now wiser and as if – now – legitimate. The humour and slight self-deprecation masked a deep structure of
leadership performance. And the performance itself would become the
'proof' of the assumption of 'authority'. Miliband's use of humour and
ability to speak without notes while walking about the stage, as if convers-
ing with party members, created a sense of proximity to the audience. The
entire speech thereafter was performed without notes or a teleprompter.
During the first 12 minutes of Miliband's extended opening of his keynote
speech, he reasserted his identity as party leader, but through humour and
a series of highly personalized insights into his family, his feelings, and his

education. He shared himself with his audience by bringing it, as if, into his private life. More personalized and humorous references followed, a humour which in previous speeches had not been used. Humorous references to his son Daniel and dinosaurs brought hilarious laughter; very early on in the speech, therefore, there is a kind of endorsement of Miliband by the audience, thus legitimating a highly personalized speech thereafter. There was even humour about the act of speech writing itself:

> [...] the Leader's Speech [...] can be a bit of a trial. You get all kinds of advice from people. Say this, don't say that. Smile here, don't smile there. Stand there, don't stand there. [...] And so the other day, and this is an absolutely true story, I decided that to get away from it all, the speechwriting, all of that, I'd go for a walk with my three year old son, Daniel. It was an absolutely gorgeous late summer day. So we went out, I wanted to go to the park. Here's the first thing he said to me: 'Daddy, I can help you with your speech.' [...] and I said [...] 'Daniel what do you want in my speech?' He said 'I want dinosaurs! I want dinosaurs, I want flying dinosaurs! I want dinosaurs that eat people daddy!' I said, 'No Daniel. We tried predators last year.' (Miliband 2012)

Miliband offered insights into first his family and then his political 'education' as it were, and then *mixed* the two:

- I want to do something different today. I want to tell you my story. I want to tell you who I am. What I believe. And why I have a deep conviction that together we can change this country. My conviction is rooted in my family's story, a story that starts 1,000 miles from here, because the Milibands haven't sat under the same oak tree for the last 500 years.
- And you know my parents saw Britain rebuilt after the Second World War. I was born in my local NHS hospital, the same hospital my two sons would later be born in. As you saw in the film I went to my local school. I went to my local comprehensive with people from all backgrounds. I still remember the amazing and inspiring teaching I got at that school, and one of my teachers, my English teacher, Chris Dunne, is here with us today. Thank you Chris and to all the teachers at Haverstock. It was a really tough school, but order was kept by one of the scariest headmistresses you could possibly imagine, Mrs Jenkins. And you know what? I learned at my school about a lot more than how to pass exams. I learned how to get on with people

from all backgrounds, whoever they were. I wouldn't be standing on this stage today without my comprehensive school education.

- So of course there were the normal things, but every upbringing is special, and mine was special because of the place of politics within it. When I was 12 years old, I met a South African friend of my parents, her name was Ruth First. The image I remember is of somebody vivacious, full of life, full of laughter. And then I remember a few months later coming down to breakfast and seeing my mum in tears because Ruth First had been murdered by a letter bomb from the South African Secret Police. Murdered for being part of the anti-apartheid movement. Now I didn't understand the ins and outs of it, but I was shocked. I was angry. I knew that wasn't the way the world was meant to be. I knew I had a duty to do something about it. It is this upbringing that has made me who I am. A person of faith, not a religious faith but a faith nonetheless. A faith, I believe, many religious people would recognise. So here is my faith. I believe we have a duty to leave the world a better place than we found it. I believe we cannot shrug our shoulders at injustice, and just say that's the way the world is. And I believe that we can overcome any odds if we come together as people. (Miliband 2012)

Paradoxically, when he then became 'serious' and as if 'getting down to business', the co-existence of the two – humour and seriousness – still complemented one another all the time, each and both enhancing his personal status and the character traits of the insightful leader who was nevertheless very human. And we can stress here that the juxtaposition of Miliband's seriousness and humour were constant, not just in this speech but throughout the Conference. Miliband devoted approximately twenty per cent of the speech to humour, mainly at the beginning. Humour was then contrasted with seriousness as Miliband offered a series of very personal insights into first his family and then his emotions, each formative of his political worldview.

Miliband referred to his upbringing as 'special because of the place of politics within it'. But the justification was not his family background, but an irresistible personal recollection that served as a parable and founding moment. So, as we have said, at 12 years old, he had met Ruth First, a friend of his mother and an anti-apartheid activist. He then recalled – coming down to breakfast, his mother in tears – his feelings of shock and anger, hearing that she had been murdered by a letter bomb sent by the South African

Secret Police. A young Miliband subsequently felt 'a duty to leave the world a better place than we found it. I believe we cannot shrug our shoulders at injustice, and just say that's the way the world is.' (Miliband 2012). This use of 'moment' and 'decision' is one of the fundamentals of story-telling. We have in the opening minutes of the speech the telling of a story: the evocation of an ordinary childhood ('I was born in my local NHS hospital, the same hospital my two sons would later be born in. [...] I went to my local comprehensive'), with elements of founding moral moments (Jewish refugees, commitment to Britain, Ruth First and the struggle against apartheid, not walking by on the other side). The personal, moral, and the highly emotional, therefore, set the scene for the theme of One Nation. In sum, the beginning of Miliband's keynote speech was humorous, emotional, evoking of (in a very visual way, moreover 'it was an absolutely gorgeous late summer day') a very *ordinary* British yet *special* childhood; the opening minutes bristled with insights, and – tellingly – were completely focused upon himself; the child as the father of the man, living – and recounting – the formative inspirations of an adult quest.[5]

KEYNOTE THEMES: ONE NATION POLICIES (JUSTICE, EFFICIENCY, AND EMOTION)

'One Nation' was the theme of Miliband's keynote Conference speech. One Nation is part of the tradition of Conservatism that existed arguably up until Thatcherism, a tradition informed by the ideas and the memory of figures such as Edmund Burke and Benjamin Disraeli, later Churchill, and then shared by Labour as part of the 'Butskellist' post-war settlement. Miliband's use of the term 'One Nation' was part of the construction of an overall holistic narrative that would also allow for interlocking narratives, all of which would align with his personalized image. I shall return to this in the conclusion of this chapter. Miliband introduced One Nation Labour thus:

> Friends, I didn't become leader of the Labour Party to reinvent the world of Disraeli or Attlee. But I do believe in that spirit. That spirit of One Nation. One Nation: a country where everyone has a stake. One Nation: a country

[5] One barely perceptible reference to 'David' was made at the beginning of the speech when referring to their childhood 'I believe that their experience [Miliband's parents as post-World War II refugees in Britain] meant they brought up both David and myself differently as a result.' That was it.

where prosperity is fairly shared. One Nation: where we have a shared destiny, a sense of shared endeavour and a common life that we lead together. That is my vision of One Nation. That is my vision of Britain. That is the Britain we must become. (Miliband 2012)

And here is the genius of One Nation. It doesn't just tell us the country we can be. It tells us how we must rebuild. We won the war because we were One Nation. We built the peace because Labour governments and Conservative governments understood we needed to be One Nation. Every time Britain has faced its gravest challenge, we have only come through the storm because we were One Nation. But too often governments have forgotten that lesson. (Miliband 2012)

The keynote speech was not used by Miliband to promote policy *per se*, but to indicate the general thrust of a (personalized) One Nation Labour policy approach, and to 'rhetorize' future policy developments with both *logos* and *pathos*:

- We can't carry on as we are, two nations not one. The banks and the rest of Britain. We must have a One Nation banking system as part of a One Nation economy.
- So in education there really is a choice of two futures. Education for a narrower and narrower elite, with the Conservatives. Or a One Nation skills system as part of a One Nation economy with the next Labour government.
- To be a One Nation economy we have to make life just that bit easier for the producers, and that bit harder for the predators.
- And here is the thing, ladies and gentlemen, I invite British businesses – work with us in advance of the next Labour government. Let's refound the rules of the game so we have a One Nation business model as part of a One Nation economy for our country. (Miliband 2012)

These four quotations offered less policy detail than a One Nation policy *approach*. He summed up: 'so friends, in banks, in education, in the rules of the game for companies – One Nation gives us an urgent call for change. But One Nation is not just about the things we need to change, it is about the things we need to conserve as well. Saying that doesn't make me a Conservative. Our common way of life matters'. (Miliband 2012) Policy 'detail' did follow from the One Nation approach. The three quotations below on the technical baccalaureate, the minimum wage and immigration, and the NHS illustrate emotion-related and 'him'-related policy allusions/propositions, thus bringing the 'self' *and* policy centre stage:

- Here's the choice that I want to offer to that 14 year old who is not academic. English and maths to 18 because rigour in the curriculum matters. But courses that engage them and are relevant to them. Work experience with employers. And then culminating at the age of 18 with a new gold standard qualification so they know when they are taking that exam they have a gold standard vocational qualification, a new Technical Baccalaureate. A qualification to be proud of. You know, we've got to change the culture of this country, friends. We can't be a country where vocational qualifications are seen as second class.
- The next Labour Government will crack down on employers who don't pay the minimum wage. We will stop recruitment agencies just saying they are only going to hire people from overseas. And we will end the shady practices, in the construction industry and elsewhere, of gang-masters. So we need a system of immigration that works for the whole country and not just for some.
- The next Labour government will end the free market experiment, it will put the right principles back at the heart of the NHS and it will repeal the NHS Bill. (Miliband 2012)

Much of Miliband's speech was a kind of (emotional) echo of Sandel's philosophical prescriptions of the previous day. It was also a kind of practical follow through. The near-corporatist sounding approach to banking ('a One Nation banking system'), education ('a One Nation skills system'), and economics ('a One Nation economy', 'a One Nation business model'), all of which were intended to have decisive repercussions in vocational education, wages policy, immigration, and the NHS, were introduced in the speech as the beginnings of what we can call a 'policy narrative'. 'One Nation' became both an umbrella (for future narratives) and a justification for policy initiatives as part of a wide-ranging but integrated social project; and all this 'imagined' in the speech unfolding (without notes) by the leader/speaker. The One Nation theme and its elaboration became the rhetorical framework of a mission, shared by all and led by the speaker.

Through performance of himself or, rather, the introduction and performing of a *new* self, as it were, Ed Miliband began to alter his preceding, received image and persona; and his manner and body movements, humour and style contributed to this. Not having a lectern, Miliband walked around the (low) stage, in proximity to his audience, 'entertaining' them; this was not just a different Miliband, but also a new kind of leader's speech; speaking without notes and not appearing nervous or hesitant illustrated real self-confidence; here, a kind of new-found self-confidence, a coming of age, as if the speech itself were, in an Austinian performative sense, a rite of passage (van Gennep 1961). It also more than implied 'authorship' of the speech, Miliband therefore appearing genuine and truthful and, in this way, in a relatively intimate and new relation to his audience. Miliband had long enjoyed the dubious attribute of 'nice man' alongside other negative qualities ascribed. Now he was constructing a notion of competence through the demonstration of confidence. I cannot underline too strongly, moreover, how much more interesting a speaker is to listen to when not reading from a script (David Cameron had done the same in 2005 in a much shorter speech, 20 minute). Whilst walking about, Miliband sometimes stopped and looked directly at party members; physically, Miliband's comportment was relaxed; he walked around casually, often with one hand in his pocket. He conveyed accessibility, youthfulness and dynamism; traits that contrasted dramatically with his immediate predecessor, Gordon Brown (and, one might add, his truly immediate predecessor, himself). At the end of the speech, Miliband's exit from the conference hall, accompanied by his wife, was the now standard, congratulatory, US-style 'golden couple' who through the illusion of accessibility demarcate their difference.

Conference Day 4, 3 October

For Day 4 of the Conference let us examine: first, the morning press coverage of Miliband's speech; second, Ed Miliband's afternoon Q&A session with the party members and delegates. We should stress here that the press coverage itself was the major event of the morning of Day 4 and – until the afternoon Q&A – the only topic of conversation in and around the Conference.

Press Reaction

The press reaction to Miliband's keynote speech was overwhelmingly positive. In fact, Miliband had never known such positive comment. The following examples were indicative of media opinion: 'Game changer' (Beattie 2012); 'Rhetorical tour de force' (Milne 2012); 'a barnstorming conference speech without notes' (Dunn 2012); 'finally he looked like the boss ... the moment he became leader of the Labour Party, de facto as well as de jure' (Hoggart 2012); 'Geek-tastic Ed triumphs by nicking a Tory mantra' (Treneman 2012); 'Labour leader takes leaf out of PM's book with bravura conference speech delivered without notes' (Grice 2012); 'Ed's display of style – and substance – will worry the Tories' (Richards 2012); 'He's a real showman' (Suphi 2012); 'Geek God. Ed becomes Labour legend yesterday' (Beattie 2012a)'; 'And now it's personal – Miliband the leader steps into the limelight' (Watt 2012). 'The Labour faithful depart from the north west confident that they have not elected a dud as their party leader. This week Ed Miliband answered the doubts within his own party over whether he has what it takes to lead them back to power. Many feared they had chosen an unelectable intellectual as their leader. But he gave a good speech that showed he has grown into his role, the gawky stiffness replaced by a more relaxed style that he has thus far kept private' (Landale 2012). 'At the end of this week, Ed Miliband is safe in his job, he has shown he can rise to the occasion, he has raised morale in his party and they leave with a spring in their step' (Landale 2012). This was quite stunning approbation.

It is clear that the relaxed, confessional style, and a personal-political narrative, the use of humour, emotion, and a natural-seeming relationship with his audience, had created a new persona, at least in the immediate term. After the keynote speech, Miliband's personal poll ratings were very positive (see Beattie 2012) and reflected his new persona as – in the conference hall as in much of the media – potentially prime ministerial, and this for the first time.

Q&A Session

On the afternoon of Day 4 of the Conference, Ed Miliband led a Q&A session with approximately 3000 party delegates and party members (just as for the keynote speech, the six lines of queues started forming two hours before, this time stretching right outside the building). The Q&A session was – as if – very informal. Once again, Miliband was applauded by delegates as he walked onto the stage; this time not wearing a jacket conveying an even more relaxed and confident man. He thanked delegates and began by making reference to One Nation Labour as the Party to rebuild Britain, as if his previous day's new idea was now narratively normative. Humour, introduced the previous day as a new aspect of the persona, here became the dominant feature of the next hour and 20 minutes. He first joked that his wife had told him that their 2-year-old son's first words were 'One Nation'. One of the essential sources of the humour, in fact, were references to the previous day's speech (e.g., on the number of times he used the term 'One Nation', and the media coverage it attained). This intertextual phenomenon – the discourse referring to previous discourse either seriously or with humour (to texts and speeches of the previous day or previous year, to Sandel's textual prefiguring, to Miliband's referring to the act of speech writing itself) – all added a proximity to, almost an intimacy with, the audience (who had also been following these discourses and their media coverage), the intertextuality justifying the legitimacy of the discourse overall (and the 'veracity' of the speaker). In an Austinian sense (Austin 1975), the speech act itself was the consequent event.

In the Q&A session, Miliband debated a range of policy positions with the audience. Questions on education, banks, crime, and the economy were each answered with whatever he felt was the essential issue in each case; that is to say, he answered each question personally – party positions being barely appealed to, although nowhere contradicted. Miliband as if 'invented' policy dialogue, asking delegates for policy suggestions and experiences, thus strategically distancing himself not just from New Labour and other factions, but from the party itself as a policy-making body. Policy was being fashioned in the immediacy of the encounter between the leader and the audience, while also stressing Miliband's personal command of all subjects addressed. Miliband always referred to questioners by their first names. And the striking feature throughout was the mixture of humour and seriousness; contributing to policy debate was both interesting and fun. He moved continually – almost continuously – from humour to seriousness and back again. Very soon, the audience were doing exactly the same.

Miliband took questions in groups of three or four, gesturing and often describing his questioner with humour (and later admonishing them, ironically, as the session progressed and the umbrellas and hats and colours used to attract his attention became more and more eccentric). As the session continued, it became increasingly animated; delegates began to stand on chairs, and wave an accumulation of possessions such as several umbrellas and coloured scarves to get the attention of the leader.[6] On several occasions, women participants reminded Ed that they had met before and

[6] There were no marshals in evidence, and at times the Q&A took on a near-carnival atmosphere. In fact, one wheelchair user who tried at length but in vain to catch Miliband's eye

that he had kissed them; his slight embarrassment and references to his being a married man humanized him and spread the mirth (from which he then plunged into a serious response to the question asked). The audience was overwhelmingly positive towards Miliband. Two delegates addressed him as the 'future Prime Minister', to much applause, as if in direct recognition of his post-keynote speech persona. There were no hecklers in the crowd (although there could have been, suggesting his openness to free debate). Towards the end of the session, Miliband stated that the 'Labour Party is not me, it's you', momentarily empowering the audience via this reversal of status, and implying a new and very special relationship. Leaders often do this, but the intense interaction of the previous 80 minutes lent the statement emotional intensity.

Day 5 was the final day of the Conference. The leader had departed, and most of the delegates – and all of the media – were already heading home. At the rostrum, deputy leader Harriet Harman made some significant closing remarks: 'It's been a great week for the Labour Party and a great week for Ed Miliband' (Harman 2012). Harman's positive reaction towards Ed Miliband's performance during Conference 2012 was like an echo of reassurance, like a response to her own more quizzical remarks at the beginning of the Conference about whether Miliband was properly known – he was now – as if a true transformation had taken place.

Conclusion

In conclusion, I want to make five observations that touch on the wider theoretical issues I raised at the beginning of the chapter concerning performance, institutions, culture, narrative, and rhetoric, each observation of both an empirical and theoretical nature.

First, the Labour Party, its internal reconfiguration, and declining trade union influence, allowed the symbolism of the leader *vis-à-vis* the party to take on major political expression. The annual Labour Party Conference speech is a significant political opportunity for leadership actors to fashion or re-fashion their political persona, much more so than was hitherto the case. Miliband used not only his keynote speech, but the whole conference to modify his political identity as party leader and

(because he could neither stand nor brandish anything) was one of the victims of such merriment. If the *Daily Mail* had noticed, one can but imagine the headline.

restore his political authority and status.[7] One of the consequences of this was that the persona of the leader drew attention away from the party-as-organization, although not party-as-narrative which we shall come on to below. By bringing 'himself' centre stage, Ed also screened David Miliband out of the political narrative; and out of contention as a potential or 'imagined' rival, at least in the medium term. One of the effects of the positive response of the media and the clear enthusiasm in the hall (and the bars) was that it silenced political opponents and rivals and the narrative of rivalry and criticism. It is worth reminding ourselves that dissent and rumours of leadership challenges had been rife since his election 2 years earlier. One related point we can make here, however, is that the dramatic character of the assertion or reassertion of his persona and authority was partly dependent upon his previous poor standing as leader. A final point on this question of persona is that its modalities were those of *ethos*, *pathos*, and *logos* in Aristotelian rhetoric (Aristotle 1991), demonstrating his standing, competence and confidence *vis-à-vis* the audience, the use of emotion, and humour, and the establishing of an intimacy with the audience, and a 'reasoning' from this emotional self the beginnings of a project for the future.

Second, the events surrounding Manchester 2012 had an architecture, an architecture related to the construction of an exemplary persona: the gathering of Miliband's friends in the garden; the questions raised by both Alan Johnson and Harriet Harman about Ed's character/charisma at the beginning of the Conference (with the implicit conflating – in anticipation – of leadership and performance); the withering remarks of Andrew Marr, and especially the Conservative Party poll, on Miliband's low popularity (all these would redound to his great advantage); the arrival of the family – followed by the omnipresence of Miliband at the Conference until the end of Day 4 (and his absence on Day 5 – Ed had left the building); Sandel's oblique endorsement; the masterful speech to an overflowing conference hall (where each of the three received personae – Red Ed, younger brother, and Wallace – were dealt with); the very positive media response; the near carnivalesque bonding with the audience the following day in the Q&A; his departure before the final day; Harman's echoing at the end of the Conference her words of the beginning, as if 'catching' and answering the question launched at the beginning (in this way noting a 'promise' fulfilled). Both Ed and the party

---

[7] There was a series of strong interventions at the Conference by such figures as Ed Balls, Yvette Cooper, Rachel Reeves, and others; but the overwhelming presence of Miliband altered fundamentally the political significance of the occasion.

had indeed had a fantastic Conference, and there was a discernible structure to the series of performances, formative of a renewal of leadership persona, formative of the narrative structure of a 'story' that we identified in the previous chapter.

Third, as regards the British Labour Party, there is a paradox: since the election of Neil Kinnock as party leader in 1983, the party had been centrally concerned with image and the performance of leadership. Yet, ideologically, leadership remained the elephant in the room, because socialism, social democracy, and democratic doctrine generally posit an impersonalism: no one is indispensable; enhanced leadership posits the opposite. It therefore falls to discourse and rhetoric to (attempt to) reconcile the two drives through the complex performance of leadership persona within the matrix of a rich and textured leftist discourse, and within the culturally and organizationally fashioned institution of the Party Conference.

There is a related issue here of methodological interest. If my point concerning leadership performance within a leftist institutional setting is correct, it raises the question of the significance of my approach not only for the post-Miliband leadership of Jeremy Corbyn but also beyond the UK case. Socialism and social democracy are fundamentally European phenomena, so the interactions of leadership and ideology present themselves in every European country. This in turn raises the question of how historical and cultural differences modulate these interactions. A compelling contrast is that of France. Between 1971 and 1981, François Mitterrand 'adapted' French socialism to the presidential Fifth Republic. A comparative analysis of UK social democratic conferences with French Socialist Party conferences, with their more radical discourse and republican tradition within the wider national framework of a much stronger leadership tradition (Garrigues 2012) would offer great insights into the nature of the relationship between leadership and culture (see Faucher 2005).

My fourth point concerns narrative. The challenge now, following on from the work of Finlayson (2004, 2007) and Martin (2014, 2015) (and Vladimir Propp and Aristotle!), is to focus analysis on the construction of leadership persona, not only in terms of the 'character' of the leader, but also the connections between leadership narrative and other narratives, especially for a party leader of a social democratic type. The perpetual distinction made between 'policies' and 'personalities' is both a category mistake and a naivety, even for a party of the left with an elaborate doctrinal history. As we have seen, the 'personalized political' is quite a subtle mechanism, and we could venture here that it characterized all of Ed Miliband's leadership between 2010 and 2015 – that is, a discourse that was self-referential and 'about him', but which also informed the way 'he' talked about issues, policies, and events. This personalized phenomenon would, however, subsequently revert to its negative effects. We shall analyse this in the next chapter.

The final observation concerns emotion. Crucial to the mediation of leadership through narrative is the rhetorical use of emotion or a range of emotions. We have seen that this was one of the fundamental elements of Miliband's keynote speech, and this in two crucially linked respects: first, in terms of emotion and himself (e.g., the death of Ruth First); second, in terms of the issues discussed (e.g., immoral bankers and a dysfunctional system that brings misery and so on). Emotional appeal, *pathos*, not only drove Miliband's speech forward in terms of both himself and a Labour narrative; it linked them. One of the creative conditions of this was that the Labour narratives that had been emerging since 2010 themselves contained a significant emotional element, either based on the attraction of the place where narrative and rhetoric wished to take us, or in terms of the sense of injustice of the place we – or those who suffer – were in; both were 'carried' by the emotion of leadership rhetoric – 'felt' by the leader, as shown in his rhetoric, or interpolated by him, as the author of a wider emerging narrative.

CHAPTER 5

Narrative Collapse and the Teller Without a Tale

Manchester 2012 and its aftermath were the half-way point and high-point, the moment when the overall direction of the narrative and leadership performance became decisive factors in their own future success or failure.

This chapter is neither a chronology of the second half of Miliband's 5-year leadership, nor an analysis of why Labour lost in 2015.[1] There will be some discussion of each, but what I want to show is what was really going on from the narrative and performative points of view. It is inevitable that I shall identify elements of 'why Labour lost' in my reconstruction of what we might call the party's loss of narrative direction and the dislocation between it and performative leadership. I need, however, to be careful to avoid a false teleology: that the 'causes' determining the 2015 failure can be found in this post-2012 period. It is stretching credibility somewhat but I suspect my analysis would be no different if, for a myriad of other reasons and factors, Miliband *had* become Prime Minister in 2015. My focus is upon narrative and performance; the latter is, as I have shown throughout my analysis, by definition non-deterministic and creative (of outcomes). An analogy might be a West End theatre run. The reasons for its failure may be multiple, to do with audience, content, timing, competition, management, venue, and so on. We are concerned here with those elements which pertain to staging and performance.

---

[1] T. Bale (2015) *Five Year Mission* (Oxford: Oxford University Press) provides an analytical chronicle of the 2010–2015 period.

© The Author(s) 2017   145
J. Gaffney, *Leadership and the Labour Party*, Palgrave Studies in Political Leadership, DOI 10.1057/978-1-137-50498-2_5

Very broadly, to sum up a highly complex process, from 2013 – precisely half way through the 5-year period from September 2010 to May 2015 – the narrative and related performance began to stumble, to lose traction as it were, in terms of previous performance and intention, and they began to separate *from each other*. If we go back to our narrative analysis in Chapter 3 we can say that the intended 'arc of rhetoric' and story which 'ends in triumph' began to falter. In the wider scenario what this also meant is that the 'promise' of the (ideological) Policy Review remained unfulfilled as the party failed to develop a wider, more overarching new narrative on politics, the economy, and society. This may be because it could not, that contemporary 'social democracy' is no longer equipped to do this, or that choices were also made – perhaps for the sake of party unity – not to 'follow through' narratively on the Policy Review and elaborate policies adequate to the narrative and performance 'promise' of 2010–2012; or that, for multiple reasons related to the personal qualities and choices of the actors involved, what should have been done was not.

It became a truism in the aftermath of the 2015 defeat, voiced by all commentators[2] that two of the reasons for Labour's failure – and this was also identified in all the polls (which we have to remind ourselves were completely wrong …) – were the wide gap between it and the Conservatives on the economy and on leadership. I have to concede that this truism is true. What my analysis demonstrates, however, and which is fundamentally more consequential and explanatory is that these two were inextricably intertwined, interwoven in narrative and performance. And inextricably linked to this was the standing, the *ethos*, of the leader, as we have seen. We shall return to this in our Conclusion, but there are leadership characteristics which doubtless influenced the status of Ed Miliband.

If we consider the relationship of a party leader to his or her party and MPs, David Cameron, for example, was elected party leader with strong support from Conservative MPs. Miliband in 2010 not so (in fact, David Miliband 'won' the MPs' vote – for Corbyn in 2015 the rules had changed but the lack of support here was also of importance). It is also my view that the interminable leadership campaign of 2010 (repeated in 2015, until the Corbyn candidacy took off, under, as I said, different electoral rules) was detrimental to leadership status and standing, publicly and lengthily 'performing' internal partisan and growingly dull

---

[2] For example 'After Miliband' Conference, 5 June 2015, University College Oxford, and a gazillion articles and blogs, many from 'insiders' and official party inquiries and reports and few of them enlightening.

performances – and the discursive and rhetorical as well as doctrinal differences between the Milibands, Balls, Burnham, and even Abbot were minimal. The party talked to itself while Cameron ran the country. Such was the reality and the impression given. When Ed Miliband was eventually elected – by a whisker – his leadership image was already weakened. I shall come back to this in the Conclusion.

Having said this we should remind ourselves that Cameron was often unpopular with his MPs and at various times, Miliband popular. A further condition, however, of Miliband's confused leadership image from the start was his association with a previous (latterly unpopular) government (he had served under both Tony Blair and Gordon Brown) and – this being the double-bind – *his own* repudiation of it. Cameron had no real, or rather publicly perceived, connection to the several 'failed' Conservative leaders of the post-John Major period (he had worked as an advisor to Michael Howard). Commentators all noted the collective gasp from the audience at the last *Question Time* before the 2015 election when Miliband, in response to a question on whether he thought Labour in office had overspent, answered 'No, I don't'. The gasp was not really in response to his 'view' but to his 5-year equivocation and eleventh-hour (and 59th minute) defence of a government whose perceived profligacy had (quite wrongly) become paradigmatic in the popular imagination, and this precisely because Miliband – for reasons of narrative choice which we shall return to in our Conclusion – had not countered this Conservative mythology for 5 years. His *Question Time* remark (30 April 2015) therefore sounded like owning up to a lie. It is arguable that since Margaret Thatcher the balance had also shifted in favour of leaders who were going to *do* something – a Thatcher and a Blair – as opposed to more cautious 'conservers' like Jim Callaghan or John Major who preceded each of them respectively. Miliband's caution over policy and direction against Cameron's greater self-awareness differentiated the image of the two men. Let us now briefly describe the 'stumbling' that we referred to earlier from 2013 to 2015.

WAITING FOR NARRATIVE LIFT-OFF

In the immediate aftermath of the 2012 Manchester One Nation speech (see Chapter 4) several of the elements of what we have referred to elsewhere as a 'rally' were in place: a foundational narrative that the leader had 'caught' and – paradoxically – become the author of, a leader who performed well and who, through performance, was gathering a rally of opinion and a following around his persona. The demonstration of this, following a new Miliband One Nation speech to the Fabian Society on 12 January 2013 (although, ironically, with its many 'one liners' it was reminiscent of Blair's style) was the 'response' 2 days later by a range of One Nation MPs and others. What is striking was how the new allegiance to Miliband being expressed by a new cohort of One Nation acolytes – they set up a group of One Nation MPs, held conferences and seminars, produced publications, re-theorized – was expressed as a personal allegiance to an inspired leader.

The 'rally' however did not really take off, and this for several reasons. One was that for a rally of opinion around a new leader to work, the whole party must be, or appear to be, involved so that the party 'looks like' a rally, with a 'here we go' quality. There were deep reservoirs of scepticism towards Miliband, and this from within his own Shadow Cabinet especially (one could almost 'see' the scepticism of Balls and Cooper, and one could certainly not 'hear' allegiance). This, coupled with a gradual return to his former, pre-Manchester 2012 image in public opinion, saw further negativity towards him in the party; and being treated almost like a boy by older Blairites, by Blair himself and certain trade union leaders further undermined Miliband's standing. The real 'failing', however, was narrative. The whole of the build up to 2012 was the gradual 'assembly' of a narrative that Miliband could use to take forward as his own to then inform the development of policies: a 'discursive site' already prepared for him by Jon Cruddas and the Policy Review. For reasons which remain obscure, the next narrative phase never took place. Some held the view that George Osborne's 'Omnishambles' Budget of 2012 (Miliband used the term (PMQs 18 April 2012) – taken from a 2009 political satire) had caused the party leadership to begin to back away from its own developing narrative and – for the sake of party unity – do little, in the belief that the party would now coast home in 2015 (with retail offers like lowering energy prices (2013)), given government unpopularity. If this was true it was a dreadful miscalculation for, irrespective of its riskiness, it meant the beginnings of narrative collapse and the – again paradoxically – accidental creation of a concerted image of Miliband as rhetorically proposing little and embodying less.

The second narrative consequence was perhaps even more significant, and I shall come back to this in the Conclusion in a comparison of the same issue in Labour's French sister party, the Parti Socialiste, in the 1970s. Here we can say that reconciling the various wings of the party around Miliband's leadership was one issue, and besides, the

Labour Party – like all parties – has various traditions, wings, and factions whose friction, competition, and rivalry is necessary for the forward movement of the party. However, the discursive reconciliation of various 'voices' of and within the party is a prerequisite to leadership success. As we have seen, the revival of an (imagined) older pre-war narrative which was rhetorically effective with its fulfilling the requirements of a foundation myth, its Arcadian overtones, and notions of wrong paths taken and 'return' to a doctrinal origin had been painstakingly elaborated from 2010 onwards. Nevertheless, once this had 'become' Miliband's own One Nation discourse he still had to realign other discursive strains within the party (back) into it. In fact, he did begin to do this. One Nation, born of Blue Labour, began to shift away from it (partly as a result of the somewhat eccentric interventions of Blue Labour's original author, Maurice Glasman, and the contentiousness of some of its proposals). There were, as we have seen, many doctrinal and policy-related contributions from New Labour Blairites, certainly early on, and the 'conversion' of former Blairites like Caroline Flint and Tristram Hunt. One Nation, moreover, was further 'irrigated' by other influences. More European social-democratic thinking was being introduced (partly through the input of Miliband's close adviser, Stewart Wood, and the journal *Renewal* edited by Ben Jackson); ideas that flourished in the German SPD (and CDU, in fact) regarding regional banking being more responsive to regional communities, an emphasis upon training an appropriate workforce through developed apprenticeship schemes; more synergized management–trade union relations, a 'contributive' health and welfare service, and so on. Further social democratic-style and innovative thinking was being developed at a high level by the IPPR in a study that would be published in June 2014 (Lawton et al. 2014); it had already developed compelling ideas around the idea of the 'relational state' and its emphasis upon devolving power to local government – with practical examples – echoing much of the One Nation narrative (Cooke and Muir 2012). This in turn was encouraging the input into mainstream party discourse of ideas about innovative and efficient left local government. Devolution of power to local communities/local government became one of the main themes of One Nation. This encouraged further emphasis upon (effective) politics at the local level, particularly local councils who could claim major successes in Hackney, Lambeth, Newham, and a range of provincial towns – in particular concerning 'joined up' welfare systems.

We can see, therefore, that a whole series of 'tributaries' were flowing into the One Nation discourse. It was thus all the more startling that this was not developed into a triumphalist rhetoric/doctrine that would give the impression of the party being carried to power and give Miliband a stronger persona. One of the reasons was, doubtless, caution. This kind of undertaking carried risks – of division, of wrong directions, of a potential radicalism unpopular with the electorate. However, the deeper explanation was the rhetorical choice of constructing One Nation as a *rejection* of New Labour rather than a reconciliation with or transcendence of it. We shall return to this discussion in the Conclusion, but can say here that One Nation – paradoxically – was divisive. It remained a slogan rather than what it should have become, namely the expression of a new rhetoric. During 2013 it was gradually abandoned, certainly by Miliband himself who by the end of the year had dropped the term from his speeches. A major consequence of this was that now he only had a rhetoric 'about him' (e.g., as a potential Prime Minister) which meant that the focus became increasingly upon his character in general, and this without a commanding narrative to draw upon. Let us look briefly at the developments in 2013 and 2014 from this perspective, namely, the fortunes of the One Nation narrative and its performance by the leader as the 'embodiment' of the party.

ONE NATION-AVERSE: FROM TELLING A STORY TO AD-LIBBING

One Nation was in part a victim of its own success. In the aftermath of Manchester 2012, it became almost the 'official' narrative of the party, triggering as we have seen acts of allegiance, seminars, conferences, and a lot of literature, well into 2013 (Carr 2014). In January 2013 certain related policy proposals were made. The idea of a Technical Baccalaureat echoed the ideas put forward in the 2012 speech surrounding apprenticeships. The idea of a 'Mansion tax' was put forward too and was presented as a kind of One Nation idea of the well-off making a greater contribution to funding health and welfare. The Mansion tax was an early example of One Nation as a *policy* process not being properly developed *narratively*. First, it was not part of an integrated programme. In fact, one feature of policy announcements throughout 2013 and 2014 was that none of them was integrated into an overall 'project', so that an overall social and economic project under the umbrella of One Nation – incorporating ideas from the 'relational state', for example – was abandoned. In part, this was in order to not develop policies too soon, but the Policy Review itself seemed to lose momentum dramatically in the course of 2013. Also, One Nation was about social harmony rather than social confrontation, but the means to harmony involved an overall policy narrative that would fashion this desired Nation. The Mansion tax could, with its Robin Hood flavour, have been part of this, but in reality it was not clear if it would work or indeed be fair (e.g., hit people who had properties whose value had risen but who had little income); more tellingly, it would not raise much revenue, and certainly not enough to fund, for example, even a fraction of the NHS. This meant that the economic narrative was not developing, an absolutely central element to an effective narrative.

This in turn raised the question of whether proposals emerging from One Nation would be radical and if so how? Or, rather, was One Nation – in its non-confrontational appeals to social harmony – masking a *lack* of commitment to developing a range of proposals. This gradually became the prevailing view. By the summer of 2013 inaction led – once again – to criticisms of the leadership and a growing sense of dissatisfaction. In these circumstances the nature of the leader's speech at Conference began to change subtly. Because 2012 had been so successful and had been pre-ceded by a period of severe leadership unpopularity, a pattern was estab-lished whereby the Conference speech (Brighton in 2013, Manchester in 2014) became the central performance upon which success depended. By September 2013, however, very little on One Nation had been developed (it remained the background slogan in Brighton, but that was all). This was in part because the environment within which a narrative could be constructed was extremely hostile. First, the economy generally, accord-ing to the standard indices, was 'picking up' and unemployment falling. The party's response to this view was to develop the idea of the 'cost-of-living' crisis, namely, that things might *appear* to be better but the lived experience of this was different. The truth or rhetorical advantage of this was one thing, but it was an indication of a deeper narrative problem: it was *reactive* rather than proactive. It criticized the government rather than offering an alternative, which is what One Nation was designed to do rhetorically; and this was compounded by what we might call One Nation-as-aversion.

Because of a reluctance or incapacity to develop a matrix of proposals that would 'draw a picture' of One Nation, throughout 2013 and into 2014, the party's narrative began to deliberately *not* describe One Nation. This was in part because the prevailing climate, comprising other narratives, was incompatible with the direction of the party's narrative. All contentious areas – each of which was filling the public space, the media, the polls, the 'national conversation', as it were – were problematic, particularly for a party without a narrative, allowing 'old' ideas about the left in general to return. Immigration, benefit fraud, Euroscepticism, and the *costing* of the party's intentions in the realm of welfare, education, pensions, and so on, pushed the party into trying *not* to talk, or trying to channel the 'conversation' towards its comfort zones (e.g., criticizing banks), now of little rhetorical advantage. Part of this was due to the narrative choice the party had made in rejecting New Labour (without rejecting it completely). This meant that One Nation Labour's attitude to the previous Labour government was unclear and so the public was unclear: 'had it overspent?' (and would it again?). There was a lot of (muted) criticism of the 'we made mistakes' type (on Polish immigration, for example – itself an absurd and strategically pointless *mea culpa*), but One Nation's having been constructed on a rejection of New Labour meant that its confused relationship was implied but could not be thoroughly addressed without major disruption within the party.

Thus One Nation became a way of not talking about issues, and Miliband's own voice was increasingly countered. One 'voice' that increasingly countered Miliband's throughout the spring and summer of 2013 was that of the Unite trade union leader Len McCluskey (e.g., *New Statesman* 29 April, just before the mediocre results in the local elections on 13 May). The effect of this was twofold. First, McCluskey's real verbal aggressiveness was very personalized, depicting Miliband as a weak or potentially weak leader. Second, it further drained One Nation of its rhetorical potential by depicting Miliband (and Douglas Alexander) as *not* left, in fact closet Blairites, near-social traitors who had to be denounced. Also, as I said earlier, the sight of the older and 'rough diamond' union leader threatening (in March 2015 he would suggest that Unite disaffiliate from the party) the much younger, university educated Miliband served to intensify the focus on the latter's 'weak' image as well as the public's image of Labour. On 13 July the Prime Minister taunted Miliband at PMQs, referring repeatedly to McCluskey. In April 2013 the Falkirk scandal had emerged (was Unite rigging the selection process there?). Miliband actually turned this to his advantage, soon proposing what seemed like a 'Clause IV' type moment, whereby trade union members would opt in to party membership, and he went on to link this via a special conference in March 2014 to further party reform, giving party members the right to elect the party leader (and the candidate for Mayor of London (see Bale 2015: 216–217)).

The 'Clause IV' moment, however, did not really happen given that the unions retained much of their influence in the party (at Conference, on the NEC, for example), and the party arguably became much *more* dependent financially upon the unions whose generosity was now discretionary. And of course these changes set the conditions for Jeremy Corbyn's election in 2015.

In August 2013 Miliband successfully led a House of Commons opposition to military involvement in Syria. All had expected the UK to join the US and France in air strikes against the Assad regime (Gaffney 2014). Miliband's view, however, reflected the national mood. In terms of 'character' and persona more of these kinds of 'acts' would have helped a great deal. He did have a history of 'standing up' to people and this on 'righteous' issues: Rupert Murdoch, the banks, loan sharks, the energy companies, now over Syria (and its helpful foreign policy dimension adding kudos to the leader and perhaps even signalling a new post-Iraq party identity). Given all the other narrative challenges that we have shown here, a coherent 'joined up' character of this kind did not emerge; it became things he did rather than memorable character traits. He remained vulnerable to opinion both in the party and amongst Labour's electorate. On 18 August in his *Mirror* column John Prescott criticized Miliband's leadership. The *Mirror* published a poll on 19 August claiming almost half of Labour voters did not want Miliband to lead the party into the next election. In the same paper on 20 August David Blunkett and Alistair Darling also weighed in with advice; and the critical pieces from a range of senior figures started appearing in the serious papers like *The Observer* throughout the summer.

Miliband, therefore, began the Brighton 2013 Party Conference in much the same way he had begun the Manchester 2012 one, without a narrative and still with his, as it were, 'unintegrated' persona which was not expressive of a compelling narrative, but now with, as we mentioned above, a heightened performative *expectation* for the Conference speech. The speech itself was perfectly adequate, and rhetorically striking policy proposals were announced on housing, childcare and, right at the end of the speech, on freezing energy prices. This latter, in particular, was arresting, and Miliband enjoyed another lift in the polls, but the 'bounce' was short-lived (Sylvester and Thomson 2013). The replacement of a narrative with a series of policy offers reflected a kind of consensus within the party but lent the leader no lyricism. There was a flurry of media interest – and support for Miliband – on the Saturday after the Conference when *The Daily Mail* published an unfounded report on Miliband's father's wartime patriotism. By this time, however, the party (and especially the leader) had less of a lead in the polls than before the 2012 Conference. 2014 would be decisive. All the things that should have begun after Manchester 2012 would have to come together: a narrative which brought the other 'strains' within party doctrine back into the fold, a wide-ranging policy offer which looked like a social and economic project which followed from the new narrative, and the leader-as-author *and* protagonist, as the party advanced towards the elections.

None of this happened. There was a series of speeches in January 2014 with One Nation themes – regulating the big five banks and six utility companies – but the general thrust of Labour discourse remained evasive. This was mainly because the other topics and narratives Labour so hated – on immigration and benefits, for example – were still dominant in public and media discourse, as was in particular another of Labour's least favourite topics, Europe. The European elections were held in May and the build-up of anti-Europeanism was striking (UKIP would go on to gain a breath-taking 27 % of the vote). Labour's pro-Europeanism held its tongue. An overall narrative would have involved a 'view' – like New Labour or 1945 Labour – on *everything*. But now it was silences, muted responses, and so on. The rhetorical awkwardness over issues such as Europe demonstrated that by 2014 the party was not constructing a narrative but avoiding one – on, *inter alia*, Europe, welfare and immigration – which all seemed to be going the other way, in the opposite direction to Labour's traditional views.

This is why the focus upon the leader himself was so relentless; there was no narrative for him to refract through, to interpolate. And on the day before the European election came the highly embarrassing 'bacon sandwich' incident (21 April) where Miliband was caught on camera eating one less than elegantly. (There was a famous photo of JFK in a diner on the campaign trail, but – and this should be advice to all public figures – he is not eating anything.) This was compounded nearly 2 months later when Miliband had to apologize (13 June) for posing with a copy of *The Sun* newspaper (which was promoting the England football team), *The Sun* being scorned by many in Liverpool because of its coverage of the 1989 Hillsborough disaster. These gaffes – described by the media as 'school-boy' errors – made the Labour leader look foolish. The latter incident also damaged Miliband's moral stand against *The Sun*'s owner, Murdoch.

In terms of Miliband's overall image by 2014 there were many rumours and the growing audibility of serious dissent within the party. Much of this would not have reached the wider public but there was an impression of barely concealed disunity. Rivalries seemed to abound within the leader's office, between the leader's office and party HQ, between the leader and the Shadow Ministries, the leader and the PLP, up to half of whom seemed near rebellion, and so on. There was also a great deal of off-the-record briefing of journalists, and some reports of a kind of hysterical paranoia and mutual suspicion within and around Team Miliband (see Steve Richards in *New Statesman*, 10 April 2014, and *The Times*, 18 October and Dan Hodges in *The Spectator*, 16 May 2015 on the 'Milibunker'; see also Cowley and Kavanagh (2016); Hodges (2015); Ross (2015); Watson (2015)). Coupled with this there seemed to be a lack of coordination on and definition of tasks. Various figures rose and fell on the scale of attention (often by undermining one another) – Liam Byrne, Peter Hain, Arnie Graf, Douglas Alexander, Andrew Adonis, and Alastair Campbell (some of whom were New Labour, bringing accusations of reverting to, without the rhetorical advantage of blending, New Labour's narrative). There was some 'rallying' to Miliband, and loyalty – Caroline Flint, Emma Reynolds, Gloria de Piero, for example. However, in spite of all this activity, Miliband often seemed isolated. This was in large part because of the very transactional relationships Miliband had with his most important Shadow Ministers. Few of them ever used the expression One Nation. Moreover, it was clear in the way Balls talked that he was utterly unsympathetic to the lyrical efforts of Jon Cruddas, for example, and subscribing to such was a *prerequisite* to a leader being perceived as a rally leader.

In the same month of June the IPPR's *Condition of Britain* was launched. It formed the doctrinal and rhetorical basis for all the 'social' elements of an election manifesto/social democratic project. And yet at its launch Miliband referred almost exclusively to the party's intended withdrawal of Job Seeker's Allowance from 18–21 year olds who were not properly seeking jobs. It was also becoming clear that the architect of the Policy Review's ideological revisionism, Jon Cruddas, was becoming disillusioned. A report in *The Sunday Times* (29 June) reported his saying as much in an unguarded moment. The 2-day National Policy Forum (18–20 July), the crystallisation of all Cruddas' work, went ahead but without fanfare (and without a narrative), and he and Jonathan Rutherford published *One Nation: Labour's Political Renewal* in September 2014 to coincide with the final Conference before the election. Unlike some of the previous documents in the 2010–2015 period, it made little impact. It was as if One Nation was over. And if One Nation meant the whole of the United Kingdom, it almost was.

The Scottish referendum on Independence took place on 18 September just before the 2014 Labour Party Conference (22 September). These were Miliband's two last main performances before the General Election campaign. Each of them was seriously disadvantageous to Ed Miliband's leadership image. As regards the Scottish referendum, there were five reasons for this, each related to perceptions of character. First, he did not see the strength of the 'Yes' vote coming, and behind it lay the virtual collapse of the Scottish Labour Party, which he also seemed to have been unaware of (yet as Bale pointed out (in Clarke and James 2015: 322) the 2011 election to the Scottish Parliament was a clear warning – Labour's worst defeat in Scotland since 1931). This idea of being unaware is related to character in that it is part of the mythologizing of leadership that leaders can 'see', are Cassandra-like in their prevoyance. Second, in a virtual panic the three main party leaders went *together* (just for the day) to Scotland to appeal for a 'No' vote. Being seen with David Cameron in this way Miliband compounded his image of an out-of-touch *English* politician. Third, when he did campaign in Scotland he had to be unceremoniously bundled in and out of places for his own safety. Fourth, immediately after the campaign, Cameron raised the question of English Votes for English Laws, catching Miliband by surprise and again making him seem unprepared (this constant wrong footing was a tactic of George Osborne too). Fifth, in performance terms, he was – as was everyone else – upstaged by, of all people, his old boss Gordon Brown whose barnstorming, impassioned speech may well have saved the union.

The Manchester 2014 Conference took place immediately afterwards. It was quite clear that Miliband was exhausted. His speech, once again memorized rather than read from the teleprompter, was less well rehearsed, and less memorable than the Brighton and earlier Manchester speeches. Once again, rather than being inspired by a 'vision' like One Nation, it was a list of proposals (all of them, however, containing 'emotion' so they could still have been part of a more inspirational narrative: zero-hours contracts, a raised minimum wage, controlling 'outsourced' contracts, childcare and, of course, the NHS). The media, however, pounced on two omissions from his memorized speech. He forgot to mention both the deficit and immigration (they appeared later in the written version). The omissions took on the character of Freudian slips; the two most contentious issues for Labour, both forgotten in the speech. It was clear Miliband was tired, but what this meant was that the rhetorical innovation of using no notes for his hour-long speech had turned against him, and now rather than enhance his image damaged it. A week later at the Conservative Party Conference, David Cameron gave a good speech. In the polls, the popularity of the couple Cameron–Osborne still easily distanced the couple Miliband–Balls. Moreover, Cameron's individual popularity was rising while Miliband's was falling.

This meant that Ed Miliband went into the 2015 election after 5 years with virtually the same leadership persona and even less of a narrative than when he was elected leader in 2010. This was not the case for the persona of UK Opposition leaders generally; most – Wilson, Heath, Thatcher, Smith, Blair, Cameron, Kinnock (although not Hague, Duncan Smith, or Howard) – had *changed* and *become* other than they were (i.e., potentially prime ministerial). Ed Miliband's persona in 2015 was identical to that of 2010.

The abandonment of the Policy Review-as-story which would have led to an emotional policy offer of a One Nation Britain (and Northern Ireland…) was replaced, as we have seen, by a 'retail' (and eminently forgettable) policy offer, the only real 'emotional' and memorable element of which was the defence of the NHS, a wasted rhetorical effort given that this was the sole policy area that the Labour Party did not need to convince on – and warning of what a returned Conservative government would do to the NHS rhetorically strengthened the idea that the Conservatives would indeed return to government. Miliband, therefore, went into the election campaign itself with only notions of *himself* as a rhetorical resource – did he have the calibre? Was he convincing? Did he have a supportive team (some journalists believed members of his Cabinet were already jumping ship).[3] Essentially, was he prime ministerial? Let us look briefly at how, thus disadvantaged, Miliband fared during the campaign itself, from early March, 2 months from the General Election, bearing in mind that this is not an account but a commentary on narrative and performance.

THE 2015 ELECTION CAMPAIGN, 7–13 MARCH

It was a week of difficulties for the Miliband camp. The background to the on-going campaign (that had really begun immediately after Christmas) was a further narrowing of the polls – Labour were slightly in the lead but the Tories were not far behind (an average of 33–34 % according to UK Polling Report – and there were a few polls showing a Conservative

---

[3] Remarks by Isabel Hardman of *The Spectator*, 'After Miliband' Conference 5 June 2015, University College Oxford.

lead).[4] More broadly, there was a general sense in the media that Labour was on the back foot. Key moments of the first week included discussion of a possible Labour–SNP coalition, debates about the composition of the TV debates, and a live discussion with young people.

Miliband in Salmond's Pocket

The Conservatives released a poster showing Miliband in Alex Salmond's jacket pocket, in order to bring home the message of a possible Labour–SNP coalition if Labour won the greatest number of seats in a hung Parliament after May. The Miliband response went down poorly – describing the prospect of a deal as 'nonsense' but refusing to rule it out entirely. Even Alan Johnson, normally a firm public supporter of Miliband, expressed puzzlement that Miliband did not rule out a deal and neutralise the issue.[5] It was as if Miliband was again walking into a Conservative trap – needlessly. Lucy Powell MP, a Miliband adviser, said on *Question Time* on Thursday 12 March that Miliband did not want to discuss the SNP option because it could be interpreted as conceding that Labour might not attain a majority. But Powell – as had Miliband – gave a confused performance, pouring cold water on the idea of a pact yet at the same time refusing to rule out any Labour–SNP deal, explaining that she was not senior enough to make such decisions. The impression was given that the leadership and everyone else lacked a clear stance on the issue.

The Debates Debate

Miliband tried to corner Cameron on the argument with the broadcasters over the upcoming TV debates. This could have been an easy Miliband win – but (even aside from his PMQs performance – see below) it appeared that he snatched defeat from the jaws of victory. Labour called for a 'legal framework' to ensure that future election debates happened; this was lampooned by many commentators.[6] This was a remarkably common feature

---

[4] For clarity the newspaper sources are listed here. http://ukpollingreport.co.uk/ (accessed 13 Mar 2015).

[5] http://www.theguardian.com/politics/2015/mar/13/alan-johnson-ed-miliband-rule-out-snp-coalition-labour

[6] http://news.sky.com/story/1440757/labour-plans-legal-framework-for-tv-debates

of the Miliband approach – upon the identification of an often procedural problem he argued for an inquiry or a piece of regulation.

New Promises on Energy

Miliband sought to take back the agenda on Friday 13th (ominous) with an announcement on energy policy, proposing that Ofgem's powers be increased to ensure domestic prices were fair and to cut bills by up to 10 % (£100 p.a.) by the end of 2015.[7] Miliband wanted to fast-track the legislation through Parliament to make sure it came into effect by winter 2015. The announcement was part of Labour's focus on the cost-of-living crisis throughout March. This policy was crucial for Miliband's leadership – after all, one of his most memorable moments in the previous 5 years was his 2013 speech, when he outlined his energy freeze promise at the party's Brighton Conference. The policy was now, however, criticized as irrelevant as the falling oil price had driven down energy prices anyway.[8] Moreover, Labour's argument about the cost-of-living crisis was itself becoming undermined, with wages now rising faster than inflation.

'Two Kitchens' Miliband

The second week of March saw efforts to once again present the 'human face' of Ed Miliband to the public, with a video of his wife Justine discussing the campaign. She recognized the personal attacks on Miliband, saying that:

> I think over the next couple of months it's going to get really vicious, really personal, but I'm totally up for this fight... because I think this goes way beyond Ed as an individual, I think it's about whether decencies and principle count for something in political life, wherever you are on the political spectrum.[9]

[7] http://www.ft.com/cms/s/0/fa356652-c8d1-11e4-bc64-00144feab7de.html#axzz 3UGezFoCw, http://www.theguardian.com/business/2015/mar/13/ed-miliband-energy-firms-price-cut-powers-ofgem-labour-freeze-bills

[8] http://uk.reuters.com/article/2015/03/13/uk-britain-politics-energy-idUKKBN0M90YJ20150313

[9] http://www.theguardian.com/politics/2015/mar/10/ed-miliband-faces-vicious-election-attacks-says-wife-justine-thornton

The move, however, backfired as the Milibands faced an onslaught of criticism for a series of apparently innocuous photos of the couple in their kitchen. After a stinging personal attack on the couple and their somewhat uninteresting-looking kitchen in *The Daily Mail* by columnist Sarah Vine (who was suitably harangued by Michael Portillo on the *Daily Politics* programme),[10] Miliband's friend Jenni Russell clumsily sought to defuse the affair by saying that the room in question was not the Milibands' main kitchen. This led to the usual tirade of accusations of hypocrisy and champagne socialism in the right-wing press.[11] Miliband responded, saying that: 'I think Justine would probably say she wishes I'd spend more time in the kitchen. The house we bought had a kitchen downstairs when we bought it. And it is not the one we use. We use the small one upstairs.' As in the past, Miliband's response seemed broadly relaxed and unruffled – there was perhaps a sense of bemusement at the media's obsession with such a trifling matter, although as we have seen trifles can have more than trifling effects.

Apart from these stories, there was a general 'grinding down' of Miliband in the media and a broad focus on his personal failures: from Peter Mandelson's critique of the 'wrapping' of Labour and his disagreement with Miliband on the Mansion tax/TV debates to critiques from business leaders that Miliband would be bad for the economy.[12] The Mandelson intervention was particularly interesting. In response to a question about Miliband's performance as leader, he stated:

> Do you think your product would be better if you changed the wrapping? It depends what you think people are voting for. People are voting for more than simply the personification of a party. Of course that is important, but they are voting for the party's values and the party's relevance, the quality of that product and whether they think that product – or in our case as politicians, that policy – will do for them. Of course, the leader has a responsibility for being the chief brand carrier of that product or policy.[13]

[10] http://www.huffingtonpost.co.uk/2015/03/13/ed-miliband-kitchen-vine_n_6862288.html

[11] http://www.dailymail.co.uk/news/article-2992073/Two-kitchens-Miliband-Labour-leader-posed-SECOND-functional-kitchenette-2-5m-mansion-interview-wife.html

[12] http://www.cityam.com/211546/ed-miliband-bad-britains-economy-say-61pc-business-leaders

[13] http://www.theguardian.com/politics/2015/mar/11/mandelson-undermines-ed-miliband-stance-on-mansion-tax-and-tv-debates

Mandelson's language here – full of marketing metaphors, deliberately bland and clinical (in spite of the reference to values) – displayed a striking difference from Miliband's own discourse of promise and change. To some degree this reflected their different profiles: the behind-the-scenes adviser and the leader. But it also revealed a fundamentally different philosophy of how an election is won and how a political party should be led. Did Miliband believe he was the 'chief brand carrier' for the party? Irrespective of the marketing-speak, greater reflection upon this issue would have been welcome.

On Saturday, Labour outlined its five key campaign pledges at a rally in Birmingham.[14] The following week was the Budget; rumour had it that Osborne would use the rise in real wages and the subsequent increase in the tax intake to promise more public spending than expected as a means of neutralizing Labour's 'back to the 1930s' argument. This would spell trouble for Labour's central economic argument in the upcoming campaign.

PMQs

Miliband was much criticized for a performance that focused too heavily on the TV debates – focusing all six questions for David Cameron on why he would not debate Miliband as the broadcasters had suggested.[15] This left other MPs (notably Stella Creasy) to ask about more substantive issues such as defence spending.[16] One commentator even went as far as to say that Miliband's decision to focus on the debates could have cost him the election (this is far-fetched, but is worth reflecting upon in terms of the effects of performance).[17] Miliband and Labour appeared stoic and serious at PMQs; by contrast, Cameron and the Conservatives appeared gleeful and raucous. To some degree this was probably due to a conscious effort on the part of Labour to appear calm and resolute; but

---

[14] http://www.birminghammail.co.uk/news/local-news/labour-launch-election-pledges-major-8688345

[15] http://www.bbc.co.uk/iplayer/episode/b055f0lr/prime-ministers-questions-11032015

[16] For commentary, see: http://www.newstatesman.com/politics/2015/03/pmqs-review-miliband-wastes-opportunity-going-tv-debates-again; http://www.theguardian.com/politics/blog/live/2015/mar/11/cameron-and-miliband-at-pmqs-politics-live-blog; http://www.independent.co.uk/voices/comment/prime-ministers-questions-milibands-mps-have-to-do-his-job-for-him-10100771.html

[17] http://blogs.spectator.co.uk/coffeehouse/2015/03/pmqs-sketch-miliband-could-have-lost-the-election-today/

it also reflected the buoyant Conservative mood. Cameron specialized in brutality during PMQs – he accused Miliband of trying to crawl through the gates of Downing Street on the coat-tails of the SNP, of being 'weak and despicable' (twice). In contrast, Miliband's language was considerably more measured; he referred to the Prime Minister as 'useless' at one point, but when interrupted by heckling and John Bercow's intervention, he repeated the sentence with the word 'useless' removed. While Cameron appeared to revel in the ruthlessness of PMQs, Miliband appeared uncomfortable with going for the jugular. This was an arguably legitimate rhetorical strategy (particularly as YouGov polls consistently showed public disapproval of the PMQs style) on condition it *always* prevailed, thus 'constituting' Miliband's character. This was not, however, the case.

I'm Ed Miliband, Ask Me Anything

In a live show filmed on 12 March[18] Ed Miliband was quizzed by young people (the other main party leaders would also have their own shows in the coming weeks). Miliband's performance in this context was strong: he came across as relaxed, intelligent, and respectful. The audience appeared broadly liberal-leaning and supportive, and Miliband seemed comfortable in this environment. In particular, at the heart of his message here was his belief in the importance of dealing with inequality. Addressing a Conservative voter in the audience, he argued that inequality affected all aspects of society. This betrayed a slightly simplistic view of voter choice – after hearing that the audience member was a Conservative, his pitch to the voter was effectively 'as a Conservative voter you might be well-off, but you'll benefit with the whole of society from higher levels of equality'. It is striking that Miliband did not seem especially interested in trying to understand what drove centre-right views – which was possibly why some on the Blairite wing of the Labour Party were opposed to him. Miliband tried the Cleggite approach of asking individuals for their names before answering their questions. He also encouraged the audience to use his first name. Miliband displayed a notable (and largely unnecessary) tendency towards self-deprecation – for instance, admitting that he had not read all of Thomas Piketty's *Capital in the 21st Century*, referencing the bacon sandwich episode, saying that he would not win the election if it

[18] *I'm Ed Miliband, Ask Me Anything*, http://www.bbc.co.uk/iplayer/episode/b055tx34/free-speech-series-4-1-im-ed-miliband-ask-me-anything

was a beauty contest, and so on. Miliband's 'personal pitch' to the electorate seemed clear: I'm not good-looking or particularly smooth, but I am decent, empathetic and principled, and that's what matters. In response to questions about his ability to lead, Miliband referred to a very specific example of his experience during the 2009 Climate talks, in order to make clear he was able to represent Britain on the international stage. This felt like an adequate response, but could perhaps have been stronger – he kept narrowing things down to specific policy examples, when people really just wanted to know whether he had the capacity to lead. Miliband was directly asked if Labour would be in a different position if his brother David were in charge. Miliband responded by setting out how he wanted to move on from New Labour (mentioning Iraq and again inequality in particular). He was then asked if he regretted stabbing his brother in the back. 'That's not the way I'd describe it', he said, emphasizing that they both stood and that he won the leadership election on a different platform. Miliband issued a succinct but effective response when asked what he would say to people calling him a weak leader. 'They're wrong', he said (somewhat tongue in cheek). Miliband's language was remarkably restrained, even when faced with the more ludicrous propositions from the audience. When an audience member proposed a 'people's bank' to replace private banking, Miliband said he was 'not sure' about the idea. Miliband used his default response to a question on immigration – beginning by saying that he was the son of immigrants and that he recognized the benefits of immigration – and then went to make his point (in this case, about the exploitation of migrant labour and the impact of EU migration on wages). A notable refrain that Miliband used here was a variation on 'People have to make a judgement about that', 'You're going to have to judge me...'. This was all necessary but not sufficient.

The 2015 Election Campaign, 14–20 March

In the second main week of the campaign, Budget week, there was a new set of difficulties. As the election neared, the momentum was with the Conservatives, who were edging slightly ahead in the polls (the Conservatives were on an average of 33 % to Labour's 32 %[19] – though the latest Polling Observatory forecast put Labour 20 seats ahead of the

[19] http://ukpollingreport.co.uk

Conservatives!).[20] Key moments of the week were the announcement of Labour's pledge card and Miliband's PMQs attack on the Conservatives' NHS record.

Labour's Pledge Card

On Saturday 14 March, Miliband announced Labour's pledge card, borrowing an idea from Tony Blair. In 1997, the five Labour pledges were on cutting class sizes, waiting times for young offenders, NHS waiting lists, getting young people into work, and tough rules on spending and borrowing; in 2015, the pledges were (roughly) cutting the deficit, raising living standards, boosting the NHS, controlling immigration, and cutting tuition fees (the pledges had been announced one by one over the previous few months). The inclusion of immigration was a little surprising given the lack of focus on the issue during the campaign so far. What was striking from Miliband's speech on the pledges on the Monday was his cursory reference to Labour's proposal to stop migrants claiming benefits for their first 2 years in the country. On all of the other policies he took time to explain the context; on this issue he referenced it and then moved straight on to how to deal with migration lowering wages. It gave once again the impression that he was uncomfortable with this topic, a topic which Labour was mistrusted on. (Something similar happened when the pledge was referred to in December 2014.)[21] The somewhat confusing thing behind this move was that Miliband had had a pledge card before. In 2012, he launched a pledge card (or 'action plan card') for protecting family budgets, which included promises to cap rail fare increases and force energy firms to cut gas and electricity bills for the over-75s. This had long faded from the public and media memory, so there was little risk of any confusion but, along with the multiple slogans, it nevertheless suggested a certain degree of inconsistency in the Miliband campaign, linked to the idea of the textured narrative being broken up into a list of proposals, some being highlighted and some being dropped. On the other hand, it was an attempt – one of many late attempts – to firm up policy;

---

[20] http://www.huffingtonpost.co.uk/robert-ford/labour-20-seats-ahead-19-3-2015_b_6874222.html

[21] http://press.labour.org.uk/post/105262118234/launch-of-labours-second-election-pledge

in 2012 the pledge card was still vague; it is arguable, however, that the 2015 pledges remained so.[22]

The Budget

Osborne's Budget posed a set of challenges for Labour and Miliband. First, the positive economic news – continued growth, falling unemployment, a falling deficit, low inflation, rising wages – created a context that forced Labour immediately on the defensive. Second, the good economic news, together with the planned sale of state-owned bank assets, gave Osborne the room to promise an earlier end to austerity by cutting the targeted surplus by 2019–2020 from £23 billion to £7 billion.[23] This planned increase in public spending, compared to the original plans set out in the Autumn Statement, undermined Labour's 'back to the 1930s' attack; once again, Miliband was outfoxed by the Conservatives.[24] Third, while the Budget was broadly seen as a 'steady as she goes' affair, with only a few pre-election treats for voters, some of the measures introduced continued to squeeze Miliband's message that, despite the return to growth, Britain was still stuck in a low wage, unbalanced economy (which arguably it was). In particular, Osborne's increase of the personal allowance to £11,000, increase on the bank levy, and promise of more powers for Manchester were all clear attempts to triangulate Miliband's plans.[25] From start to finish the Budget was full of politics – indeed, one or two of the policies such as the consultation on deeds of variation seemed purely designed to irritate Miliband.[26] And it is without doubt that Osborne did a similar triangulation in his first Budget after the election in July 2015 with promises of a Living Wage, fewer cuts than planned, and so on. All of this threw into high relief first, the idea that the Labour Party was following a Conservative lead but simply trying to slow it down to make it

---

[22] http://labourlist.org/2012/03/return-of-the-pledge-card/

[23] http://www.bbc.co.uk/news/business-31942068

[24] http://www.independent.co.uk/voices/commentators/andrew-grice/budget-2015-tories-look-like-they-won-economic-argument-but-nasty-party-image-remains-10123268.html

[25] http://www.economist.com/news/britain/21646764-george-osborne-aims-kick-labours-strongest-economic-argument-ed-milibands-one-legged-stool

[26] http://www.independent.co.uk/news/uk/politics/budget-2015-george-osbornes-three-jokes-that-cost-the-taxpayer-41-million-10117998.html

less damaging and second, the idea that the Conservatives were indeed slowing it all down thus making the left irrelevant...

In this second week, Miliband decided to focus his PMQ debating points (18 March) on the NHS, the centrepiece of Labour's campaign. Specifically, he asked Cameron about promises he had made before becoming Prime Minister (e.g., 'no top-down reorganization of the NHS', reduction in cancer treatment waiting times) and compared them with his record in government. Of course, Miliband was mocked by Cameron about the previous week's 'two kitchens' fiasco. Miliband came prepared and responded with the line 'at least I paid for my kitchen, unlike the government chief whip!' (referring to Michael Gove, who was accused of 'flipping' homes during the expenses scandal and who also, perhaps not coincidentally, was married to Sarah Vine, the journalist who set off the whole kitchen debacle in the first place). Miliband's PMQ performance was overshadowed, however, by the Budget.[27] Miliband was generally perceived as giving an adequate, perhaps even a good response, particularly given the challenging political circumstances outlined above. Miliband's primary critique of the Chancellor's Budget was that it 'cannot be believed' – that, despite their denials, if the Conservatives were to return to power they would increase VAT and cut the funding to the NHS. But with the positive economic news, the shift in approach by the Chancellor and the lack of preparedness, Miliband had few options open to him. His was certainly a rousing speech, criticizing both the Conservatives for their deceptions and the Liberal Democrats for their broken promises. In response to the more personal insults and jibes by Osborne in his Budget, Miliband responded as follows: 'We're not going to take lessons in fairness from the Trust Fund Chancellor and the Bullingdon Club Prime Minister.' This was somewhat hackneyed, yet there seemed to be visible discomfort from David Cameron, George Osborne, and Nick Clegg throughout the speech.

One of Miliband's strongest lines in his response was his rebuttal of Osborne's claim that living standards were improving:

> The Chancellor knows that on the official measure from the ONS people are clearly worse off under him. So he's had a bright idea, Mr Deputy Speaker! To invent a new measure of living standards to improve what in fact people know, in their wallets and their pockets, somehow isn't true. But, Mr

---

[27] *Budget response – 18/3* http://www.bbc.co.uk/iplayer/episode/b05gxcml/budget-2015-live-budget-2015

Deputy Speaker, people don't need a new measure, which pretends they're better off, they need a new government to make them better off!

The disagreement was in fact much more nuanced than Miliband made out – the Labour figures were based on gross earnings, whilst the Conservative figures were based on disposable income.[28] But Miliband was able here to frame the figures in a convincing narrative of Conservative deception and incompetence. The final line was well delivered – with a mocking emphasis on 'new measure' and a short pause before 'they need a new government' to magnify the effect of the repetition of the phrase 'better off' – and it received a big cheer from the Labour side of the House. As is perhaps natural in a speech given in haste, Miliband's argument was somewhat diffuse – at one point he criticized Osborne for failing to get the deficit down as he had promised; at another he warned that the spending plans were extreme and that there would be 'secret cuts' to the NHS; elsewhere he attacked the government for pretending to be the friends of the low paid and the North. Of course, none of these things was mutually contradictory, but the speech still came across as somewhat confused. Due to continual interruptions and shouting from within the chamber, Miliband had to stop and repeat himself many times over. This had an unfortunate effect of undermining the strength of his message through its at times laborious delivery.

THE 2015 ELECTION CAMPAIGN, 21–27 MARCH

Miliband's third week in March was dominated by two performances – the last PMQs of the Parliament and the Cameron/Miliband showdown with Jeremy Paxman. The two performances and their receptions sharply contrasted with one another.

PMQs, 25 March

The last PMQs before the election were a clear victory for Cameron over Miliband.[29] Seemingly tricked – once again – by George Osborne who

[28] http://www.telegraph.co.uk/finance/budget/11484316/George-Osborne-Ed-Milibands-cost-of-living-election-pitch-has-been-demolished.html
[29] http://www.bbc.co.uk/iplayer/episode/b05nf4kz/prime-ministers-questions-25032015

had feigned uncertainty over whether the Conservatives would raise VAT if they returned to power by evading questions at the Treasury Select Committee on the Tuesday – Miliband focused his opening question on the VAT issue. 'So here's a straight question', Miliband asked: 'Will he now rule out a rise in VAT?' Cameron responded with a simple 'Yes'. This was clearly not what Miliband expected, and his response appeared weak – 'nobody's going to believe it' and Conservative spending plans were 'extreme'. Commentators and sketch-writers accused Miliband of failing adequately to prepare for any potential response to his question. And Cameron sailed through the 'straight answer' test which nearly all politicians fail. The simple 'Yes' was therefore a rhetorical setback for Miliband. Miliband then moved on to a series of other questions designed to catch Cameron out, but there was a sense that these were 'back of an envelope' alternatives that Miliband did not think he would need to use or, indeed, may have even come up with on the spot. One of these questions, for instance, was whether Cameron had broken his promise of no top-down reorganization of the NHS, something Miliband had asked in PMQs 2 weeks before. Cameron then turned the tables on Miliband by asking him whether Labour would rule out a rise in National Insurance Contributions. Because Miliband would not answer – using an 'I ask the questions' approach – it was easy to call these final PMQs a Cameron victory. (Ed Balls did rule out the NI Contributions increase shortly after PMQs. The rhetorical opportunity, however, had passed.)

The First (Non-)Debate, 26 March

Before analysing Miliband's performance in the first 'debate' of the election campaign, it is worth looking at the context.[30] As Steve Richards set out in *The Independent*, Miliband had been preparing for the debates for a long time – he really believed they could be a game-changer. Cameron clearly shared a similar view; he had done his best to undermine the debates and prevent them from going ahead in the form they had in 2010. In the end he refused a head-to-head and only agreed to participate in one seven-way debate. Miliband, for his part, seemed desperate to participate in any debate he could, even asking (perhaps unwisely) to join a 'Challengers' debate with the smaller non-Coalition parties. The first 'debate', broadcast on

[30] http://www.channel4.com/programmes/cameron-miliband-live-the-battle-for/

Thursday 26 March, consisted of a conversation with Jeremy Paxman followed by questions from a studio audience for each of the two leaders (without them meeting, hence the inverted commas). Going into this non-debate, the expectations were generally high for Cameron, who was seen as a polished media performer, and low for Miliband. This, Miliband and Cameron both thought, played to the Labour leader's advantage in that he might be able to unexpectedly impress.

And so he did to a certain extent, but there were several rhetorical mistakes. Cameron appeared uncomfortable and stiff in both the Paxman interview and the audience exchange (though he did begin to loosen up towards the end), while Miliband came across as more relaxed and assured than expected. While the immediate post-interview poll showed that Cameron edged the debate, with 54 % of people thinking that he did a better job, this was still a strong showing for Miliband given his generally poor personal ratings. A number of commentators issued glowing reviews of Miliband: 'On trust, the underlying theme of the night [Miliband] was the winner by a head' said *The Telegraph*'s Mary Riddell; he was 'light and breezy and charming with Joe Public – and disarmingly frank with Paxman' said the same paper's Tim Stanley; 'it was the Labour leader who came across as the more comfortable and more fluent performer' said *The Guardian*'s Jonathan Freedland. Nigel Farage gave Miliband the thumbs up, saying he thought Miliband the 'clear winner' and that 'What the guy showed tonight is he can weather it'. Even the pro-Blair *Independent on Sunday*'s John Rentoul gave Miliband credit, noting that he was 'more effective than Cameron against Paxman, leaning forward and disrupting Paxman's flow'. Others were less kind: 'the Labour leader seemed callow and tetchy' said Matthew d'Ancona. *The Sun* described Miliband as 'squirming', and a focus group run by *The Guardian* was broadly negative, with one participant saying 'Ed Miliband doesn't seem to speak as confidently as David Cameron. Also not as ready with the numbers as David Cameron.'

Four things stood out from Miliband's performance overall:

1. Miliband gave a significantly more genuine, normal, human performance than Cameron. This had its positives and negatives. On the one hand, he got far more applause than Cameron and appeared to elicit sympathy from the audience when Paxman repeatedly fired questions at him on his character – it seems that people genuinely liked him more than Cameron. But on the other hand, in a segment

of the programme hosted by Kay Burley, he appeared to be given less respect – audience members fired direct, sometimes quite rude, questions at him; Burley herself interrupted him on a number of occasions (which she did not do to Cameron), and the audience repeatedly laughed at his answers. While Miliband came across as likeable, he was still not seen as a Prime Minister in waiting.

2. Given that he was meant to have prepared so thoroughly, Miliband had a surprisingly poor grasp of policy. He struggled to answer Paxman's question on whether Britain was 'full' and what his net migration target would be, despite this being a very obvious question to prepare for. He did not give clear answers on how Labour would reduce public spending and get the deficit down in office. As *The Times* editorial said: 'The central weakness of the Labour Party's campaign – the sense that it cannot be trusted with economic policy – was left intact by this encounter.' This was in part the result of the gradual focus, from 2014, of the *whole* narrative upon the 'character' of Miliband, as I have argued throughout this chapter.

3. As usual, at the centre of Miliband's performance was a reiterated focus on his decency and integrity, his concern about inequality, his commitment to keeping his promises, and his willingness to stand up to powerful interest groups. He used his commitment to cutting tuition fees to illustrate his commitment to keeping his promises – but this was not a great example because of course he had not yet been able to implement these changes. And the experience he had had in the last Labour government he did not exploit; in fact he had been silent on this for 5 years, another rhetorical disadvantage of rejecting the New Labour administrations.

4. Miliband's harsh treatment of New Labour in the Paxman interview was striking. He was at ease with criticizing his old government, saying they got it wrong on the liberalization of the banks, on inequality, on spending, on immigration, on foreign policy (Iraq). When asked what else the former Labour government did wrong other than give poor migration estimates ahead of the A8 accession (of Eastern European countries to the EU in 2004), Miliband responded: 'I think there are two things I would mention in addition to that – by the way, I'm proud of many of the things we did – but two things I would mention...' The reference to the positives of New Labour was so cursory as to be almost meaningless – Miliband seemed entirely happy undermining the record of the previous

Labour administration (which included himself). I shall come back to this in the Conclusion, because it is in my view one of the reasons for the 2015 defeat.

Apart from these general points, four specific exchanges were of particular interest:

1. The EU referendum. Miliband gave his standard answer to an audience question on why he did not want to hold an in–out referendum in the next Parliament; the presenter, Kay Burley, unimpressed, said 'that's a politician's answer'. Her remark was unfair – Miliband had a clear policy on this (no EU referendum unless there was a transfer of powers). But Burley undermined Miliband, who answered by saying 'not sure, not sure' in an irritated manner, a response that left little positive impression on viewers. Miliband was unfairly treated here (and as we have suggested she was markedly nicer to Cameron), but he was also unwilling to get into the policy details and make the case for his proposals. The problem was that by emphasizing that it was 'unlikely' that there would be a referendum in the next Parliament, he implied that he just was not sure what to do, when his real point was that his policy depended on the decisions of other EU member states. His wording here was far from ideal.

2. Miliband was asked by an audience member 'Do you not think that your brother would have done a better job? He was better qualified and better positioned.' (He was asked a similar question at the 'free speech' event with young people a couple of weeks before so would have been well-prepared for this.) Miliband's response was to say that he was the right person to move the party on from New Labour – he therefore explicitly tied his own political leadership and personal relationship with his brother with Labour's overarching narrative and shift away from New Labour. We shall come back to the possible, perhaps disquieting psychological reasons for this in the Conclusion. Asked by Burley about regrets for creating divisions within his family, Miliband said the contest between him and his brother was 'bruising' but that it was 'healing'. He then said 'I wouldn't have gone through all of that [falling out with his brother] if I didn't have pretty strong convictions about how we need to change Britain.' This statement, while ostensibly ideological, hinted at a peculiarly tragic Miliband – again tying Labour's political vision

with his own personal narrative, but in a way that suggested a man forced to justify his acts by connecting them to something with a wider and sadder significance. His justification actually underlined the seriousness of the rift with his brother (as well as raising further questions about his motives), particularly as the first clause of the sentence actually suggested a follow on to the phrase: if I had known what the consequences would be... .

3. Miliband was told by Paxman that virtually all his forecasts on the economy had been wrong. Miliband hit back firmly by saying that wages had fallen. But he stumbled (this is the kindest way I can put it) when Paxman then asked him what his spending cuts would be when in office. Miliband's response was the following:

> The figure is – is at least hundreds of millions – more than a billion pounds – but look that's not the point. Let me explain: we are going to make – we are going to have to make these decisions when we're in government, but I've got to set out an overall approach. And I have set out an overall approach. I've set out an overall approach which says, as I said earlier, it's about fair taxes, it's about – I'm a Labour leader going into an, the, an election saying we're going to reduce spending outside a small minority of areas – Tony Blair never went into an election saying that!

This meandering response, and again on fiscal issues, and finishing with an unnecessary reference to the former Labour leader, significantly emphasized Miliband's weakness in this area. A 'vision' of the first 100 days could have been rhetorically stunning. Here Miliband's 'avoidance' suggested there *were* no policies, no envisioned 100 days....

4. The final section of the Paxman interview was, once again, on Miliband's character. 'You know what people say about you', Paxman began, before asking him if he was tough enough to be Prime Minister. Miliband then underwent a shift in posture and tone – he started to use the word 'right' after every sentence and his voice became sharper. At first, the audience laughed a little, somewhat bemused by this shift. But Miliband then gave the most memorable line of the evening – 'Am I tough enough? Hell yes, I'm tough enough!' This Americanism got a round of applause. This author wonders if 'Oh yes, I'm tough enough' would have sounded

more authentic, and therefore been more rhetorically effective. Opinion was divided on whether the 'Hell yes' was a good move; it sounded unnatural and a little odd, but in a way that did not really matter: expectations were so low that the surprisingly firm response had a positive impact regardless. Similarly, later in the discussion Miliband delivered the line 'I'm a pretty resilient guy, and I've been underestimated at every turn', another slightly artificial (and presumably well-rehearsed) but strong retort. Common refrains here were: 'Let me explain why' and 'Let me make this point'. The final moments of the show, as the camera zoomed away to prepare for an advert break, revealed an odd exchange between Paxman and Miliband. Paxman asked Miliband if he was alright, to which Miliband, confused, replied 'Yeah, are you?' Again, this was a good example of the slow drip-drip – some of it perfectly well-intentioned – undermining Miliband's credibility. 'What a bizarre question, Jeremy' would have been a better response.

THE 2015 ELECTION CAMPAIGN, 27 MARCH–3 APRIL

The Campaign Launch

Miliband officially launched the Labour Party's campaign on 27 March, with a speech at the Olympic Park. He announced a new policy on capping private profits in the NHS and went over Labour's five campaign pledges. The slogan of the Labour campaign – used repeatedly in the speech – was 'Britain can do better than this' and was an expression Miliband had often used before. It was also, however, reminiscent of Drew Westen's critique of the John Kerry campaign in 2004 in his book *The Political Brain: The Role of Emotion in Deciding the Fate of the Nation* (Westen 2008). Their slogan was 'Together, we can do better'. Westen's analysis is instructive: he wrote that the Kerry slogan was decided as a compromise between a positive appeal and a negative attack, but ended up doing neither very well. It neither bruised the Republicans – implying that things were going well enough under George Bush – nor sold the Democrats, implying that they were just 'slightly less bad than the GOP'. The same could be said of the Labour campaign slogan.

This was also the week of the main seven-way debate (Miliband, Cameron, Clegg, Sturgeon, Farage, Bennett, Wood), one of the main events and certainly the main media event of the campaign. Miliband did well enough and Cameron badly enough for Miliband to close the popularity gap still further. He reduced Cameron's lead here to 10 percentage points. It was at this point that the Conservative campaign began to panic. Cameron became much more animated and 'up for it', as it were, in an attempt to add dynamism to the Conservative campaign, taking his jacket off and rolling up his sleeves... . But this 'consequence' was an indication of the effect of Miliband's performance in the debates. It is perhaps worth mentioning here that Clegg's performance was as lacklustre as Cameron's, and post-debate Clegg's ratings collapsed. Farage did badly too, tactically badly, playing loudly and somewhat boorishly to his core support. Miliband therefore stood in strong relief to the other three male politicians. The problem for Miliband was that the real star of the evening was Nicola Sturgeon, at that time relatively unknown to the English audience. And she came across as passionate, informed, engaging, and fluent. Her poll ratings, as well as the SNP's as a whole, rocketed, making her rather than Miliband the star of the show.

Miliband's reduction of Cameron's 'prime ministerial' lead underlined further the now neck-and-neck idea of the competition (whose effect may paradoxically have put many floating voters or lukewarm Conservative voters *back* with the Cameron camp). By this time in the campaign, moreover, Labour's constant ambivalence about its attitude to 'business' lent it a kind of 'irresponsible' quality. It, therefore, began a concerted effort to respond to this handicap. But here too was a further illustration of a narrative/rhetorical response which came far too late in the 5-year period. The 'anti-business' element in the party's narrative and certainly the *public's* perception, had been developing since 2010. Changing public perceptions at this eleventh hour was not feasible.

THE 2015 ELECTION CAMPAIGN, 4–10 APRIL

The second week of the official election campaign was a promising one for Labour, with a number of positive stories, a series of (mostly) backfiring right-wing attacks, and a few polls.

Ratings Rising

Perhaps suggesting a tilt in Labour's direction, Miliband's personal ratings had been rising since the first two leader debates.[31] Lord Ashcroft released

---

[31] http://uk.reuters.com/article/2015/04/09/uk-britian-election-poll-idUKKBN0N01VB20150409

some positive-looking polls in marginal seats (notably that Labour had now pulled ahead in Harrow East),[32] and there appeared to be greater momentum in the Labour camp. Yet it is clear that the fundamental perceptions of the election remained: a Labour wipe-out was expected in Scotland and, so it seemed, neither main party would have enough seats to form a majority. A Labour–SNP (/Lib Dem?) arrangement of some sort was looking slowly more likely. This affected Labour and Miliband's image as being not in any real control of the outcome, and even less in control of the consequences of the outcome, as it were.

The Easter weekend was dominated by allegations that Sturgeon had told the French Ambassador that she preferred a Conservative victory in the elections. Labour made full use of the story, describing it as 'astonishing'.[33] Miliband said 'these are damning revelations'.[34] Given that much of the story was up in the air, with Sturgeon and the French Ambassador both denying she made the statement, it was perhaps unwise for Labour to make so much of the story (partly because a lot of people doubtless agreed with what Sturgeon was reported to have said). But in the end responding to the rumour was irresistible for Labour: they helped make the point that voting SNP in the General Election was most likely to benefit the Conservatives in Parliament. The electoral dynamics here were confusing, with Sturgeon also saying she would 'help make Miliband PM',[35] and the Conservatives suggesting that Miliband could get rid of Trident as part of a post-election deal with the SNP. The main concern was that Labour seemed unprepared for what was, then, a plausible outcome on 8 May; a hung Parliament with the most feasible governing arrangement being a Labour–SNP deal. Also that weekend, *The Sun on Sunday* for its 5 April edition got hold of some of Ed Miliband's notes from the previous week's seven-way TV debate. There were no major surprises but a certain trivializing of the Miliband persona: he wrote 'Me vs DC: Decency Principle Values', 'Relish the chance to show who I am', 'Calm never agitated', 'Negative → Positive' and 'Happy Warrior. These were the ones which the

[32] http://lordashcroftpolls.com/2015/04/back-to-the-con-lab-battleground/

[33] http://www.telegraph.co.uk/news/politics/SNP/11514933/Nicola-Sturgeon-secretly-backs-David-Cameron.html

[34] http://www.theguardian.com/politics/2015/apr/04/ed-miliband-nicola-sturgeon-allegations-damning-labour-snp-david-cameron

[35] http://www.bbc.co.uk/news/election-2015-scotland-32212940

press ran with the most, Happy Warrior in particular.[36] The 'Happy Warrior' phrase was originally from a Wordsworth poem, but Miliband most likely borrowed it from Obama's description of Vice-President Joe Biden in a 2012 speech.[37] It confirmed a fundamental difference in approach between Cameron and Miliband for the debates and, in fact, for the course of the campaign as a whole. While Cameron was following a steady-as-she-goes strategy primarily focused on the message of 'finishing the job', negative attacks, and avoiding mistakes, the Miliband method was one of the plucky underdog, savouring any opportunity to communicate with the electorate. Cameron appeared uncomfortable during this campaign, certainly at the beginning of it; Miliband looked, at least, like he was enjoying himself. Ironically, both of them were wrong in their interpretations.

On Monday 6 April, Tony Blair gave a speech as part of the Labour campaign, supporting Miliband's position on the EU referendum.[38] This speech was widely seen by commentators as perfunctory. It was an open secret that Blair was no fan of Miliband. But it did raise the question of what the relationship between Miliband and Blair should have been and how it affected Miliband's image and status. The issue is a complex one. Miliband staked his leadership on a break from New Labour, but while in many quarters the former PM was reviled for taking Britain into the war in Iraq, Blair still commanded considerable respect for his electoral achievements and personal leadership qualities. Miliband had been unwilling to reconcile these tensions, instead appearing simply to 'weaponize' Blair to build support for Labour where there was agreement between the two politicians (e.g., on Europe) but minimizing his interventions on other issues.[39]

One of Labour's big policy announcements in week two of the official campaign was the abolition of Non-Dom status (a tax loophole): it should not be the case that 'we are powerless in the face of the richest and most powerful' – Labour should act to ensure that the economy worked for

[36] http://www.dailymail.co.uk/news/article-3026869/Happy-Warrior-Ed-s-TV-debate-cribsheet-Miliband-s-motivational-notes-telling-relish-chance-scripted-downs-against-rivals.html

[37] http://blogs.spectator.co.uk/coffeehouse/2015/04/where-did-ed-miliband-get-happy-warrior-from-clue-not-wordsworth/

[38] http://www.tonyblairoffice.org/news/entry/tony-blair-europe-a-very-good-reason-to-vote-labour/

[39] http://www.telegraph.co.uk/news/general-election-2015/politics-blog/11519277/Is-Tony-Blair-an-asset-or-a-liability-to-Labour-Ed-Miliband-needs-to-decide.html

working people.[40] Crucially, it also was recognized as a sensible, modernizing move, winning support from unlikely figures such as *Dragons' Den* businessman Duncan Bannatyne[41] and Blairite *Times* columnist, Philip Collins. Yet, as with other Labour policies in this campaign, this seemed to be a sensible proposal that was then in part fluffed in the communication, with confusion over whether Labour actually wanted to scrap Non-Dom status entirely or just limit its use. To confuse things further, an old video emerged of Ed Balls saying that abolishing Non-Dom rules would lose the government money, and in an unfortunate interview on the BBC Shabana Mahmood, Shadow Treasury Minister, said that the plans would save 'hundreds of millions of pounds', but was unable to explain where this figure came from.[42]

Personal Attacks

Later in the week, Labour faced a series of attacks from the Conservatives and the right-wing press. First, Michael Fallon, then Secretary of State for Defence, attacked Ed Miliband for not ruling out a post-election deal with the SNP and risking Britain's nuclear deterrent as part of an agreement.[43] He also said Miliband had 'stabbed his own brother in the back' and was 'willing to stab the UK in the back' over Trident.[44] *The Telegraph* then followed with a story about Miliband's relationship with former *Newsnight* journalist, Stephanie Flanders, suggesting that he had concealed the time of their relationship because it would have been inappropriate for a Special Adviser to be dating a journalist.[45] Both these stories smacked of desperation: Labour had already ruled out sacrificing Trident as part of a deal with the SNP and the only new piece of information in *The Telegraph* story was the timing of the relationship (which was revealed by Justine Thornton in

[40] http://www.theguardian.com/politics/video/2015/apr/08/ed-miliband-labour-abolish-non-dom-tax-status-video

[41] http://www.independent.co.uk/news/uk/politics/duncan-bannatyne-says-hell-vote-labour-because-of-ed-milibands-courage-in-taking-on-nondom-tax-status-10161411.html

[42] https://www.youtube.com/watch?v=0A1KjRPBvnU

[43] http://www.theguardian.com/politics/video/2015/apr/09/michael-fallon-ed-miliband-trident-video

[44] http://www.bbc.co.uk/news/election-2015-32231115

[45] http://www.telegraph.co.uk/news/politics/ed-miliband/11526188/Ed-Miliband-was-dating-senior-BBC-economics-journalist-Stephanie-Flanders-when-he-was-at-the-Treasury.html

an interview in *The Independent*). Miliband's response to the first attack was to try to rise above it – he said that Fallon was a 'decent man' but that he had 'demeaned himself' and that 'national security is too important to play politics with'. He then went on to use more striking language:

> I think David Cameron should be ashamed. He's got nothing positive to say about the future of the country, he's got no forward vision for the country, and he sends out his minions like Michael Fallon to engage in desperate smears. I mean, I think Conservatives today, decent Conservatives right across our country, decent Conservative Members of Parliament, decent Conservative Party members, decent people right across Britain, will say 'Come on, we're better than this kind of politics'.[46]

As a response to Conservative attacks this was one of Miliband's strongest: it showed magnanimity towards his opponents, it accurately captured one of the fundamental Conservative weaknesses in the campaign (the lack of a positive narrative), and it focused on *ethos* as a mode of rhetoric to turn the tables on Conservative attacks (with a repetition of the word 'decency', a term regularly used to describe him in the past).[47] Indeed, the Labour strategy did appear to be having some positive effect, with some rumours that Cameron was starting to avoid talking about Miliband's personality (instead focusing on the election being a choice of 'team') amid strengthening personal ratings for Miliband.[48] Here were stellar examples of 'elements' of a real and persuasive 'character' for Miliband which should have been developed from the start; and as regards the Stephanie Flanders

[46] http://www.bbc.co.uk/news/election-2015-32231115
[47] http://www.theguardian.com/politics/2015/mar/06/ed-miliband-dont-mistake-my-decency-for-weakness
[48] Campaign speeches, debates, and interviews:

Ed Miliband Speech at the London Business Manifesto Launch, 30 March 2015 https://www.youtube.com/watch?v=MsoNWhrPqLI
Q & A following Labour Business Manifesto Launch, 30 March 2015 https://www.youtube.com/watch?v=1S6wugrsOMI
Ed Miliband on Absolute Radio: Full Interview, 1 April 2015 https://www.youtube.com/watch?v=14Wy4Vh-4bM
Ed Miliband Q & A in Yorkshire, 1 April 2015 https://www.youtube.com/watch?v=BW5OZbJMNqk
Leaders' debate, 2 April 2015 https://www.youtube.com/watch?v=7Sv2AOQBds
Clip from Ed Miliband speech in Bury, 2 April 2015 https://www.youtube.com/watch?v=v-XPNspy0d0

story, the general attitude on social media was simply 'some guys have all the luck', thus enhancing – reversing – the former aspect of his image as unattractive and nerdy aspects of his character he had himself encouraged on *Desert Island Discs* (see Chapter 6).

THE 2015 ELECTION CAMPAIGN, 11–17 APRIL

In the third week of the main election campaign the stalemate seemed to continue. After the Manifesto launches and the third TV debate, there had been no clear failures or victories and the polls continued to 'show' that the parties were more or less neck and neck, albeit with a tiny Labour lead (in terms of seats, of course a huge miscalculation). But this week was still an important one for Miliband with a number of key tests: most notably the launch of Labour's Manifesto and his response to Nicola Sturgeon's offer in the 'Challengers' Debate' on Thursday 16 April.

Labour Manifesto Launch

Labour was the first of the main parties to launch its Manifesto (it also launched its Women's Manifesto,[49] Youth Manifesto,[50] and Scottish Manifesto[51] later in the week). While there were no major surprises – most of the policies had already been announced – the overall packaging of the Manifesto stood out: Labour introduced a triple 'Budget Responsibility Lock', comprising (i) no additional borrowing for Manifesto commitments, (ii) a Budget each year that cut the deficit, verified by the Office for Budget Responsibility (OBR), and (iii) a fall in the national debt and a surplus on the current budget as soon as possible in the next Parliament. Given the lack of Conservative counter-attacks in the previous few days, Labour's promise that all its Manifesto commitments were costed appeared watertight. There were also some new policies in the Manifesto, including a fully funded freeze on rail fares for a

---

Clip from Ed Miliband speech announcing end to non-dom status, 8 April 2015 https://www.youtube.com/watch?v=oQ9QTLxg5N0,   https://www.youtube.com/watch?v=rWRoHHCSI3Q

[49] http://www.telegraph.co.uk/women/womens-politics/11539963/Labours-womens-manifesto-Launched-from-a-sand-pit.html

[50] http://www.theguardian.com/politics/2015/apr/17/labour-pledges-four-week-limit-unpaid-internships

[51] http://www.bbc.co.uk/news/election-2015-scotland-32339883

year[52] and the introduction of a National Primary Childcare Service.[53] The
'triple lock' was clearly a rhetorically effective attempt to win back economic
credibility and block the Conservative/Liberal Democrat critique of Labour's
spending during its last period in office. But, once again, Labour had left it
very late in the day seriously to challenge this view of Labour's economic
and fiscal laxity, an accusation which had hounded the party throughout the
2010–2015 Parliament. It was unlikely that the Budget Responsibility Lock
could have a serious impact on public opinion at this late stage. Still, the
move by Miliband diminished Conservative attacks on Labour spending for
the remainder of the campaign. Miliband hoped to go further by comparing
Labour's Budget Responsibility Lock with the Tories' unfunded spending
promises on the NHS. But this would always be difficult, and his line that the
Conservative promises were 'unfunded, unfair and unbelievable' suggested a
lack of focus – were the Conservatives being irresponsible ('unfunded', 'unbelievable') or were they being cruel ('unfair')? Was he attacking the fact that
there were impending cuts or that there were not? How could a 'promise' be
both unfair and not believed? Overall though, Miliband delivered a confident
speech at the Manifesto launch. As with Labour's weakness on fiscal responsibility, Miliband aimed to address the issue of leadership head on, contrasting
Cameron's unwillingness to challenge vested interests with his own record in
Opposition. It was at the end of the speech where Miliband made his most
striking pitch, recalling three former Labour reformers:

> And today we follow in the footsteps of those who have built the great
> institutions of our country. All of them called time on the old way of doing
> things. In 1945, Attlee called time on the dark days of the Depression. He
> said 'never again'. In 1964, Harold Wilson called time on the fusty, old ways
> of doing things. He beckoned in the white heat of the scientific revolution.
> In 1997, Tony Blair called time on a decaying public realm. He said our hos-
> pitals, our schools, and all our public services could once again be the best in
> the world. I do not offer a government that tries to carry on from where the
> last Labour government left off. I will lead a government that seeks to solve
> the challenges of our time. Over the last four and a half years, I have been

[52] http://labourlist.org/2015/04/labour-announce-a-fully-funded-fare-freeze-in-their-
manifesto/
[53] http://www.theguardian.com/politics/2015/apr/13/labour-election-manifesto-
key-points

tested. It is right that I have been. Tested for the privilege of leading this country. I am ready. Ready to put an end to the tired old idea that as long as we look after the rich and powerful we will all be OK. Ready to put into practice the truth that it is only when working people succeed, that Britain succeeds. If you elect me as your Prime Minister in just over three weeks' time: I will work for that goal. I will fight for that goal. Every single day. In everything I do. In every decision I make.

Three key things stand out from this section of the speech. First, Miliband's references to Attlee, Wilson, and Blair (also mentioned in his *Independent on Sunday* interview)[54] supported a narrative of reform and progress ('call[ing] time on the old way of doing things') that differed in tone from other Miliband interventions. Miliband portrayed himself here as taking on the mantle of Labour's heritage – helping both to develop his stature within the party and depict himself as one of Labour's political 'winners', and as an inevitable force for change in the country as a whole. Second, Miliband's assessment that he had been 'tested' (in a near chivalric/Luke Skywalker way) was both a recognition of the challenges of his period as leader but also an attempt to frame the election campaign as the final stage of a 5-year journey as Leader of the Opposition ('I am ready'). Third, and quite simply, there is an enormous and repeated emphasizing of the speaker by the speaker.

BBC Challengers' Debate

The Challengers' Debate was a risky move for Miliband – entering a debate with a series of minor party leaders, where there was a risk that he would be rhetorically outflanked by anti-establishment and left-wing lyrical alternatives. But the risk appeared to have paid off: Miliband delivered a strong performance; polling suggested he 'won',[55] and the media were broadly positive (on the left) or at worst indifferent (on the right). Polly Toynbee wrote in *The Guardian* that 'Calm, relaxed, even laughing sometimes, he hit

---

[54] http://www.independent.co.uk/news/uk/politics/generalelection/general-election-2015-ed-milibandDOUBLEHYPHENbuoyant-labour-leader-says-hell-be-as-radical-as-attlee-wilson-and-blair-10170294.html

[55] http://uk.reuters.com/article/2015/04/16/uk-britain-election-debate-poll-idUKKBN0N72QQ20150416

all the buttons',[56] while Toby Young in *The Telegraph* described Miliband as
'workmanlike'.[57] In fact, Miliband's personal image and overall 'credibility'
seemed to be improving steadily and embedding itself (at long last). But
the real coup for Miliband was his ability to appear prime ministerial in
the absence of the Coalition partners, something he had struggled to do
successfully since becoming leader. Rachel Sylvester in *The Times* said that
Miliband 'looked prime ministerial while still having a bit of Opposition
zeal'.[58] Damian McBride, also in *The Times*, argued that by facing down the
smaller parties and rejecting their calls to stop austerity and scrap Trident,
Miliband 'was trying to show the whole of Britain that he is a credible, cen-
trist Prime Minister, not a chaser of cheap applause. And he succeeded.'[59]
He began to appear as the 'sensible' leader of *all* the Oppositions. Opinion
was divided on whether Cameron was wrong to sit out the debate or not –
and Miliband's final challenge to Cameron to appear in a one-on-one
debate, which had been straightforwardly rebuffed by the Prime Minister,
certainly gave Miliband a rhetorical flourish to close the evening.

There was a number of ways in which Miliband gradually enhanced
his prime ministerial stature during the course of the debate. First, he
repeatedly said 'no' to questions from the other leaders – specifically,
when asked about whether he would sign Britain up to a European army
('I think no is the answer', 'There's not going to be a European army'
and, most ambitiously 'I'm not going to have a European army'), as
well as when asked about the possibility of working with the SNP in the
event of a hung Parliament ('It's a no, I'm afraid' to Nicola Sturgeon).
This sounded a different note to Miliband's previous and recent performances, helping to mark him out as a direct, firm, and hard-headed
leader. This was reinforced by Miliband's efforts to dismiss the smaller
parties through both his words (e.g., claiming without explanation
that '[Farage's] sums don't add up') and his body language and facial
expressions – sighing, dropping his shoulders, shaking his head, raising
his eyebrows and occasionally laughing.

[56] http://www.theguardian.com/commentisfree/2015/apr/16/challengers-final-tv-debate-general-election-columnists-verdict
[57] http://www.telegraph.co.uk/news/general-election-2015/politics-blog/11542513/BBC-challengers-debate-Who-won-Who-lost-Who-got-their-message-across.html
[58] http://www.thetimes.co.uk/redbox/topic/broadcast-battles/might-david-cameron-regret-his-absence
[59] http://www.thetimes.co.uk/redbox/topic/broadcast-battles/ed-milibands-sister-souljah-moment

Second, Miliband enhanced his standing with an emphasis on centre ground policy solutions that highlighted the importance of sensible and responsible government. In the opening discussion on the deficit and spending cuts, he emphasized the need for 'balance and fairness', triangulating between the left-wing leaders' demands for an end to austerity and the Conservative and UKIP plans for 'extreme' spending cuts; on immigration, he sought to find a middle path between Farage's critique and the other leaders' wholehearted defence of migration levels, noting that 'people's concerns [about immigration] are real and we have to address them'; and on Trident Miliband said that 'the first duty of any Prime Minister is to keep our country safe, and that's why I'm going to keep our independent nuclear deterrent'. This line appeared carefully worded to inspire reassurance and to draw a direct line between Miliband's personal qualities (note the use of 'I') and Labour's commitment to security.

After facing (some) criticism for his passivity in the earlier leaders' debate, this time Miliband took Farage to task on a number of occasions. Toby Young suggested that Miliband's decision to target Farage was a mistake given that UKIP split the right-wing vote,[60] but this was beside the point: the confrontation with Farage helped to bolster Miliband's credentials within the party (as well as with other left-wing leaders) and position himself as a credible centre ground option for the wider audience. Miliband's critique of Farage broadly consisted of three components. First, he sought to portray Farage as a Conservative-in-disguise, a secret Thatcherite who would go further than the Tories in UKIP's proposed spending cuts and privatization. This was most clear on the NHS (but also on housing) where Miliband quoted Farage's previous apparent support for privatization: 'But Nigel, the thing you've got to answer is this, because people at home need to know this: you don't want the National Health Service, you want a private insurance system of healthcare. You've said it on the record...'. Second, Miliband suggested that Farage was not a serious candidate, unable to offer solutions to the problems he raised. In one clearly pre-planned line, Miliband quipped, 'Here's the problem I have with you, Nigel, is you want to exploit people's fears rather than to address them.' Third, he accused Farage of being fundamentally untrustworthy, of having ulterior motives, and of failing a basic test of decency. This he did by detailing Farage's former position on the NHS – but also

[60] http://www.telegraph.co.uk/news/general-election-2015/politics-blog/11542513/ BBC-challengers-debate-Who-won-Who-lost-Who-got-their-message-across.html

by other means. When Farage – in a fit of irritation – dismissed the audience as being too left-wing, Miliband joked that 'it's never a great idea to attack the audience, Nigel, in my opinion'.

Miliband's challenge came at the end of the debate, when he was forced to respond to an offer by SNP leader Nicola Sturgeon (whose image as a rising star and 'exemplary' leader had been growing daily since the wider UK audience had become familiar with her) that she would be prepared to support a Labour minority government in order to stop the Conservatives returning to power if it pursued more progressive policies, arguing that she could help Labour 'be bolder': appear to accept the offer and he would infuriate the English media and large swathes of the public, not to mention the Scottish Labour Party; reject it and he could potentially lock himself out of No. 10 in the event of a hung Parliament. Under these severe political limitations, Miliband opted to rule out a formal coalition and to attack the SNP as untrustworthy – accusing Sturgeon of hypocrisy over her anti-Tory rhetoric:

> Oh no, Nicola – look, here's the situation: you've got a very odd approach, because you claim you want a Labour government, but you're saying 'anyone but Labour'. In England you're saying vote Green, in Wales you're saying vote Plaid Cymru, and of course in Scotland you're saying vote SNP … You want to gamble on getting rid of a Tory government; I can guarantee that we can get rid of a Tory government if you vote Labour in this election.

Miliband delivered a powerful response here in challenging circumstances (regarding in particular his 'standing' *vis-à-vis* the other candidates), emphasizing the strength of a Labour vote with his use of the (alliterative) 'gamble' and 'guarantee' to contrast the consequences of a Labour and an SNP vote. But he could not lay this issue to rest (how could he? The looming tsunami of an SNP Scottish landslide made it impossible) and with the polls remaining remarkably stable it would dog him for the rest of the campaign. An Ashcroft poll (17 April) revealed a dire situation in Scotland, with both Scottish Labour leader, Jim Murphy, and Labour General Election Strategy Chair, Douglas Alexander, predicted to lose their seats by significant margins (they did).[61] Scottish politics and the prospects of a Labour–SNP deal would continue to dominate

---

[61] http://lordashcroftpolls.com/2015/04/latest-scottish-constituency-polling/

the election campaign in the coming weeks, seriously impacting upon and countering the meticulous prime ministerial 'authority' Miliband was at last beginning to convey.[62]

THE 2015 ELECTION CAMPAIGN, 18–24 APRIL

This was the week that Ed Miliband was transformed for a while from awkward geek to media teenage heart-throb – at least in part of the Twittersphere and the tabloids. The Conservatives continued to focus their fire on the prospects of a Labour–SNP deal, but the polls were proving stubbornly close (34 % for both Labour and the Conservatives, according to UK polling report averages). Highlights of the week were discussion of a Labour–SNP alliance, growing media interest in Miliband's personality, the Evan Davis *Newsnight* interview, and foreign policy issues.

Health Week

The plan for Labour in the fourth week of campaigning was to turn the focus once again to the NHS, with Miliband accusing the Conservatives of a 'double deceit' over their 'extreme' public spending cuts and their commitment to £8 billion extra funding for the NHS.[63] While some announcements received coverage, including promises to increase the numbers of nurses and GPs and a commitment to cut waiting times for cancer tests, many of the policy details were drowned out by the Conservatives' forewarning of a Labour–SNP (or 'SNP–Ed Miliband') alliance. Besides, as I have pointed out, the NHS was already an *acquis* for Labour; developing the economic narrative would have been more profitable. Miliband responded by accusing

---

[62] Campaign speeches, debates, and interviews:

Labour manifesto launch – Miliband Speech (13 April 2015). Video of speech: https://www.youtube.com/watch?v=K8S28J5TjRs

Transcript of speech: https://www.politicshome.com/party-politics/articles/story/ed-milibands-full-speech-launching-labours-manifesto

Video of Q&A: https://www.youtube.com/watch?v=Zntp7xvPn68

Challengers' debate, 16 April 2015: http://www.bbc.co.uk/iplayer/episode/b05r87pr/bbc-election-debate-2015#group=p02n2pb1

Labour youth manifesto launch – Miliband Speech (17 April 2015) https://www.youtube.com/watch?v=5DqccOWHRzs

[63] http://www.bbc.co.uk/news/uk-politics-32380982

the government of trying to stir up both English and Scottish nationalism for political gain. In a speech earlier in the week, he stated:

> [Cameron] is demeaning his office; he is demeaning himself … and I think it says something about his campaign. Because his has become a campaign where he will say anything and he will stop at nothing. And I don't think that's what people want in a Prime Minister.[64]

This mirrored some of the language of moral disapproval he used about Michael Fallon's 'back-stabbing' remarks earlier in the campaign. But it was the Conservative agenda that continued to dominate, amid Labour fears it might be engulfed by a problem of 'dual illegitimacy' (taking power with the second highest number of seats *and* being reliant on the SNP to pass legislation applying to England only) come May 8.[65] The confusion of purpose and perceived outcomes, and the leadership style relevant to it were becoming significantly confused and confusing.

'Milifandom'

The fourth week of the campaign saw a renewed media interest in Miliband's personality, with a series of detailed portraits in the media[66] and, more bizarrely, a growing fan base on Twitter among teenage girls. Early in the week, Miliband's 'Battle Bus' was mobbed by a hen party – the clip, where the women posed for photos with Miliband, was widely circulated online, adding a sense of carnival to a long, somewhat tedious campaign.[67] A report in *The Evening Standard* also gave a detailed account of Miliband's earlier love life (including photos of three or four attractive women, mainly women he knew from Oxford or the party), although with one anonymous Labour source describing him as a 'nerdy commitment-phobe'.[68] And to top it off, A level student Abby Tomlinson led a group of teenage girls on Twitter to form a fandom for Miliband, using the hashtag 'Milifandom'. Tweets using the hashtag included declarations of infatuation, photoshopped images

[64] https://www.youtube.com/watch?v=FbZuzD-CWYk
[65] http://www.newstatesman.com/politics/2015/04/even-if-miliband-second-placed-prime-minister-it-would-still-be-victory-labour
[66] E.g. http://www.telegraph.co.uk/news/politics/ed-miliband/11545453/Ed-Miliband-so-what-is-he-really-like.html, http://blogs.channel4.com/gary-gibbon-on-politics/ed-miliband-profile-gary-gibbon-meets-labour-leader/30643
[67] http://www.standard.co.uk/news/politics/moment-ed-miliband-is-mobbed-by-screaming-women-during-hen-do-in-chester-10187771.html
[68] http://www.standard.co.uk/lifestyle/london-life/political-poldark-how-ed-milibands-life-loves-and-university-circle-resemble-the-world-of-the-bbc-bodiceripper-10189082.html

placing Miliband's face on the bodies of scores of cult figures (Superman, Rambo, Beckham…), a Vine with the song 'Careless Whisper' playing over a camera shot of Miliband's face, as well as a number of more substantive discussions about the marginalization of young people from politics. While Milifandom would have little impact on the General Election, it did suggest something interesting about the nature of leadership in the context of the rapidly evolving, impatient, forgetful, and at times incoherent world of social media. Previous Labour leaders struggled to adapt to the changing media landscape – in particular the importance of radio and later television – until Blair mastered the art form of TV and radio appearances under New Labour. But the now dominant form of media strategy as practised by Blair and his successors – carefully rehearsed, micromanaged, full of soundbites – was itself somewhat out of step with the new media context which now thrived on spontaneity, creativity, and disorder. Miliband's attempt to portray himself as a radical reformer, as a man committed to transformative social justice, was continuously countered and undermined by the chaotic, unpredictable media world he inhabited (as well as a sustained campaign against him by the right-wing press). But in these spontaneous, unrehearsed moments (the hen party, meeting members of the public, young people, party workers) he was often at his best. The Miliband team would have done well to develop this phenomenon. The stories – of attractive and intelligent women and now a female fan club – had a positive edge in the 'fashioned' persona of Miliband. But mainly because it came so late it did little to counter the now 'received view' of Ed. It did, however, support the argument that Miliband was having a better-than-expected election campaign and that the Conservative hope that voters could be dissuaded from Labour by putting Miliband at the front and centre of their campaign seemed to be slowly dissolving in the light of Miliband's apparent positivity, determination, and resilience.

The Evan Davis Interview

Ed Miliband again gave a confident performance in his *Newsnight* interview with Evan Davis, continuing his run of above-average media appearances for the duration of the campaign.[69] This was a more substantive discussion than the Paxman interview earlier in the campaign. Three things stood out. First, Miliband did show resilience under pressure. Pushed by Davis on Labour predictions on the economy, crime and tuition fees earlier in the Parliament that

[69] https://www.youtube.com/watch?v=Lklwne_3C-g

had turned out to be wrong, Miliband was unwilling to cede any ground, noting that 'You're definitely right that there are a number of statistics that the Government cites to say "Everything's fine in the country and everything's doing well" … but let's go to the big argument at this election: is the country fixed or is the country not fixed?' Similarly, on the spending cuts, Miliband refused to give the details Davis wanted to squeeze out of him (at one point using two glasses of water to represent borrowing and capital spending in an attempt to get clarity from Miliband on his spending plans), saying simply that Davis was not asking 'a sensible question'. Neither of these issues showed Labour in an especially positive light: on some of the big predictions (particularly with respect to growth and employment) the figures were on the government's side, and while it did appear that Labour's plans did have provisions for greater borrowing for capital spending, Labour were clearly unwilling to specify this. But from our leadership performance perspective Miliband showed a clear and confident response to Davis' questioning, using a plethora of firm expressions ('I'm not going to play your game with the glass of water', 'I'm not going to do what you're asking me to do', 'Let me make this point', 'I don't agree with Nicola Sturgeon'). All this gave the impression of directing the conversation and projecting gravity and sincerity. Davis was clearly frustrated with the repetitive nature of Miliband's answers – at one point pulling out a piece of paper listing all of Labour's standard lines on the deficit and the debt and ticking off the ones that Miliband had mentioned – but they indicated a tightening of the campaign around Labour's key messages.

Second, on the question of an SNP–Labour deal Miliband strengthened his response further after days of Conservative anti-SNP messaging. Davis raised the possibility of the SNP 'calling the shots' on a Labour government's agenda. Shaking his head firmly, Miliband answered 'That ain't gonna happen'. While a firm response (albeit not enough to stop this line of questioning from the Conservatives or the media), Miliband's language here was reminiscent of his 'Hell yes' response to Paxman's questioning earlier in the campaign – somewhat artificial in its casualness.

Third, Davis finished the interview with a couple of questions on Margaret Thatcher. He asked Miliband about her 'levelling down' argument about inequality.[70] Would Miliband trade a poorer but more equal society for a richer but more unequal one? This may have been a mistaken line of questioning for Davis (who was much more aggressive than his usual I'm-nicer-than-Paxo persona), because of course it fitted naturally into Miliband's wider argument about inequality – that inequality is inherently damaging to prosperity for all. Perhaps more importantly, Davis also asked Miliband whether he saw any

[70] Original clip here: https://www.youtube.com/watch?v=BnOGaQX04Cs

parallels between himself and Thatcher (noting generously that Miliband too was a 'conviction politician'). Miliband, of course, could not favourably compare himself to such a Conservative icon, but instead rehearsed the lines he used at the Manifesto launch the previous week – comparing himself to the Labour reformers Attlee, Wilson, and Blair.

Miliband Turns to Foreign Policy

With the situation in the Mediterranean reaching crisis point in this third week in April (on 19 April 800 refugees drowned when their boat capsized), the election campaign turned to focus on foreign policy. At a Chatham House event on 24 April, Miliband set out his foreign policy vision. There were murmurs from critics that it was odd for Miliband to focus a speech on foreign policy so close to a General Election. But there was an obvious strategy behind the intervention – namely, a renewed effort to build Miliband's prime ministerial appearance, addressing one of his main perceived weaknesses as Labour leader. The speech drew a sharp distinction between the 'small-minded isolationism' of the Conservative-led government and the Labour Party's 'outward looking' vision – with a particular focus, of course, on the Conservative promise of an in–out EU referendum. (Miliband's case was helped by news that HSBC was thinking of removing its headquarters from the UK due to fears over Brexit.) Miliband identified three central challenges for foreign policy – the transnationalism of growing issues like terrorism, migration and climate change, the current strains facing international institutions, and the internal economic, social, and political limitations of individual states. The 'Miliband Doctrine' outlined at the event centred on a 'hard-headed multilateralism' that involved learning the lessons of the Iraq war, restoring commitment to international institutions such as the EU, working with regional actors to tackle Isis, seeking a two state solution for the Israel/Palestine conflict, addressing global inequality, working with China on issues like climate change, stepping up sanctions on Russia, and committing to multilateral disarmament.

The Conservative counter-attack centred on Miliband's claim that the government did not commit to enough post-conflict planning in Libya and that this contributed to the deaths of migrants in the Mediterranean. The Conservatives argued that this was an attempt to politicize the tragedy and blame Cameron for the deaths of the migrants. Cameron said that Miliband's remarks were 'ill-judged' – clearly an attempt to diminish the Labour leader's stature and question his ability to operate on the world stage. Questioned on this after the Chatham House event, Miliband sounded uncertain: he said

that all governments were responsible for the failure of post-conflict planning in Libya but that it was the people traffickers who were to blame for the
migrant deaths – and yet at the same time drew a direct connection between
Libya and the refugees. This led to continuing accusations that Miliband was
cynically exploiting the crisis in the Mediterranean (his responses were also
quite confusing).[71] The major disadvantage to Miliband here was his lack
of interest in post-conflict planning in Libya up until this Chatham House
announcement. It was as if everything that was policy-related and persona-
related was emerging too late. He had no foreign policy persona, thus risking
the undermining of the very purpose of the speech, and heightening the sense
that this was simply an attempt to firm up his credentials as a Prime Minister-
in-waiting. In terms of our analytical perspective, this incident, almost on
the eve of a domestic election, drew out the failure of Team Miliband to use
foreign policy to nourish the Labour narrative as it pertained to Miliband's
persona. And of course, there had been a previous Foreign Secretary in the
family, his older brother David.[72]

---

[71] http://www.telegraph.co.uk/news/general-election-2015/politics-blog/11561427/
Ed-Miliband-should-be-proud-hes-used-dead-refugees-to-bump-David-Cameron-off-the-
agenda.html

[72] Campaign speeches, debates, and interviews:

Ed Miliband on the campaign trail in Crouch End (17 April 2015) https://www.youtube.
com/watch?v=EHYb9rW30RE

Ed Miliband on the SNP's plans – extract (18 April 2015) https://www.youtube.com/
watch?v=OJ0bBFDnb4Q

Ed Miliband speech on immigration (18 April 2015) https://www.youtube.com/
watch?v=Vcy_Orf16jw

Ed Miliband mobbed by hen party in Chester (19 April 2015) https://www.youtube.com/
watch?v=yKWMViBmJNo

The Leader Interviews – Ed Miliband (20 April 2015) https://www.youtube.com/
watch?v=Lklwne_3C-g

Ed Miliband on BBC Breakfast (21 April 2015) https://www.youtube.com/
watch?v=cDCxJ88zLvw

Ed Miliband on Lorraine – extracts (23 April 2015) https://www.youtube.com/
watch?v=ThJpIMc71S4, https://www.youtube.com/watch?v=S2UhwOfLkOI

Ed Miliband speech on NHS – extract (23 April 2015) https://www.youtube.com/
watch?v=iXapj8ZsTUg

Ed Miliband speech on foreign policy at Chatham House (24 April 2015) http://labourlist.
org/2015/04/full-text-of-ed-milibands-foreign-policy-speech-
at-chatham-house/

THE 2015 ELECTION CAMPAIGN, 25 APRIL–1 MAY

The final full week of campaigning brought out a series of last-minute measures from the Labour and Conservative campaigns – from an additional sixth pledge on housing on Labour's pledge card (immortalized – for 4 days – from 3 May as the 'Edstone', a major PR miscalculation) to David Cameron's 'pumped-up', 'bloody lively' electioneering. A highly personalized – and actually quite effective – response to a sense that the Conservative campaign was poor and Cameron bored. The sudden shirt sleeves rolled up cliché still seems to have resonance in image terms. Miliband dominated the news midweek with his surprise interview with comedian Russell Brand – yet the polls were starting to show a small but clear shift in the Conservatives' favour. Highlights of the week were the Brand interview and the Question Time, Election Leaders' Special.

Milibrand

Miliband's decision to agree to an interview with the comedian Russell Brand at his home in East London for his online show 'The Trews' was the subject of much comment in the last week of April. Had Miliband made a mistake by reaching out to an eccentric, non-voting comedian? Or had he made an intelligent strategic decision to engage with Brand's millions of young admirers?[73] Cameron poured scorn on the meeting, describing Brand as 'a joke' and saying that he didn't have time to 'hang out' with him.[74] But the interview – which could have been a car crash given Brand's erratic conversational style – played out in Miliband's favour. Brand allowed Miliband to set out his political economy ideas and his plans to address tax avoidance. Brand agreed emphatically with him at various points and avoided pushing him on other major issues where there may have been disagreement (e.g., Labour's spending plans or its immigration proposals) coming close, at the end of the interview, to endorsing

---

[73] http://www.telegraph.co.uk/news/general-election-2015/politics-blog/11570185/Russell-Brand-is-absurd-and-stupid-but-hes-also-popular.-Ed-Miliband-was-right-to-talk-to-him.html, http://www.thetimes.co.uk/redbox/topic/labour-election-campaign/ed-miliband-was-right-to-sit-down-with-russell-brand, http://www.telegraph.co.uk/news/general-election-2015/politics-blog/11568285/Meet-Ed-Miliband-Labours-leader-and-pound-shop-Russell-Brand.html

[74] http://www.theguardian.com/politics/video/2015/apr/28/david-cameron-russell-brand-is-a-joke-miliband-video

him (although Brand also appeared to endorse the Green Party later in the week).[75] Miliband himself gave a relaxed performance, often challenging Brand on his scepticism towards electoral democracy and the ability of politicians to make change happen. (Miliband interjected a number of forceful statements throughout the interview – on three separate occasions using variations of the phrase 'That's just totally wrong'). He was criticized by some for putting on a faux-Cockney accent during the interview (use of glottal stop à la Tony Blair) – but Miliband at least managed to get through the interview unscathed by Brand's eccentric manner.

The Brand interview highlighted the importance of the populist 'common touch' impulse underpinning Miliband's leadership, and its near absence throughout 5 years as a rhetorical and performative strategy. Let us dwell on this point here (particularly as it has relevance also for any analysis of Corbyn). While Miliband clearly hoped to tap into populist sentiment at least during his 5 years as leader, it would be misleading to apply the label rigorously to Miliband himself. According to Fieschi, there are three core components of populism: 'The perception of a fundamental, unbridgeable fracture between the real people and the elite'; 'A conviction that ordinary people in their common sense and emotionally direct relationship to politics have all the answers'; and 'An unreflective diagnosis of problems and quick-fix solutions'.[76]

Brand encompassed these three principles of (in his case left-wing) populism – with (1) his belief in 'unelected powerful elites' operating from behind the scenes; (2) his identification with ordinary people (notably through his use of 'we' throughout the interview) and his argument that 'ordinary people pushing politics', rather than politics itself, ensured progressive change; and (3) his tendency to identify the solutions to Britain's problems as simply a matter of targeting bankers and tax avoiders (e.g., 'what the people of Britain need is someone that's gonna say "You lot, don't you worry about HSBC, don't you worry about bankers, I'm your man, I'm going to go in there and take care of this stuff"'). In contrast, while Miliband used populist language ('ordinary people', 'the richest and most powerful'), he fell short of Fieschi's three-part characterization as he needed to appear as a plausible alternative to Cameron, while in the context of having 'understood' Brand. The Brand interview made this clear. First, while Brand attacked the 'unelected powerful elites' – bankers and multinationals – and argued they were untouchable by politicians, Miliband

---

[75] https://www.youtube.com/watch?v=OISY8hFVPVI
[76] https://www.opendemocracy.net/catherine-fieschi/plague-on-both-your-populisms

made the case for 'politics and people' working together, rejecting the idea of an unbridgeable gap between ordinary people and the elite. (He also took a more nuanced view on bankers, noting that 'we need banks ... banks are a good thing, not a bad thing'). Second, while Brand appeared willing to give ordinary people all the credit for progressive change, Miliband fully (and rightly) recognized the importance of politicians too – making reference, for example, to Barbara Castle and the Equal Pay Act in the interview. On *Question Time* later in the week, Miliband also gave a distinctly non-populist argument for his decision against an in–out EU referendum, claiming that taking leadership on a political issue sometimes meant going against the most popular option. Third, while Brand pointed to a narrow set of quick-fix solutions in the interview, Miliband brought in a range of other issues – the NHS, zero-hour contracts, and energy bills – and emphasized the need for 'practical change', which he admitted would not be easy to achieve. Miliband's diagnosis of policy problems was hardly unreflective, given his coterie of academic advisers, and he was perhaps too much of a policy wonk to offer quick-fix solutions – even emphasizing in his interview with Brand that as a political leader he was 'not looking for euphoria'. Taken together, Miliband did not meet Fieschi's criteria for populism. Having said this, there was a populist edge to Miliband's image here in that he was *engaged in the exchange* and in a friendly manner with one of the country's populist icons; although Miliband's discourse was not here populist, his *being there* was a response to it.

It is true that Miliband was keen to mobilize populist opinion in his electoral direction throughout his time as leader – and his focus on inequality clearly had the potential to appeal to followers of Brand. It is also true that he favoured certain interventionist policies that had been labelled as populist by more hostile parts of the media. But – at least, on the Fieschi definition – these things in themselves do not constitute authentic populist politics, but in leadership terms they point towards a kind of potential discursive, doctrinal, and rhetorical 'reconciliation' of populism and, say, social democracy. A proper development of One Nation could have achieved this. In his Canning Town Special Conference speech in March 2014 Miliband was able to use a much more populist tone than he usually did. We shall return to this topic in the Conclusion when we examine this and also what other leadership styles were available to Miliband.

Question Time, Election Leaders' Special

The last of the four election debates/interviews proved difficult for Miliband. While Cameron who faced the BBC *Question Time* audience ahead of Miliband put in a smooth performance, whipping out Liam Byrne's infamous 'I'm afraid there is no money' note from 2010, Miliband struggled with a set of gruelling questions about Labour's economic record and its 'offer' to business. *Independent* columnist (and Blair biographer) John Rentoul noted that Miliband fell back onto Blair-ish glottal stops at times as the questions got more troublesome (as he did in his interview with Russell Brand too, see above).[77] Miliband's slight trip while walking off the set at the end of the half hour was taken by some of the media as symbolic of his political stumble (*The Daily Mail* talking of a 'Kinnock moment').[78] Jenni Russell in *The Times* was more forgiving, describing Miliband's performance as 'plausible, passionate, authoritative'. Still, only four million tuned in to watch the programme, far fewer than for the 2010 debates.[79] Two particular exchanges for Miliband are worth noting: the questions on the deficit and the questions on post-election deal-making. First, Miliband was cornered repeatedly on Labour's spending before the crisis. Asked whether he accepted that when Labour was last in power that it overspent, he responded:

No I don't – and I know you may not agree with that ... Let me tell you: because there are schools that have been rebuilt in our country, there are hospitals that were rebuilt, there were Sure Start centres that were built, which would not have happened – and so, look I don't agree with that, and let me just explain to you the way I see it. There was a global financial crisis, which caused the deficit to rise. Now look, President Obama isn't dealing with a high deficit because we built more schools and hospitals. He's dealing with a high deficit because there was that global financial crisis. But spending has got to fall – I said to this gentleman here – spending has got to fall. And that's why we will reduce spending.

[77] http://www.independent.co.uk/voices/comment/question-time-special-cameron-is-up-to-speed-now-while-miliband-hit-a-bump-10217330.html

[78] http://www.dailymail.co.uk/news/article-3063264/Ed-stumbles-TV-debate-Miliband-TRIPS-leaves-stage-Question-Time-grilling.html

[79] http://www.thetimes.co.uk/redbox/topic/broadcast-battles/only-4-million-tune-in-to-watch-final-leaders-debate

This met with a disastrous audience response – from gasps of disbelief to angry accusations of Labour deception. Miliband's weakness here was twofold. First, of course, was the long-term strategic decision to not address the issue of Labour spending earlier in the 2010–2015 Parliament. With this issue left unaddressed, it was – as Dimbleby noted – a 'millstone around [Miliband's] neck'. Green and Prosser (2015) have pointed out that one of the reasons for Labour's defeat in 2015 was that it was still being blamed for the pre-2010 crisis. We can see that this was in part because the post-2010 narrative did not address the issue. Second, Miliband's rhetoric here was defensive and inconsistent, and therefore lacking a coherence to bring together Miliband's historic explanation of Britain's high deficit (via the financial crisis) with Labour's current promise of fiscal credibility. Moreover, Miliband's explanation for why he would reduce spending was tautological ('we will reduce spending' because 'spending has got to fall'), giving the impression that Labour's promise of fiscal credibility was vacuous. This point was also linked to the early 'narrative choices' of the party under Miliband which screened out *both* his condemnation of the previous government's spending *and* his defence of it. We shall come back to this also in the Conclusion. Second, Miliband was again pushed on the prospects for a Labour–SNP deal. This time, however, Miliband went further than his previous comments, stating:

> If it meant that we weren't going to be in government – not doing a coalition, not having a deal – then so be it. I'm not going to sacrifice the future of our country – the unity of our country – I'm not going to give in to SNP demands around Trident, around the deficit, or anything like that. So I just want to repeat this point to you: I'm not going to have a Labour government if it means deals or coalitions with the Scottish National Party … If the price of having a Labour government was a coalition or a deal with the Scottish National Party, it's not going to happen.

Miliband's language here is interesting and contrasts sharply with his prevaricating answer on the deficit, and especially earlier responses on the SNP question. While Miliband had made the point about not working with the SNP before, here his rhetoric was considerably more laden with emotion – he repeated his statement three times in a row, with references to 'sacrifice', the 'future', and 'unity' of Britain, the 'price' of a Labour government, and multiple uses of the phrase 'I'm not'. By personalizing the issue, Miliband made the question of a Labour–SNP deal a matter of his personal integrity as leader. This was effective rhetoric – conveying the notion that he would sacrifice victory for integrity; but it should have been the immediate response to the SNP issue weeks before, the view of Labour at the mercy of the SNP having already taken hold.

This made for a convincing performance for this moment of the election campaign. But because there was a danger of the strategy backfiring post-election, so the pre-election perception of a post-election crisis if a Labour minority government needed the support of the SNP underwent constant scrutiny by the media, particularly as there was considerable confusion over what would count as a deal with the SNP and what would not. Moreover, with Miliband's Shadow Cabinet colleagues suggesting that they would talk to the SNP to pass a Labour Queen's Speech if Labour were in the position to form a minority government after the election, the scope for accusations of illegitimacy and hypocrisy was vast.[80] It never happened, but the probability of support from the SNP on legislation was in part the reason for this tardy and confused, and then principled, but because tardy and confused, ineffectual refusal of a 'deal'.[81]

[80] http://www.cityam.com/214985/andy-burnham-opens-path-labour-talks-snp
[81] Campaign speeches, debates, and interviews:

Ed Miliband: Live On LBC (24 April) https://www.youtube.com/watch?v=RvB6duPjnng
Ed Miliband interview with Andrew Marr (and exchange with Boris Johnson) (26 April). Transcript: http://news.bbc.co.uk/1/shared/bsp/hi/pdfs/26041504.pdf, http://news.bbc.co.uk/1/shared/bsp/hi/pdfs/26041502.pdf. Full video: http://www.bbc.co.uk/programmes/b05t3j3f
Ed Miliband speech on international development (26 April). Transcript: http://press.labour.org.uk/post/117438512869/ed-miliband-speech-on-international-development
Ed Miliband speech in Stockton-on-Tees on new housing pledge (27 April). Transcript: http://press.labour.org.uk/post/117508448409/ed-milibands-speech-in-stockton-on-tees Short clip: https://www.youtube.com/watch?v=z7AoAWyFOI0
Short clip of Q&A (Miliband asked about his childhood dream): https://www.youtube.com/watch?v=tcAbhgLXtd0
TOWIE's Lydia Bright interviews Ed Miliband (27 April) https://www.youtube.com/watch?v=Eexqwuqpjh0
Labour campaign video – 'Ed Miliband: A Portrait' (28 April) https://www.youtube.com/watch?v=6ac_pbq-zHc
Ed Miliband On His Russell Brand Interview (28 April) https://www.youtube.com/watch?v=QGefXp4Ovbw
Ed Miliband speech – The Tories Secret Plan (29 April). Transcript: http://press.labour.org.uk/post/117675481409/the-tories-secret-plan Full video: https://www.youtube.com/watch?v=fHQ-6VlYL4w

CONCLUSION

We can see from our, as it were, annotated summary of the Labour leader's performance during the campaign itself several factors that bear on our analysis. Miliband's personal campaign was generally creditable, in fact it was much better than many had anticipated. We can also say that the 'personal' attacks themselves, that is, personal attacks as a Conservative strategy, were not particularly successful. However, we can make three points related to our approach and each underlines that 'the personal' and its failings came from within rather than from without and were related to the question of (lack of) leadership performance of a narrative.

First, the personal references and attacks were many, and Miliband was on the whole quite successful at coping with these, either ignoring them or trying to deal with them. The problem was that he was coming from such a low point in public estimation and notions of competence and confidence. The overall reasonable performance was, therefore, the result of mild surprise that he was less *gauche*, more competent than he had been depicted as being by his adversaries, and in particular the rightist press.

The second point to note is that these revisions of view appeared far too late to affect voting intentions. Perceptions of 'character' take time to bed down in public consciousness. We should remember that in contrast to Miliband, the persona of Tony Blair had been relentlessly and positively constructed for certainly three and arguably 5 years before the 1997 victory.

Third, and this point is related to the above, Blair had a narrative – New Labour, Third Way, Modernization, all of which resonated across the political spectrum. One of the reasons Ed Miliband went into the election campaign with 'only' the personal, and underwent a kind of appraisal of his character (which as we have said was more positive than had been expected) was because the wider and potentially rich narrative of a 'Milibandism' had been virtually abandoned and was certainly

Ed Miliband on This Morning (29 April) https://www.youtube.com/watch?v=sKUT8EtytSk, https://www.youtube.com/watch?v=POcXFMi1BAo

Ed Miliband interview with Russell Brand (29 April) https://www.youtube.com/watch?v=RDZm9_uKtyo

Ed Miliband: There Are Seven Days To Go To Change How Our Country Works (30 April). Short clip: https://www.youtube.com/watch?v=ICddhYPn-7k

Question Time – Election Leaders Special (30 April) http://www.bbc.co.uk/iplayer/episode/b05t2k80/question-time-election-leaders-special

underexploited in the aftermath of 2012. So, to a large degree, entering the election campaign with an (incomplete) persona without a rally narrative was *chosen* by Miliband/Team Miliband as a performed strategy and rhetoric.

A fourth point I might add here, and return to in the Conclusion, is the question of leadership style. Was there another style of leadership, another persona available to Miliband, one that was not a (failed) attempt to develop a new narrative and perform it as a rally leader? It is arguable that the 'campaign' style of 2015 was relatively successful because it posited a different kind of leadership: the leader of a social democratic party, almost un-ideological, practically minded yet more decisive ('Hell yes') than before; unpretentious, with a lesser retail offer, but one which had been prepared, given a narrative, and performed over previous years, and which would have linked Miliband more to a kind of Northern European leadership style. But this was like an afterthought at a minute to midnight on the quinquennial clock.

CHAPTER 6

Conclusion: Narrative, Rhetoric, and the 'Personalized Political'

The aim of this book was to take the period 2010–2015, the period of the Labour Party in Opposition under the leadership of Ed Miliband, and identify and examine it as a discursive, rhetorical, and performative event or series of events. In this 'arc', the rhetorical performances of the leader drew upon the party's evolving narrative with the intention of enhancing leadership (both within the party and *vis-à-vis* other party leaders), giving 'voice' to the party, and advancing it and the leader's position and status, and gaining advantage in the elaboration and presentation of policies to the wider public, in the context of the imagined 'endpoint', the UK General Election of 2015. In order to show this, I divided the analysis into five parts and the Conclusion here.

I first, in Chapter 1, addressed key theoretical developments in and approaches to the relation between rhetoric and politics, agency and structure, and language and change. What I was particularly interested in demonstrating was that (and how) language and rhetorical performance were not simply a reflection or discursive emanation of political practice and process but an essential part, arguably *the* essential part, of the political process; that rhetorical expression and agential performance fashion, affect, and change – arguably *are* – the political process.

Then, in Chapter 2, I addressed the question of former leaders to see whether the performance of leadership in the Labour Party influenced party identity and direction and whether this 'past' was formative of leadership performance in the period we were studying; if for example there was

© The Author(s) 2017
J. Gaffney, *Leadership and the Labour Party*, Palgrave Studies in Political Leadership, DOI 10.1057/978-1-137-50498-2_6

a range of types of leadership (desired or disdained), of styles of leadership, and how these related to the narratives of the party and the specific conditions of political exchange: the party organization, mass membership, the trade union connection, the PLP, and evolving media and, not least, leaders' influence upon process in a party that has always pretended that personal leadership is not an essential – even desirable – issue, even concept. In mythological terms, one point worth noting here is the virulence in the party of what we might call the Pied Piper myth: the figure who took us away from our rightful place through artifice and deception, whether it is a MacDonald, a Blair, a Miliband, or a Corbyn. Choose your Piper. The personalized nature of leadership now also valorizes dramatically another Labour myth: that there are 'wrong roads'; today, however, it is not just wrong decisions (e.g., widespread nationalizations after 1945) but wrong leaders 'followed' down those wrong roads travelled.

In Chapter 3, I identified the evolution of party discourse after the 2010 electoral defeat and Miliband's election to the leadership of the party, and how he used this 'new' narrative rhetorically and how, over time, he laid rhetorical claim to authorship of the party's narrative, and used it to project his leadership persona and inflect the party's identity and purpose. In many ways One Nation – potentially – was a masterstroke; it caught a growing wave of 'identity politics', and had the potential to conflate left and right in a new venture.

I then, in Chapter 4, took just one 'performance', the 2012 Manchester Party Conference, and analysed it in great detail to demonstrate our underlying thesis of the fundamental relationship between narrative, performance, and leadership.

Then, in Chapter 5, I examined in some detail how the leadership and the party coped with and responded to the challenges of the second half of the period, the two-and-a-half year period after the Manchester Conference and the preparation of an election manifesto and a 'credible' leader and Shadow Team, that is to say, the period where the party and leadership elaborated/attempted to elaborate a 'narrative of government' with two parts: (a) a party narrative, image and rhetoric, and (b) a related leadership narrative, image, and rhetoric. I also demonstrated that ideationally and discursively – for example, building upon both *The Purple Book* and *The Labour Tradition and the Politics of Paradox* and, say, IPPR output, an imaginative set of proposals was easily within reach, the one problematic area being an economic narrative; but that the whole effort was more or less abandoned – which had the dramatic effect of turning the spotlight *even more* upon the leader. I also showed in this chapter how in such circumstances good performances (Gaffney 2012; Gaffney and Lahel 2013) can become hostages to fortune in that they become the focus of attention, and then there is a poor performance... .

In this my concluding chapter I appraise what my analysis demonstrated, and some of the practical and theoretical issues it raised. I also appraise the narrative limits of One Nation rhetoric, performative issues, particularly during the 2015 election campaign, and the relationship between Ed Miliband's rhetoric and the persona projected, the unresolved nature of the 'two brothers' issue upon the persona, and how the election of Jeremy Corbyn to the party leadership in September 2015 was intimately bound up with the narrative and performance of Ed Miliband's leadership.

Rhetoric and Its Effects

We saw that there is an emerging body of scholarship on the role and effects of rhetoric in the political process (*inter alia* Finlayson 2004, 2007, 2012; Gaffney 1991, 2001, 2014; Krebs and Jackson 2007; Martin 2014). The authors stressed the centrality of rhetoric in contemporary political life, each offering a method for analysing rhetoric, each drawing inspiration from the Aristotelian triptych of *ethos* (the person), *pathos* (use of emotion), and *logos* (use of logic/enthymeme) as in *The Art of Rhetoric*. In Chapter 1 I suggested an adaptation of classical rhetoric. Aristotle stressed the role of language in the public realm and its deployment to effect; the importance of the act of communication and its significance in terms of audience, followership, and character. However, when I used *ethos*, *pathos*, and *logos* in order to help us understand rhetoric and its contemporary use, some aspects of the triptych were problematic. For example, *ethos* referred to the importance of moral credence; Aristotle stresses age and social status as determinants of the moral credence of a speaker. 'Proofs from character are produced, whenever a speech is given in such a way as to render the speaker worthy of credence – we more readily and sooner believe reasonable men on all matters in general and absolutely on questions where precision is impossible and two views can be maintained' (Aristotle 1991: 74).

Contemporary authors modernize the concept of *ethos* by alluding to a series of leadership traits, for example, vision, judgement, articulacy, decisiveness, and ability to work well with colleagues. For my purposes, *ethos* also includes the personal and political background of a speaker, for example, an evoked 'trajectory' and its effects upon rhetoric. Regarding *logos*, for Aristotle this is arguably the most important element; how through 'argument' persuasion is achieved. Yet we have seen that, however 'necessary', it is 'insufficient'. I place emphasis upon the structure of the speech, as if it were a musical score. As regards *pathos*, what I was interested in were the techniques a speaker (Miliband) evoked and created in order to appeal to the emotions of the audience and these to persuasive purpose. The use of *pathos* by political leaders in the contemporary context includes, though is not limited to, the use of compelling metaphors, emotionally charged language, biblical references, and a whole range of other discursive/communicative techniques – for example, alliteration, rhetorical questions, use of opposites – all of which may or may not contribute to positive endorsement and persuasion/followership. One of the major uses today, as we saw in Chapter 4, was to 'emotionalize' the speaker himself. Aristotelian *ethos, pathos,* and *logos* offered a starting point for examining the role and use of rhetoric in contemporary political life. Our case study demonstrates that (a) rhetoric has major effects upon the political process and political outcomes and (b) leadership performance uses rhetoric and now is crucial to it.

Most of my empirical work has drawn upon case studies of France and the UK and analysis of the leadership performance of French Presidents and UK Prime Ministers (and would-be Presidents and Prime Ministers). My research on leadership studies has drawn attention to the personalization of politics and its complex structure, and to the role of rhetoric in the political process and to the way in which rhetoric and performance are fashioned by political culture and institutions. The empirical case study here combines inquiry into the personalization of leadership and the way in which a leadership actor uses rhetoric to political effect, for example, in the construction of a 'character'; *ethos* is viewed as a series of character traits which constitute a political persona. Aristotelian *ethos* modified to the 'rhetorical persona' can be deployed within a range of cultural and institutional contexts – each offering a series of opportunities and constraints. Culture and institutions are thus formative conditions of rhetoric and of the construction of 'character'/persona through political performance. Let me summarize my theoretical contribution to research before examining my findings in the Miliband case:

- Aristotelian *ethos* is modified and viewed as 'rhetorical persona'.
- The speaker's depiction of the world, of the self and of others is central to leadership rhetoric.

- Proximity (a sense of) to the audience is a condition which affects imagined relationships between leaders and audiences.
- The institutional and cultural frameworks of leadership performance are the conditions of production of rhetoric.
- Rhetorical performance and the deployment of image – individual style and its public reception – are moments of agency in the political process.
- The way in which leaders create an image of themselves, a 'character' with a style, and apply it to a range of leadership purposes (public mobilization, agenda-setting, coalition building) is part of the political process.
- The stress upon the elements and role of *ethos* or persona in the projection of the political 'character' accompanies the rhetoric; it is not simply how he or she persuades through emotion and argument, but who is the he or she 'seen' in the rhetoric, and also imagined as existing outside it, and possessing a particular character and style.

I lay great stress, therefore, upon the relationship between leadership performance, language, and the 'rhetorical persona', and upon culture and institutions as the essential conditions of performance. Content (rhetoric and leadership performance) is not divorced from context (culture and institutions), is not a function of it, but is a performance that takes place upon the 'stage' of context.

THE PARTY'S NARRATIVE

We saw from our analysis that one of the central issues for a political party, particularly after a defeat, was how to develop a new narrative and one that would enhance the new leadership. For the new leader in 2010, Ed Miliband, the task was to produce one, as is the case for any new leader. The 'Third Way'/'New Labour' Blairite style and narrative had dominated Labour and politics generally for 20 years (Naughtie 2002; Atkins 2011). Miliband's task in replacing it was eased by the altered image of 'Blairism' in the aftermath of the Iraq war, and by its final days as 'Brownism', and the descent into deep unpopularity just prior to Labour's worst electoral defeat and the resignation of the sitting Prime Minister, Gordon Brown. The whole Blair–Brown narrative had also been severely weakened by the economic crisis of 2008 and its aftermath.

It is of course arguable that the criticism directed at Third Way thinking as regards the economic crisis was unfair. Bogdanor[1] has argued that overall as regards growth, prosperity, income, child poverty, and so on, the 1997–2008 period was a major success, one of the best in the modern period. The association, however, of the economic crash with the Gordon Brown government offered to a Miliband narrative the opportunity to reject a previously dominant party narrative, labelling it as neoliberal, and creating rhetorical opportunities for its replacement. As we saw in Chapter 3, this narrative shift, although advantageous in that it offered Miliband a new voice, posed problems in the longer term in that the resulting eclipse of the Blairites between 2010 and 2015 had to be countered not only in terms of policy elaboration for 2015 but also and importantly in terms of personnel, and the need for their experience in the elaboration of policy and the organization of the 2015 electoral campaign. In the earlier period (2010–2013), however, the party leadership tried to move away from the Blairism of 1997–2008 (although not that of oppositional Blairism of 1994–1997, for reasons that we shall come on to) from the party's discourse, depicting it as the road that should not have been travelled. In fact, the ideas informing Blairism as a narrative – supply-side economics, targets, national level decision-making, working with the markets to increase growth and therefore state revenues for redistribution, bringing the culture of capitalism into the running of public services, and so on – were depicted, not as a Third Way (between Old Labour and Conservatism) but, far worse, as a direct continuation of Thatcherite neoliberalism (Wood 2013). In this way, a dramatic opposition could be displayed between the period 1997–2010 and an emerging 'Milibandism' by making the period 1979–2010 a single movement or moment of a neoliberal undertaking which ultimately failed by showing its inadequacy: that is, by being unable to domesticate the monster it unleashed and being then savaged by it in 2008. As we saw, some apologists for a new post-2010 approach indeed took the 'wrong road' motif back to 1945 not 1979, seeing the whole Labour (and Conservative) state project of the post-war period as a betrayal and abandonment of a true devolved community socialism of the 1930s and earlier.

---

[1] Vernon Bogdanor presentation at 'The One Nation Labour Debate. Labour and the new era in Politics'. Organized by One Nation Labour at the House of Commons, 19 March 2013, Committee Room 10.

For most involved in developing a post-2010 narrative, such a fundamental revisionism was too extreme, although the overall sense that post-2010 Labourism was about finding the true, original source of a left that had lost its way became the dominant rhetorical 'space' in the evolving party narrative. For some, Blair's 1994–1997 period as Opposition leader was seen as the moment when the right road had been found (then lost after 1997), particularly as it had developed a 'One Nation' approach, even using the expression (as had Neil Kinnock).[2] It is also worth stressing that this period was exemplary for the party in terms of the dramatic rise in popularity, membership, and the image of its leader, Blair. Reigniting that enthusiasm by revisiting the 1994–1997 narrative might have been beneficial to Miliband's narrative – and indeed was much closer to him ideologically than pre-war socialism.

Two final points on this are worth making. First, that 'cleavage' discourse – whether between a post-1945 or post-1997 narrative – was rhetorically advantageous but also problematic because Miliband's own personal new narrative was dominated rhetorically by notions not only of 'return' but also reconciliation, unity and a collective purpose. An oppositional rhetoric within the overall Labour narrative was antithetical to this. At some point, moreover, for the practical reasons of policy, personnel, and real reconciliation, as we have already mentioned, a Third Way narrative or something resonant of it would have to be brought back in. IPPR was an exemplary expression of this doctrinal, rhetorical, and narrative attempt at such an ideational reconciliation. There were also attempts to do this after Brighton 2013, and we shall return to the consequences of this below for the fortunes of an overall Miliband rhetoric and narrative. Before revisiting what became of the One Nation narrative and its rhetorical exploitation by Miliband, I make two points. First, it was not only the perceived inadequacies of Third Way Blairism: its not foreseeing/contributing to the 2008 crisis (the first point was true, few did – the second was debatable, as we have seen with our reference to Bogdanor) that enabled it to be screened out as another narrative emerged; its 'character' had also changed since its inception. After taking office in 1997 the general thrust of New Labour had been associated with the modern, even the trendy (e.g., 'Cool Britannia'), but it also became associated with 'money' and people (e.g., Bernie Ecclestone) who were not seen as the ordinary working or middle-class people Labour should

<hr/>

[2] I owe this insight to Mark Wickham-Jones (2013a).

represent. This aspect of New Labour eventually became personified in Peter Mandelson, linked in the popular press and significant sections of the party to yachts, Russian oligarchs, and dodgy finance. This might just be seen as a kind of logical 'power corrupts' aspect of politics, but this aspect of a New Labour aristocracy, as it were, tells us something about the narrative that followed it, in that the emerging post-2010 narrative would go on to define itself as not only 'returning' and 'reconciling', but also as being highly moral; and this would also later attach itself to the 'character' of the leader himself (Fairclough 2000).

Second, the depiction of New Labour as having lost its way, disillusioning those striving for a true collective purpose and a just society, and even being associated with corruption and money, would characterize the dramatization of the emerging One Nation rhetoric into not only a moral repudiation of New Labour but an emotional one too. This too would be associated with the leader's own character, and would cause problems when, by 2014, it was clear that some kind of realignment of One Nation and New Labour, lyricism and social democratic pragmatism, was seen as desirable, imperative even. I now turn to the development and 'enactment' of the central 2010–2015 narrative: One Nation.

As I pointed out above, theoretically and strategically, the Labour Party in 2010 'needed' a new narrative, first to create a new rhetorical 'offer' after the 2010 defeat, and second to provide the new leader with a narrative of 'his own' which he could rhetorically deploy. On this latter, I should make two points which bear upon Miliband's leadership image. The first is that Miliband's own personal image was extremely problematic when he took the leadership. He was the younger brother of the expected winner, former Foreign Secretary, David Miliband. Apart from the mark of Cain which, in fact, arguably constituted the only 'dramatic' aspect of his persona throughout the 5-year period, the public persona of Miliband was quite restricted; he was seen as a bit of a policy-wonk from North London/Oxford, rather 'nerdy', undramatic in rhetorical terms: European social democrat in background and style, and in terms of New Labour, if anything, a 'nice' version of a Brownite (the 'nasty' version being his soon partner and near-silent rival, Ed Balls). There was little 'to' his public persona beyond this. It is worth remembering that previous leaders had a richer heritage to draw on: Welshness or Scottishness (Kinnock, Brown, Smith), other major portfolios (Callaghan and, although not leaders, Healey, Jenkins, Castle, Williams etc.), or youthful trendiness (Blair), or radicalism (Foot), and so on. I discussed this in detail in Chapter 2. There is both an irony and a logic, therefore, in Miliband's encouraging the development and later 'adoption' of the narrative of One Nation, with its appeal to the past and to emotion, uncharacteristic of his 'persona'. In fact, the emotionalism and moralism that would develop around One Nation rhetoric can best be seen in this 'need', this 'lack' of what we might call an identifiable personal background discourse. Might one have been fashioned to better advantage? My own sense is that of course it could.

The second point to note concerns the 'operationalizing' of a rhetoric of Labour leadership. Labourism – like all left thought – cannot invent a narrative that has no links to the past. It has to go back to somewhere. It used to be able to go back to *someone* (Bevan, Gaitskell, Lansbury, and so on), but this is now seen as too limiting (and arguably divisive); but left leadership has to draw its legitimacy from *somewhere* – hence the emergence of a narrative Miliband could use. The focus today upon leadership and personalization across the political spectrum is all-pervasive. The challenge for Labour in this situation was to respond to such an exigency by making Miliband himself the 'author' of a narrative that, in fact, preceded him. I looked at this in detail in Chapters 3 and 4 and shall return to it briefly below. Let me turn now though to the leader's new/old narrative.

THE LEADER'S NARRATIVE

The One Nation narrative that Miliband 'authored' in 2012 (at the Manchester Party Conference) predated 2012 and emerged into the political space, as we saw, in several stages. Let us briefly recapitulate its main stages and see how it lent itself to personal authorship. It began, like all narratives of renewal, *before* the 'event', that is, before the 2010 electoral defeat, in the form of an attempt at beginning a renewal of party thinking. Examples were James Purnell's 'Open Left' project with Demos in 2009, and Jonathan Rutherford and others organizing seminars in Oxford and London (*Labour's Future*). Underlying these 'projects' (projects which were themselves related to deep myths of renewal within the left) were further notions of more democracy, a rejection of Blair-Brownism, and a search for a deeper 'truth' to the Labour project.

After the 2010 election, as was to be expected, a wealth of debate and output began, including a new Policy Review commissioned by the newly elected leader. This produced several texts and emphasized more party reform, more democracy, interaction with the grassroots, and so on. The wider/ deeper revision of the party's ideas and thinking was gathering momentum, in fact *overtaking* the Policy Review. Rutherford and others became much more prominent and, along with the community activist Maurice Glasman (promoted to the Lords by Miliband), a powerful and widespread narrative began to spread across the 'discursive space' within the party, in particular with the ideas around Blue Labour (BBC Radio 4, March 2011) which gained wide media coverage and debate within and beyond the party.[3]

The significant thinking about Blue Labour and other activity was that the party and whole Labour movement was being invited to return to its (imagined) roots and find again the lost road to the broad sunny uplands of Labour's true envisioned 'destination'. Great emphasis was placed on community, devolution, and older Labour values of cooperation and mutualism. Earlier writers and philosophers such as G.D.H. Cole and R.H. Tawney regained currency and a great deal of emphasis was placed upon Labour history up until World War II. Thus a 'story', a 'Labour tale' was being rediscovered/rewritten. As we have seen, a profoundly Arcadian feel emerged from the texts. It was, nevertheless, also promoted as an answer to current problems; that is to say, an antidote to the things that had gone wrong, the implication being that had the wrong road (e.g., Blairism) not been taken, these problems would not exist: alienation, community strife regarding housing and education, immigration and integration, a lack of a sense of belonging, and a pervasive *anomie*. All this lent the emerging narrative marked rhetorical power. In order, therefore, to put this emerging narrative to purpose, it informed much debate about contemporary politics and the elaboration of *policy* (e.g., banking, community life, local healthcare), as well as party organization, and strategy.

Many political narratives do this, namely, legitimate a myth by stressing contemporary relevance. The 'tale', a conflation of myth and realism, produced widely read texts: for example, *The Labour Tradition and the Politics of Paradox*, and *The Purple Book* (2011) to which many of the then rising

[3] *'Blue Labour'*, *Radio 4 Analysis*, BBC Radio 4, 27 March 2011. Transcript available at: http://news.bbc.co.uk/nol/shared/spl/hi/programmes/analysis/transcripts/21_03_11.txt

'My Blue Labour vision can defeat the coalition'. *The Observer*, 24 April 2011. Available at: https://www.theguardian.com/politics/2011/apr/24/blue-labour-maurice-glasman

'A conversation with Maurice Glasman', 11 November 2011. *Independent Labour Publications*. Available at: http://www.independentlabour.org.uk/main/2011/11/11/a-conversation-with-mauriceglasman-part-1/

Glasman (2013). See References.

stars and soon a major cohort of One Nationers contributed.[4] What was striking about the rhetoric of these texts was not simply that they applied often older ideas to new problems, but they brought into the rhetoric and policy elaboration the metaphors and similes of earlier times (rampant capital as evil, working conditions like Satanic Mills) and their solutions (cooperation, small is beautiful, time to reflect and learn, harmonious communities, 'joined up' living, and so on). This meant that a reservoir of emotional appeal, Aristotelian *pathos*, lay in the emerging rhetoric, a *logos* in the service of *pathos* rather than the other way round. There were also in the discourse, of Blue Labour particularly, elements of a populist rhetoric that would facilitate its acquisition and use by the leader's rhetoric. A 'modern' illustration of this idea of (forgotten) community was the commissioning of the respected community campaigner from Chicago, Arnie Graf. His task from 2011 was to suggest a whole series of reforms and actions for the party to become a 'bottom–up' movement, and a larger one, open to input from its members, open to the outside, positive (and fun!), and to create in the revitalized party a microcosm of a revitalized One Nation nation. As we have seen, this too was not to last, and carried within it the irony of the party's massive increase in membership in the *aftermath* of the 2015 defeat.

By early 2012, the Policy Review process had been completely overtaken by this new narrative, its own focus having been almost exclusively on policy and even more so in a second phase on organizational issues. In response, Miliband made Jon Cruddas, who shared many of Rutherford and Glasman's views and was himself one of the authors of this emerging narrative, the new Chair of the Policy Review. This brought the new narrative to the centre of the party. The Review was no longer one of policy – this essentially put on hold until much nearer the 2015 election, ideally 2013–2014; one of the major rhetorical failures of this was, as we have seen, its not being properly used as a *consequence* of a rhetorical conflation (post-2012) of *pathos*, *logos*, and *ethos*. The new Policy Review chaired by Cruddas was actually a process of ideological revision of the party towards and by means of the new narrative, and would remain so into 2014 (here its dynamic would falter as other priorities contested it and drained it of its momentum; as Hopi Sen wrote (*Progress*, 23 September), by 2014 the 'cathedral' had become a 'chapel').

[4] *The Purple Book: a Progressive Future for Labour* (2011), edited by Robert Philpot, was the last major contribution of the Blairites to the developing narrative after 2010.

In this climate of what we might call 'narrative fervour' and significant textual and ideational output, the image of the leader – crucial to success – generally remained static beyond the party. Miliband himself saw little evolution in his personal image. It had remained much as it had been when he was elected, and in opinion polls he always failed the 'prime ministerial' test. This is what made the Manchester Party Conference of 2012 so interesting. Let us revisit this moment of rhetorical and formative potential.

Two Authors, One Protagonist

As we saw in Chapter 4, it was at the Manchester Conference in 2012 that Miliband developed his One Nation theme, making it the central organizing theme of the speech and of the subsequent evolution of the party's rhetoric for around the following 12 months. This is significant for two reasons. First, One Nation was a refinement of the narratives and ideas developed by Glasman, Cruddas, Rutherford, and others over the previous 2 years, so that the One Nation 'philosophy', as it were, that he made the central element of his Conference speech was also the (new) narrative of the party. It was more 'practical', more social democratic, a little less lyrical, a lot more personalized. Second, through the speech itself, he became the author of the party's narrative, and in fact in terms of One Nation as a 'story', the protagonist of the tale is its hero. He spoke for over an hour without notes; he referred to himself, his family, his political 'calling', his intentions, his vision of the future throughout the speech. He used all the standard rhetorical devices for creating a bond – humour, sadness, indignation, analysis, understanding, and so on – throughout the speech, so that by the end it had become 'his performance' of the One Nation philosophy. At the Q&A the following day all of these motifs and themes were deployed again and the One Nation themes reasserted, and here in a lighter, 'informal', friendlier and more interactive 'enactment' of the relationship: listening to, participating with, yet leading the new party.

The following January (2013), *One Nation Labour – Debating the Future* was published by LabourList.org – an independent progressive e-network. Edited by Cruddas, *One Nation Labour – Debating the Future* was the first textual expression of the Policy Review under Cruddas' leadership and the development of One Nation as a 'post-2010' Labour Party narrative. In chapter after chapter the contributors – Shadow Ministers, MPs, and others – picked up the theme of One Nation, but in nearly all cases, made direct reference to Miliband as the inspiration of their commitment or as the originator of the idea, and so on. In this way, the narrative of the party became the rhetoric of the leader and it, in turn, became the narrative of the party. What we saw in *One Nation Labour – Debating the Future* was not policy elaboration but the reimagining of society, inspired in great part now by Ed Miliband. Under Cruddas' leadership, the Policy Review ceased to be a Policy Review and resembled a rhetorical and ideological exercise until well into 2013. Over the next year, many of Miliband's closest collaborators – for example, Cruddas, Rutherford, and a range of 'One Nation' MPs – went on to refer to him and to the One Nation theme again and again. The question was whether this narrative rebirth could be, or how it might be, given resonance beyond the party, and how it might be given depth *within* the party, and in the persona of the leader.

I called this – the rhetorical phenomenon of eliding a narrative and 'the self' in an individual's rhetoric – the 'personalized political', that is to say, the rhetorical use of the 'self' of Ed Miliband (childhood experience, intimacy with audience, references to his children, wife, father, use of humour, communication of his passion, and so on) to mediate (or enhance, or stress, or oppose, or refute) other doctrinal or policy ideas that are not normally linked to personal interpolation. This interrelation of the leader with a very particular narrative and his (literally and metaphorically) 'giving voice' to it lent itself to the notion of a gathering rally behind the leader. There was also a further development enhancing the 'status' of the leader.

As I touched upon briefly in Chapter 5, in March 2014, the Labour Party voted fundamentally to reform its relationship to the trade unions, and the way it elected its leader (and subsequently deputy leader, candidate for Mayor of London, Conference Arrangements Committee, and Policy Forum representatives). It was compared in importance to Tony Blair's abolition of Clause IV in 1995, which abandoned the party's long-held, deep-seated, and by then near-universally ignored commitment to full-scale nationalization. Blair's reform had a massive effect on the party, helping to catapult it back into power after 18 years in divided opposition. Ever since, further reform, particularly of membership, funding, and the election of the leader, had become leitmotifs for modernization, culminating in Miliband's March 2014 success in winning union, affiliate and party support for his reforms by a landslide 86 % of votes. What had started out as a bust-up in the summer of 2013 over Unite's alleged packing of the Falkirk constituency with union members for the selection of the party's candidate turned into a personal success for Miliband. It arguably cast him in the Blair mould of the visionary leader, insightful and right before his time. By carrying his party with him, Miliband completed the historic OMOV task begun by John Smith in 1992. In many ways, the Clause IV and OMOV moments were comparable, but in some ways not. In fact, their dissimilarities were clues to their real function. And the effects in 2015 upon the party leadership election were utterly unforeseen.

Blair's Clause IV reform was significant, but ultimately symbolic. Not even the Attlee government of 1945 nationalized on the Soviet scale implied by Clause IV. The real significance of its abolition was not what it told us about Labour's ambitions for the economy's commanding heights, but what it told us about the commander. The risk he took in taking on the redundant but near-sacred text (see my reference to Wilson in Chapter 2) gave him an exalted status in relation to his party, in relation to the public and to Labour history and Labour's future. The level of risk involved in Miliband's reforms was higher than that which Blair faced. The practical consequences could have been immediate. Delegates speaking against the motion warned of the potentially catastrophic consequences to Labour's finances, long-term loosening (if not severing) of the union relationship, and through a kind of atomization of the party 'will' in the name of democracy, the loss of the truly collective identity and endeavour of the party, although the overwhelming backing of the trade unions for the reform suggested that these consequences would not follow.

However, as with Clause IV for Blair, party reform was less about the party than about Ed Miliband and his leadership. The 'Clause IV moment' was about the creation of Blair's prime ministerial 'character': a man who courageously brought the crazier elements of the party to heel, and prepared it for government. Miliband's achievement was designed to serve a similar purpose. It in fact served the purpose of making Jeremy Corbyn leader of the Labour Party in 2015. At the Canning Town Special Conference, Miliband entered the conference hall to music, clips of the party's history, and footage of his previously well received conference speeches. He remained on the stage throughout the 2 hours of debate. The overwhelming majority of speakers were in favour, not only of the proposals but of the proposer. They regularly named and congratulated their listening leader, celebrating his insightfulness as he listened intently. His status was enhanced by his listening respectfully to his few critics and the one or two admonitions. Both rhetorically and visually this was Miliband's moment, the conference a *demonstration* of his leadership.

In his opening and closing remarks Miliband used the populist language of the rally leader,[5] but in his own restrained and calm manner. His desired (rather than actual) audience/constituency on this occasion was not the 'squeezed middle', the teachers and social workers, or the chattering classes who were often addressed in Miliband's speeches. He sought instead to rhetorically reach the legions of disenfranchised or 'self-disenfranchised' low-paid workers: the ambulance drivers, part-time working women, care workers, the disabled, families in poverty, the unemployed and underemployed and, as Miliband told his audience, a non-voting mum called Tracy. This populist tone also informed his depiction of his adversaries; the Tories were heartless, sexist, Eton and Harrow bullies, while the the Lib Dems were simply pathetic. The speech teemed with references to himself and his envisioned future, the guiding virtue of which was justice. Miliband's speech was personalized too in its pedagogical telling of home truths to the party: that if it did not change, both it and politics itself would become 'an empty stadium' – the reform certainly filled the stadium after May 2015. He also reminded his audience that his response to the Falkirk scandal was the origin of the reforms and therefore, implicitly, the conference itself became the realization of that personal choice. And, in a moment of classic populist rhetoric, he urged his party to become (or become again) a 'movement'. His proposed relationship to this movement was made clear: 'If I am elected Prime Minister, I want to change this country, but I can only do it with a movement behind me.'

Miliband's approach to the Special Conference of March 2014 in Canning Town cast him as the hero of the party, the leader who unleashed the popular voices of disillusioned and excluded Britain. We can see here a shift in Miliband's rhetorical emphasis. Until 2014, One Nation had, through its evocation of a harmonious society, been a relatively 'quietist' rhetoric. In Canning Town, the rhetoric was more about mobilizing a much less 'ideal' nation, a much more oppressed and alienated one. In fact, Miliband's speech was a call to the party to go out and bring this section of society – the poor, the lost, the alienated – to the party. Such a rhetoric was understandable, but it pointed to a deeper problem, that

[5] Ed Miliband's Special Conference speech is available at: http://www.politics.co.uk/comment-analysis/2014/03/01/ed-miliband-s-special-conference-speech-in-full

of whether One Nation was failing to gain traction and its spokesperson wider popularity when compared to the precedent and comparator, Blair and the Third Way in the mid-1990s. And, more prosaically, whether the Tracys were even listening and whether they would even bother coming out to vote in 2015. There is evidence that support for Labour in opinion polls by traditional non-voters did increase but that these remained essentially non-voters (Green and Prosser 2015). One final effect of this Miliband's 'Clause IV' moment may well have created the conditions – Corbyn's election – for its return.

THE NARRATIVE LIMITS AND RHETORICAL CHALLENGES OF ONE NATION RHETORIC

There were limits to the 'success' of the One Nation rhetorical undertaking. It seemed to work well in providing the party with a new (old) and inspirational discourse to replace the tired and partially discredited narrative of Third Way Blairism. The One Nation narrative was moral and practical, reflective, and 'legitimate' in left terms; as legitimate, in fact, if not more so, than any other variant of the left narrative at this time. As such, its second essential 'function' was to provide Miliband with a (personal) narrative and a 'vision' which he could (re)transmit to the party, as we have seen. The main reason why this was the case, as we saw with the Canning Town version of the rhetoric, was that within the parameters of the left, One Nation when given voice by the leader *could* become populist: emotional, idyllic, transformational, inclusive; and at one level pacifist, at another insurrectionary. In this – as with Miliband's overall management of conflict within the party 2010–2015 – his rhetorical approach within the party was exemplary. As the regular Q&As and his general interaction with the party activists showed time and again, the Miliband persona and rhetoric chimed perfectly with the 'mood' of the post-Blair/Brown Labour Party, certainly in public meetings and with local activists. The first criticism one can make is that its strengths were also its weaknesses. Let us look at these in turn. I will divide my analysis into three: cultural constraints, performative issues, and – this will form the main part of my conclusions – the narrative and rhetorical challenges and constraints of One Nation Labour. I shall then look at the post-Miliband leadership debacle.

CULTURAL CONSTRAINTS

Much of the thrust of Miliband's rhetoric involved notions of party 'revital-ization' in order to clear obstacles and give voice and vivacity to the mem-bership. The membership would, in turn, interact with the 'outside': the party sympathizers, voters, and potential voters. All of this was like the release of subterranean powers and the (near-forgotten) voice of the Nation. The emerging narrative surrounding Blue Labour – *The Politics of Paradox*, *New Politics, Fresh Ideas, Refounding Labour, The Purple Book*, and so on – were in perfect synchrony with this, offering a (partial) philosophical justification for a new way of doing politics. Party reform and the new narrative in turn became, as we have seen, a narrative that enabled Miliband to rhetorically portray/invent himself as a rally leader (transforming in discourse the ulti-mate 'harbour', 2015 and its aftermath, into a semi-mythical arrival, not 'just' an election). All of this, however, is unusual and culturally problematic in the UK, and especially on the UK left.

There is a recent and contrasting example of this central use of what is, in fact, a migration myth. In 1970s France, this was precisely what François Mitterrand and the French Socialist Party did (Gaffney 1989). In 1971, Mitterrand became the populist rally leader of an essentially social democratic party which portrayed itself as a 'rally of opinion' around the leader. And it worked. In 1981, Mitterrand brought the Socialists to power in France for the first time in the Fifth Republic – in democratic cir-cumstances and with a landslide absolute majority. The culture Mitterrand was operating in was highly personalized, indeed strongly disposed to the idea of the providential leader – even on the left – storming the gates of privilege and injustice in the name of the people. This tradition is weak in the UK. The nearest real national precedent in rhetoric is probably Chartism, itself – crucially – leaderless and, perhaps in part for that rea-son, unsuccessful. French political rhetoric is also much more disposed to populist purpose. Indeed, in the very early period (compare Mitterrand's address to the Party Conference in 1971 at Epinay) Mitterrand's rhetoric was not just populist, but insurrectionary. Mitterrand's real skill was to take millenarian myths and migration myths and align them with both the French left's insurrectionary tradition and the normative paramenters of a personalized republic. He took French Socialism and rhetorically adapted it to the exigencies of Gaullism. The UK Labour Party of the 2010s was operating in a very different culture and discourse. There is also the question of Mitterrand himself as an appropriate rally leader: he had come to Socialism – via the labyrinthine byways of French political culture – as if through a Damascene conversion (see *Ma part de vérité* (1969) Paris: Seuil). He had stood as the left's candidate against the colossus de Gaulle in 1965. He was a significant intellectual figure in French politics (in a country that greatly admired intellectuals). He brought the left to power after the heady days of 1968 and its aftermath; and so on. Does such an alignment of discourse, vision, trials, and personal quest – these chivalric allusions are not accidental – align with UK political culture and the personalization of leadership? There are precedents – mainly on the right – but few, and these are normally associated with crisis and major change. Perhaps May 2015 could have been such a moment. Let us turn our attention then from vision to the envisioner.

PERFORMATIVE ISSUES

There was a marked difference between Ed Miliband's personal image inside the party and outside. There were real tensions inside, but his general non-conflictual management of the party and his popularity with the 'rank and file' was beyond doubt (and their recognition of the need for change was also very positive), many of them joining or rejoining because of what (they thought) he represented, a leftwards moving party. In public opinion generally, however, Miliband had rarely been seen as a leader of rally proportions. His 'performances', especially his conference speeches, occasionally became virtuoso performances, as we have seen. His performances generally were good, although like all party leaders he had, in the House of Commons for example, good days and bad days. His image was arguably – still – too much that of a politician rather like most of the others; before the 1997 election, Blair's national image really began to take off in the polls. Two questions therefore were raised as to whether this rhetorical movement of the populist-friendly party narrative contributed to these difficulties in certain respects. In what sense was the One Nation rhetoric and all it carried within it in terms of Blue Labour and the rest, as well as the 'populist turn' (Tracy, essentially) Miliband and his team gave to it in early 2014, *appropriate* to the party in the first instance, and what was its significance to the leader's performing persona in the second? We have seen how it was perceived as being necessary and appropriate to him. Let us examine where the challenges came from and where it might have been inappropriate, and/or at least better defended.

The Ideational Challenges to One Nation, and All Its Opportunities Missed

We can make three substantive points here. First, why One Nation? What actually was it? At many points after Manchester 2012, both Miliband and his supporters acclaimed One Nation. And it did give, almost by definition, an umbrella quality to the presentation of ideas. It facilitated both a caring approach (to welfare, to training, for example) and an emotional one; it proceeded from a party desire and personal desire (with accompanying *logos* often in the form of *pathos*, as we have seen) to develop policies and programmes that would help heal the country and create the conditions of prosperity. It did not, however, beyond this, have a great deal of substance. And there was always an ambivalence around whether One Nation government could actually *afford* (financially and politically) to return the decision-making at the commanding heights of the state to 'the local'. It also lacked, and Blue Labour even more, an economic rhetoric. It suggested a theory of community but an ambivalent theory of power, and a poor theory of political economy. Blue Labour also attracted hostility over its ambivalence regarding what kind of communitarianism it advocated, its relative silence on women's issues, and even its parochialism. One Nation was a hugely attractive national idea. It always has been. Without substance it was in danger of remaining just that.

Over and above this, One Nation, which was in part an answer to the hesitations about Blue Labour, set out to establish itself as a rally rhetoric, but it was not rallied to by everyone. And this is highly problematic for rally rhetoric. There were two problematic categories. The first were those who opposed it, and this involved quite a broad range of personalities rather than factions. Often these were people who themselves represented Labour traditions: Roy Hattersley, for example, who as I said in Chapter 3 represented a version of the Attlee tradition. Radicals outside the party like Billy Bragg opposed it; Polly Toynbee, respected in the party and the intelligentsia, was sceptical of One Nation and hostile to Blue Labour. Earlier leaders and other figures were muted in their support, including Blair, as one might expect. Some union leaders were critical, as were some members of groups within the party, including people in the highly articulate and influential reflection group 'Progress'. When I asked one researcher of an independent think tank how she characterized Blue Labour she replied 'three blokes in a pub'. It is in this context that the active support for

One Nation and Miliband by figures like Neil Kinnock was so important. Kinnock's support, from the symbolic point of view, went beyond the simple support of an influential individual, and acted as a reference point to the overall narrative. Disapproval was not represented by any organized groups of opinion, but criticism, if not a threat to Miliband, was a threat to the credibility of the One Nation rhetoric and its status as a rally rhetoric.

A second category not 'rallying' to One Nation was arguably even more of a threat, namely, the other active figures in the party who ignored it. For a union leader or former leader to oppose was perhaps less damaging than the fact that the expression 'One Nation' rarely passed the lips of crucial members of the Shadow Cabinet, in particular Ed Balls who privately scorned the idea and almost never referred to it. This was the same for the Shadow Home Secretary, Yvette Cooper, and others. The fact that there were figures like this who did not rally to the rally discourse was perhaps one of the single most important underminings of One Nation. It is the case that after the Shadow Cabinet reshuffle of November 2013, many more 'Milibandists', and a rising generation of young women (known in the media as 'Milibabes'), and those who were signed up to the One Nation rhetoric moved centre stage. By 2014, however, one had a sense less of a rally discourse celebrating One Nation than of the drawbridge being pulled up, Miliband's closest supporters becoming an embattled group around the leader, the opposite of what should have been happening in the period before an election. There was a One Nation edited book produced in October 2013 (another in 2014), and a One Nation group of MPs set up.[6] An irony here is that this was precisely the moment where Miliband himself started to abandon the term, which ceased to be a feature of his speeches and presentations. It still appeared on projector screens and incidental party literature. It was still the slogan for the 2013

[6]At the 2013 Labour Party Conference in Brighton, *One Nation: Power, Hope, Community* (Smith and Reeves 2013) had a publication launch, despite the fact that it was not on the official Conference Programme. The hurriedly prepared publication was edited by Owen Smith and Rachel Reeves, two upcoming Labour Party figures, and contained eleven essays by a cohort of the 2010 intake of MPs – Milibandites and now One Nationers – Tristram Hunt, Shabana Mahmood, Rachel Reeves, for example. Each essay was a celebration of Miliband as the source of One Nation Labour and then a celebration of their One Nation constituency efforts e.g., a 'neighbourhood-wide engagement programme' (Shabana Mahmood). The book was an endorsement of Miliband and the One Nation supporters. It also marked the beginnings of a division between Miliband and the supporters of One Nation and his critics: for example, Andy Burnham, Ed Balls, and Yvette Cooper.

Conference but he barely referred to it; six references against 64 in 2012. One Nation was clearly not giving voice to the leadership and the party as, say, the *Changer la vie* theme had in the French PS of the 1970s.

Miliband's diminished use of the term in late 2013–2014 was partly the result of the recognition of the need for something else to replace it or, rather, add to it (such as the Canning Town attempts at the kind of populism we analysed above). It is perhaps worth mentioning here that Miliband himself 'belonged to', as it were, a different strain of the left. Through his intellectual training, choices, and experience he was more than anything else a mainline (European) social democrat. It is to his credit, therefore, that as early as 2010, he and his team recognized the discursive, ideological, and above all performative value of an alternative rhetoric.

Social democratic discourse on its own has rarely had a rallying effect – with few exceptions (and in other settings): Olaf Palme, Willy Brandt, or earlier in Léon Blum's distinctions between the conquest and the exercise of power; or when it is trying to assert its values in crises, for example, during Portugal and Spain's transitions to democracy. But it is profoundly practical and 'quiet' in its tone and, in spite of its union connections (usually), even separate from the discourse of Labour's union tradition. More of this aspect of Labour's discourse – reasonable, state-centred, technical, knowledgeable – and cognisant of other valuable social-democratic approaches – German, Scandinavian, Dutch – is probably the kind of rhetoric that would find most resonance in the UK voting public (although it too has been in something of a bad way everywhere throughout the early twenty-first century). Over and above this, yet another discursive tradition in the party which behind the scenes carried great weight (and was pro-David Miliband in its majority) and which the overwhelming majority of MPs (including Ed Miliband) had subscribed to for years, was New Labour itself – far closer to social democracy than to the neoliberalism of its accusers. In fact, in its fundamentals, it and Miliband's type of social democracy were barely distinguishable. More importantly, the Blairites had the experience and – crucially – the knowledge of how to organize, how to 'narrate', and how to win elections (Gould 2010). No leader had ever done electorally what Blair had done: three successive elections and, in spite of the ungenerous narrative about Blairism of the post-2010 period, a government record of domestic political reform that, as we suggested at the beginning of this chapter, was exemplary in terms of Labour's reforming history. More importantly still, Team Miliband needed this expertise. An inevitable inflexion of the One Nation narrative – Blue Labour, Third Way, and social democracy (on Palestine, renationalizing the railways, quantitative easing, you could even have sprinkled some Corbynism) – *intermingled* and organized around a related but separate ideational cluster would have been the necessary result. By 2014, however, the impression was of a social democratic leader 'using' a rally discourse without taking into proper consideration that such had to have what we might call rhetorical follow-through (and concomitant policies).

Social democratic and New Labour discourses (and others) therefore began to vie with One Nation, altering its direction – and its impact. It was clear that Blue Labour's central advocates, Glasman, Rutherford, and so on, became, from the autumn of 2013, less vocal and less central, much to their perplexity and concern in some cases. It is also the case that there was a stalling of One Nation and then the use of a more practical electoral discourse. There was also the incompleteness of some of the One Nation rhetoric and its discursive allies. Blue Labour for example, even less than One Nation, did not really have the complexity – did not really claim to such – in terms of developing a compelling political economy, for example, or reform agenda for public services, both compelling issues. But there was, however, another discursive, intellectual, and rhetorical resource that, although it saw itself sometimes in opposition to something like Blue Labour – through its own intellectual rigour – could have built upon it rhetorically in a major way, namely IPPR ideas and rhetoric (and Cruddas was close to IPPR, as was Stears). Some of the work of the IPPR, a think tank close to the Labour Party, published *The Relational State* (2012) and *The Condition of Britain: Interim report* (2013), and an updating of the 2012 document *Many to Many: How the Relational State will Transform Public Services* in 2014. Let us look at these very briefly in order to demonstrate how Blue Labour/One Nation were only a whisker away from having a theory and a practice.

The Relational State (2012) was an outcome of an IPPR seminar in early 2012 and was edited by Graeme Cooke (Open Left project at think tank Demos/IPPR) and Rick Muir (IPPR). In the extended introduction which set out the context for discussion, the editors stated that 'the purpose of this collection is to begin to fill this political space by introducing the idea of the 'relational state' – a new intellectual and political perspective on statecraft and the public services.' The publication featured two major essays by Geoff Mulgan (chief executive of the National Endowment for

Science, Technology and the Arts) and Marc Stears (Miliband's advisor and an academic) and a series of responses. I want to make two points on this publication and its significance for my analysis. First, in the critique of 1979–2010 (New Public Management: Markets and Targets) many of the contributions contained echoes of Blue Labour's communitarianism. This was reinforced in Mulgan's essay in which he advocated a range of personal/local measures, for example, long-term patients to decide on their care plan. Second, the contributors stressed the value of human relationships, thus promoting a narrative based upon personalism (in Mounier's sense (1947)), and localism, and strongly against both a collectivist approach and the hard individualism of the market.

The Condition of Britain: Interim Report was published in December 2013. The report was edited by Kayte Lawton and set out the first stage of findings for *The Condition of Britain* project, which aimed to answer one central question: 'How can we come together to build a better society in these uncertain times?' (p. 3). In the Introduction, Graeme Cooke, Kayte Lawton and Nick Pearce (IPPR) set out a series of post-economic crisis pressures and problems that individuals and families faced (household finances squeezed, family life under growing strain, young people's prospects increasingly uncertain, some neighbourhoods blighted by crime, a minority of people excluded from society, many people having lost faith in the benefit system, and more and more older people facing loneliness and isolation). These pressures were used as the basis for suggesting new directions for centre-left policies: for example, not hoarding power at the centre or among elites, shifting power to people and places (p. 9); rejuvenating parish or county councils; building institutions that brought people together, including more children's centres to support young people as well as social clubs and support networks, and not just relying on cash benefits (p. 10). There was more: nurturing space for relationships; enabling civil society genuinely to take the lead on tackling complex problems like long-term unemployment; preventing problems before they developed and tackling root causes; expecting everyone to contribute, and promoting inclusion and solidarity; a politics of broad alliances and popular movements rather than a politics of blame and division (p. 10). What we see in these policy suggestions was a dramatic emphasis upon personal initiative and upon localism and arguably a One Nation social project for a Labour government.

In subsequent chapters, five briefing papers discussed family, adulthood, neighbourhood, work and financial security, and getting older and staying connected. Each of the papers presented the views of people across Britain interviewed as part of the project. Policy suggestions iterated the narrative of personal initiative and localism: for example, devolving power so that local leaders had more power to solve complex social problems and improve their neighbourhoods (p. 47). This was a dramatic improvement upon previous party texts.

In *Many to Many: How the Relational State will Transform Public Services* (2014), the updated version of *The Relational State*, the authors Rick Muir and Imogen Parker set out an approach to public services that was based upon person, place, and relationships. Themes that were inherently One Nation Labour (and Blue Labour) developed at various points in the text to demonstrate a post-2015 policy programme for public services that was unlike the public services policy programmes of 1979–2010 (privatization, competition, deregulation). The publication had both a complexity and simplicity: setting out the intellectual, theoretical, and practical case for public service reform was very complicated and detailed (some of which was captured in the publication: for example, costings/financial implications). However, the authors used One Nation themes (which were the central themes of Blue Labour) and presented a simple and harmonious model of public service reform, a model which embraced individuals and relationships, localism, notions of the mobilization of civil society, the 'small state', but not in a neoliberal or individualist way, with individuals connected to one another and relationships that were not just 'transactional'.

The publication cited the inadequacies of neoliberalism as a form of governance from 1979 to 2010 (an interesting conflation with the ideas of Blue Labour and Stewart Wood), specifically its emphasis upon privatization which had led to fragmented public services (this was also in the earlier 2012 publication). It noted that bureaucracy and markets – what the authors called the 'delivery state' – were sufficient in dealing with linear public service problems such as bin collections. However, other public services were characterized by greater complexities. For example, tackling long-term unemployment was not a linear problem, and should be understood as highly complex and addressed by looking at a range of issues that could include mental health problems, low self-confidence, lack of skills or a history with the criminal justice system (p. 1). Thus, the inadequacies of neoliberalism from 1979 to 2010 were seen as a justification for changing the way in which 'we' thought about public services, by adopting the relational state approach.

The micro and macro levels were both reconsidered in *Many to Many*. At the macro level, government became the enabler rather than the manager, steering an interconnected system in which a diverse range of actors and institutions took the lead. At the micro level, the relational state meant cultivating deep relationships in place of shallow transactions. In practice, service users were linked with professionals with whom they could develop relationships over time; professionals were allocated neighbourhood-based patches, and institutions were designed to strengthen relationships between citizens and enable them to tackle shared problems together (pp. 6–7). In this publication, the authors actually aligned the relational state with One Nation Labour. They evoked the values of One Nation Labour (localism, relationships, community) in their illustration of public service reform. We can see, therefore, that something complex like an IPPR document could rhetorically 'align' with a somewhat Arcadian narrative like Blue Labour, thus dramatically enhancing the overall narrative status of One Nation. Thus the theoretical, intellectual, and practical complexities of public service reform could have been relatively easily grafted onto One Nation. And it is clear that to persuade a sceptical electorate all of these proposals would have to be costed, but it is clear even from my resumé here that this was less about money than about reorganizing social effort.

Andy Burnham (then Shadow Health Minister) used the relational state model on public services as part of the development of Labour Party Health policy. In a speech in Birmingham in February 2014, Burnham set out his policy proposals for the NHS: an integrated, whole-person care plan. The policy would provide a full integration of health and social care: councils and the NHS would work in partnership and offer a single service to patients. For example, preventive social involvement, such as a local council installing a grab rail in an elderly person's home to prevent them having a fall, ending up in hospital and then requiring aftercare at home. Burnham also proposed that power and budgets would be devolved to local commissioning groups. Despite evoking the constituent values of One Nation Labour – for example, localism (devolving budgets to local GP-led commissioning groups and a host of other allusions; although a version of this happened under the Coalition's Health and Social Care Act 2012) – there was not one mention of One Nation by Burnham. What we saw in his NHS proposals was an approach that was underlined by the values of One Nation Labour (and most other doctrinal strains), with proposals that used the relational state framework developed by the IPPR as if 'One Nation' were of no importance. A (possibly deliberately) missed rhetorical opportunity. Was no one bringing all this together into a rally discourse? Cruddas clearly was attempting to do so; but by the end of 2013 the narrative's 'author', Ed, had virtually stopped talking about it; and the 'Policy Review' now poised to generate a raft of One Nation policy proposals was like a stalled engine. Lots of meetings were scheduled, particularly a major full weekend meeting of the National Policy Forum in July 2014 to dot and cross all the i's and t's; the culmination of all Cruddas' work. No one took the blindest bit of notice.

To sum up my discussion so far: as regards the left generally, to go forward you have to go back. A left party, and even more a left leadership or leadership team, has to develop a new discourse while legitimating it within the left's past. In the case of the Labour Party during the 2010–2015 period, in order to find a way of replacing New Labour, it first depicted it as the wrong road travelled and, *in extremis*, as a kind of left neoliberal accomplice to rightist neoliberalism. It then gave voice (as if 'back') to an earlier rhetorical narrative, one that was metaphorically rich and ideologically sound – One Nation and its variants – that reignited pre-World War II British (perhaps just English) Socialism, and an Arcadian, conservative and, it has to be said, compelling view of 'This England'. Mythically, this is the rhetoric of 'return'. The role of leadership was to adopt and exploit this narrative (or series of narratives).

In order for this to be effective, two things had to happen. First, the narrative had to be given contemporary purpose, that is to say, have contemporary relevance. In part, this was done because it was current 'need' which provoked it – for example, the early search (2009) by Open Left to find an alternative to failing Blair-Brownism. Then in the thinking of all of its exponents (Glasman, Rutherford, Cruddas, and so on) its contemporary relevance was crucial, in part because they knew that if it was only backward looking it would be heavily criticized. The thrust of One Nation rhetoric throughout the 2010–2015 period was to demonstrate the contemporary relevance of its ideas. My point here is that all this is true but what is more important for us is that the real significance is the inverse: it was the older Arcadian/Utopian rhetoric that was *reignited* in the contemporary imagination. Community, the local, devolved power, and related ideas of healing, mending, strengthening, returning to older sources, harmony, well-being, and so on were given narrative and ideological justification. It is not without significance that some of the more complex developments of ideas and indeed policy had Baudelairian *correspondances* with the earlier ideas, and these often in spite of the antipathy between their sources. For example, a lot of the output of the IPPR – *The Relational State, The Condition of Britain, Many to Many* – through its very complexity (and, indeed, use of complexity theory) was a rejection of the simplicity of, say, Blue Labour's pastoral. However, it 'corresponded' ideationally through its imagining of a harmonious contemporary society (encouraging a joined-up approach between councils and the NHS, enabling civil society to tackle complex problems, rejuvenating parish or county councils) with similar ideas underpinning Blue Labour (localism, community, and so on) as well as earlier thinkers like G.D.H. Cole; and *both* sources could have become the basis of policy elaboration in the course of 2014. This is also true of Andy Burnham's narrative regarding healthcare and healthcare reform. The central motif of this narrative was the notion of return (to a fairer system) and the future (the application of a new elaborated person-related national-local mission), both compatible with the ideas underpinning the One Nation narrative.

This brings me to a second point, namely, that through the use of a range of rhetorical undertakings the old/new discourse was brought forward by its personalization in the rhetoric and performance of the leader, Ed Miliband. And two things happened: he brought it forward, and it became his personal rhetoric. This began in earnest at the Manchester Party Conference of 2012 (where *earlier* (less successful) conference speeches were treated as truths 'before their time', as we saw in Chapter 4). Throughout 2012 he was developing it. We have also seen from our analysis that One Nation – a narrative that blended several narratives of the past and, in their construction and arrangement, made claims about the present and the future – became also the personalized narrative of the leader. Miliband became the author of the party's narrative and the protagonist within its story; he literally and metaphorically became the party's voice. And he did this through his rhetoric and his – in 2012 highly and in Brighton in 2013 still effective – 'performance'. And it is worthy of note that the emergent *pre*-Manchester narrative (see Chapter 3) not only had '*correspondances*' with subsequent policy elaboration, as we have seen, but also with the construction of Miliband's persona. He took authorship of the narrative through humour, *pathos*, vision, commitment, sadness, appeal, communion, indignation, reassurance, inspiration, and so on. These in turn became the traits of his 'character', so that One Nation vision was personified in him and reinforced from early 2013 onwards by supporters of One Nation; and a book of 2013, distributed at Brighton, brought many of its supporters together; by then, however, it was already fading fast.

One Nation was one of many effective ways that Miliband kept the party 'on board' in the 2010–2015 period. It was and is generally acknowledged that Miliband managed the party's internal divisions and the demands of the party membership well throughout this period, most criticism of the leader most of the time being only on an individual basis. And with comparable periods – the Foot and Kinnock internal oppositions – it was ... incomparable. The question of how divisions are best managed remains a constant problem, but One Nation was a clear attempt to 'imagine' a party united. We can see from our rhetorical analysis that there were also rhetorical reasons for this, bearing out Martin and Finlayson's conviction of the practical effects of political rhetoric. The new narrative created a discursive space, and the leader used it to rhetorically perform a deployment, an enactment of narrative and of his rhetorical 'self', his 'character'. This, in turn, informed policy elaboration which set out to embody One Nation, with all its attributes. But a final, less positive point that we can make here concerns the narrative fortune of One Nation. As we have already noted, for a range of reasons – failure of Miliband's public popularity to really take off; perceived emptiness/ obscurity of One Nation's content; competing voices (social democracy, New Labour, IPPR complexity, and so on), and individuals' hostility or criticism (Hattersley, Bragg, Toynbee) or indifference (Balls, Cooper, Burnham) – Miliband himself began to diminish the rhetorical elaboration of One Nation and of One Nation as 'his'. The questions then became: how he might maintain the forward thrust of the party's narrative towards the General Election and the elaboration of a manifesto; and how he might develop and 'flesh out' his own persona with recourse to rhetorical resources other than the One Nation narrative (this, in my view is where it began to go irrevocably wrong). Let me turn, therefore, to how all these elements were arranged or mis-arranged as the party headed into the General Election of 2015.

Narrative, Performance, and Defeat

I said at the beginning of the book that my aim was not to detail 'Why Labour lost' in 2015. Besides, my study focuses upon only two closely related aspects of the life of the Labour Party, namely, narrative and leadership performance. I should also say in parenthesis that I am not interested here in detailing the seats lost and other leadership losers (e.g., Balls, Alexander), nor the electoral and regional breakdown of the defeat. These studies abound in both extensive and thoroughgoing media coverage and growing academic analyses, in particular the ESRC's British Election Study (since 1964). In the first part of this chapter I was concerned with appraising what the 2010–2015 'arc of rhetoric' did or intended to do. In this second part of my concluding chapter it becomes much more difficult to stick to my original and 'scientific' intention and not elaborate my own long list of 'Why Labour lost'![7]

So, bearing in mind my recognition that my own perspective is partial, let me offer an appraisal of the narrative and performance problems of the period. In a sentence, there were problems from the start, but the second part of the period 2010–2015 saw the narrative, persona, promise unfulfilled and the related leadership performance isolated. A second prefacing point to make is that in the run-up to the election the very inaccurate opinion polling meant misleading information having consequent effects. The prevailing idea that the two main parties were neck-and-neck in terms of seats and that Ed Miliband would most likely be the next Prime Minister, when in fact the two main parties would turn out to be almost a hundred seats apart, can only have influenced the way parties acted and voters voted. And we can legitimately speculate that if such a scenario had been seen as a strong possibility, the party's narratives and performance would have been very different from the start, and certainly in the 2 years or so before the 2015 election. That said, Labour's defeat was a profound one. Given the collapse of the Liberal Democrat vote, most of which should have gone to Labour, Labour still did badly – and (according to the polls) early on in the Coalition, Labour seemed to have swollen its potential vote dramatically with the huge numbers of Lib Dem voters hostile to the Coalition. So, from a narrative and leadership perspective can my approach account for such disillusion and defeat for Labour in 2015, or rather how might my perspective contribute to such an account?

A first point to note might be a narrative-doctrinal one, namely, that the national electorate, today much more aware of the UK in the European and global context, and less loyal to political parties than before, will now choose the prospect of economic growth over the traditional drive for reducing inequality, particularly if unclear about *why* an alternative should be envisaged. This is now a major issue that any left party needs to

[7] I am also prompted by the poor quality of a lot of the comment and analysis particularly from within the Labour Party itself. There is a good article by Patrick Wintour (*Guardian*, 2 June 2015), and some of the journalism (*inter alia* Steve Richards, Philip Collins, Janan Ganesh) is first class, but a lot of it is eminently forgettable.

address. There remains, nevertheless, a very strong strain within opinion about fairness and care. This is reflected in the UK population's deep attachment to the National Health Service. What is also reflected in the polls is a firm view that the Labour Party is more concerned with and protective of the NHS than the Conservative Party. Having said this, the NHS, as we have seen, became *the* central focus of Labour's campaign to the detriment of its 'economic' narrative, the theme it should have been addressing. Besides, the NHS 'vote' was already Labour's, and the over-emphasis upon it suggested a kind of discursive avoidance of other central policy areas it should have been making up rhetorical ground on. I recognize that I am flirting here with prescription (and it is going to get worse before the end of this book), but the above underlines the imperative need for the missing piece of the puzzle, Labour's economic narrative and its emergence in One Nation through Miliband's 'performance'.

We should highlight here, however, one of the enormous difficulties Labour faced on the narrative-doctrinal-policy fronts; arguably it was a difficulty it had never faced before. The Labour narrative was having to fight rhetorically on five, even six, fronts (including Plaid, seven!), certainly in the General Election campaign but arguably throughout the legislature. In terms of its policy 'offer' it had the Greens to its left, the Conservatives to its right, the Lib Dems to its right and left, and a UKIP vote eating into its working class electorate. Finally, it faced wipe-out in Scotland against an SNP firing on all the Aristotelian categories. Labour, therefore, embraced economic and fiscal caution, but without flair. This was down, essentially, to the Shadow Chancellor, Ed Balls, ensuring that none of the Shadow Ministers made bold proposals which had fiscal or economic implications that could potentially be seen as 'irresponsible'. The party was, moreover, being pulled to the left by the SNP and the right by the Conservatives on the very issues its narrative was weakest on. And as these two tensions were voiced, the party sounded insincere or cowardly on its left and 'just like Cameron' or 'austerity lite' on its right.

An issue related to the image of the leader and the leadership 'team' was that at the decisive moment team unity appeared to evaporate. At the time of writing much of it is about image and hearsay – future accounts will confirm or deny it – but there was no impression of very much camaraderie between the members of the Shadow Cabinet. The Shadow Ministers generally seemed unaware of what Miliband was doing, and mainly seemed to ignore one another. Rumours abounded of constant feuding and arguing within Miliband's office and between it and Party HQ, the PLP, and the Shadow Ministers and their teams. There was a cheerleading team in the One Nation group but few of its members were in senior posts, and by 2015 it had become directionless. The 'team image' therefore was not one of a cohort of the 'best and the brightest' on the threshold of power, but of a quite 'muted' party with its collective fingers crossed. There was even hearsay (subsequently confirmed) of post-defeat leadership challenges already organizing themselves and their teams. Miliband seemed, therefore, to have a good rapport with party members and local constituencies but there was a great deal of fighting in and around the Captain's Tower.

All of this fractured solidarity meant a whole series of opportunities missed at the rhetorical level. Let us remind ourselves of just one major opportunity missed that we discussed earlier to illustrate our general point. As I mentioned above, the think tank IPPR close to the party had been championing the notion, in particular with the work of Rick Muir, of a complex theoretical social theory which in practice meant 'joined up' welfare, devolution, a sensitive individual-friendly health service; a 'tomorrow' which had many resonances in One Nation and Blue Labour, a kind of practical yet rhetorically Utopian *project*. The IPPR also developed, as we have seen, another project led by Kayte Lawton in 2013–2014, *The Condition of Britain* (also the title of a book by... G.D.H. Cole), a long detailed 'picture' of Britain today and optimistically what it might look like tomorrow if a government committed to the common good applied its proposed policies. Taken together this all constituted a wide-ranging practical, theoretically attractive and emotional basis for a legion of reformist policies. It would need to have been reflected in a party and leadership team that reflected this spirit of the nation's head and heart acting together to create a new society. Instead, *The Relational State* and *Condition of Britain* remained just source texts. No leading figure in the party came forward with much and, as we saw in Chapter 5, at the launch of *The Condition of Britain* in Bethnal Green on 19 June 2014, Miliband made a speech welcoming the report, then concentrated (almost exclusively) on one 'positive' measure (countering Conservative depictions of the party) of stopping 18–21 year olds living at home from claiming Jobseeker's Allowance. The failure to follow through rhetorically on *The Condition of Britain*, for example, showed a party leadership (Miliband, Team Miliband, the Shadow Ministers, and the NEC) locked in mutual stasis, unable to create any dynamic movement, and unable to create emotional allegiance. Anecdotally, although perhaps not insignificantly, Miliband had just been through a very difficult period in the press, with opponents in the party briefing against him, and the question of – yet another – possible rebellion was posed. At the IPPR launch, Miliband, as he had at the 2014 Annual Conference, looked utterly exhausted.

The question of emotion is also extremely important. The case of the NHS was a clear example of how emotion underpinned politics. Given the One Nation theme and all the other potential tributaries to a new narrative – social democracy, the unions, CLPs, the 'relational state', left radicalism, local government, and so on – a set of *highly* 'emotional policies' could have been developed, a 'transformational policy offer' instead of a transactional one. All the conditions were there by 2013 in the developing narrative being shaped/led by Jon Cruddas. All of these could have seen 'Labour values' (their lack of definitional specificity perhaps at last helping the narrative rhetorically) coincide with the deeper sentiments of a less partisan culture: fairness, efficiency, welfare, prosperous local communities, justice, the eradication of delinquency, and decent education, and so on, and so on. It is possible that the 'risk averse' option prevailed against such a narrative 'adventure', or it was considered that intra-party conflict would increase; but the lack of narrative energy by 2015 was accompanied by an absence of emotional energy and excitement. And one had the impression that Cruddas was gradually being sidelined to the role of 'philosopher' rather than Policy Chair at the moment he should have been drawing up a raft of One Nation policies.

There were real attempts to respond to public responses to proposals, but often negatively; for example in mid-2013 one speech on welfare made by Miliband and another on immigration were not well received either by the public or the media. In response, the leadership 'swerved away' from these issues – instead of taking them head on (Stears at 'After Miliband' at an Oxford seminar 5 June 2015). A more positive response to the economic narrative was, as we have seen, that of bringing in the notion of 'locks' on both spending and costing so that all proposals became a clear part of the party's narrative but this only 4 weeks before the election (*The Guardian*, 15 April 2015). By this late stage, only *Guardian* readers would have become aware of such fiscal soundness, not an essential prerequisite to a more widespread public imagining of a Labour government.

It is worth stressing that just as there are – obviously, given the nature and evolution of the Labour movement – deep echoes of 'Labour values' in the wider culture, the opposite is also true, the wider culture resonates in the party; indeed they are not really opposites at all. Blue Labour's Arcadian strain is a 2000-year-old deep deep myth in UK/English culture. Nostalgia for pre-Norman England, or for pre-industrial Britain, are deep structures in our collective psyche. They are myths, in a near-Jungian sense, but probably no less true for that. Myths and fictions are other truths. Beyond the chattering classes this welcome assertion of Arcadia was, however, inaudible. Anecdotally, on this question of Labour and beyond the Guardianistas it is probably true to say – it is certainly my conviction even though I have no hard evidence – that the Labour leadership, and this throughout the 5-year period, seemed inordinately present in and preoccupied by the written press (and more positively social media) and not nearly interested enough in its presence, and Ed's performance, in the visual and audio media where most of the UK is.

What we seem to be identifying here is less a question of wrong choices made ('wrong roads') than of non-choices made. There is a puzzle here. Why is it, how is it, that Miliband and his Mensa-level team crashed so utterly? Why was so much promise not fulfilled? It is the received view now – with hindsight – that Labour could never have won, that defeat was always inevitable. I do not agree with that, and think Labour could have won but did not for one simple reason – and another (also simple) that followed on from it. Before saying what these are, let me admit that that is what I would think because the conviction that performance can alter anything underpins all my analysis. Not that there are no constraints – in Chapter 1 I quoted Simone Weil: not anything can happen but nothing is determined. With this in mind let us elaborate our two sequential 'simple' reasons. The first was the understandable but inelegant rejection of New Labour by the post-2010 leadership. This need not have involved a rejection of 'Third Way' discourse but did. The second was that by rhetorically pushing New Labour away, One Nation entrapped itself. The 'narrative attack' upon New Labour gave Miliband(ism) a (potential) identity and a distance/breathing space from the shipwreck of 'Brownism'. However, we can make five points related to those issues, two for point one (New Labour) and three for point two (One Nations's self-entrapment).

First, replacing New Labour with One Nation may have been understandable, even necessary, but it follows that One Nation needed to be 'richer', doctrinally and emotionally, than New Labour.

Second, and relatedly, once done, the Third Way, among the most successful Labour Party experiments ever, should have been folded back into the narrative – and some of the New Labour figures who had engineered three Labour victories folded back in too. One stunningly easy way of doing this would have been to make a compelling distinction between New Labour and the Third Way (i.e., John Smith, Tony Blair, and Gordon Brown via such themes as elaborated by David Marquand, Tony Giddens, and others *before* 1997), so that the latter could be picked up again to profit, and the post-1997 appraisal made in terms of a range of deviations from the norm. Instead, taking the rhetorical-emotional path chosen meant that the 1997–2010 (1994–2010?) period was rhetorically 'screened out' ideationally and rhetorically. It would have been much more helpful and reconciling (and still have kept the mythical in left thought and the personalized in the new conditions) to have found 'small' wrong roads in *all* the journeys, and bring them together in One Nation or New Nation: where 1930s Labour went wrong and right, idem 1945, idem Wilson's leadership, idem Foot then Kinnock's fight back, and so on, thus creating a 'new' ideational set (Beech et al. 2004).

The third and debilitating consequence of this was unforeseen: by 'abandoning' 1997–2010 – indeed by linking it to the 'neoliberalism' of 1979–1997 – Miliband became, among many other things, defenceless against Osborne's continuous jibing about 'not repairing the roof when the sun was shining'. Miliband could only acquiesce rhetorically in such a criticism, for – rhetorically – it was his own. And he could not refashion (though he should have) a defence of Blair (and Brown who 'saved' the UK in the financial crash) because his whole project was based upon an idea of *complete* renewal (which is to misunderstand rhetoric and ideology's mutability – and besides, many of the doctrinal differences within the Labour Party, and this forever, are of the how many angels there are on a pinhead type). Making New Labour the wrong road travelled and not integrating Third Way (and other) discourse into a new way forward was a fundamental mistake.

Fourth, it also alienated some of the earlier 'best and brightest' who were still active.

Fifth, it would also have allowed for the reconciliation of 'New' and 'other' Labour, and their integration into a vision of the future – one of the prerequisites to a bold (yet internally harmonious) vision of the first 100 days (the elements of which were there): what a One Nation government would do immediately in government – a bold and clear programme linked to decentralization (Blue Labour+), financial reform, banking, regional banks, apprenticeships (social democracy+), a commitment to modernization (Third Way+), vigorous education and training programmes (German social democracy, trade unionism+) and so on. Instead, after 5 years of narrative fashioning the party made a forgettable 'retail offer'.

THE TWO BROTHERS ISSUE

Inextricably linked to this hesitation regarding narrative – and for us this is the fundamental point – was the hesitation regarding the 'definition' of Ed Miliband's 'character' or rather, here, style. One of the options, given the relative quiescence of the narrative, might have been a more 'common sense' (European Social Democratic?) style of leadership that Miliband might have projected. It would have been closer to his 'real' character, would have prepared him for a different kind of governing style (e.g., coalition), and might have favourably impinged upon a more 'celebrity politics' style that ill-fitted Miliband. This brings us back – and finally – to the 'character' of Ed Miliband himself and its influences in this 5-year period. Could he have 'embodied' and 'performed' the party's narrative? Did he at all? And if so, how?

A first point to make is that he was a 'shock' leader in that throughout the (interminable) campaign from May to September 2010 the near universal assumption was, as we have seen, that David Miliband would win, was a kind of heir apparent. Indeed, there was a sense that in the 2010 leadership election David had in part been 'punished' for having exuded a sense of 'entitlement'. An illustration of this was his reply to a journalist asking (19 June) why both brothers were running, 'I think that's a question you would have to ask Ed.' But the 'unsaid' of the result was that he had been punished not by just a 'contender' but by his own brother. This cast the election and the leadership image of the unexpected younger brother in a very strange light. It was not Ed Balls or Andy Burnham who dished David but the younger brother of the assumed winner. And perhaps even worse from a 'legitimacy' point of view, Ed was in a minority with MPs and was pushed (inched) over the line by the trade unions. And for several weeks after there was a kind of absence of Ed from the political scene as if he was as unprepared for his victory as everyone else (there was one early PMQs (1 December) where the Prime Minister, David Cameron, drew attention to his apparent invisibility in the early months with the jibe 'when is he going to start?'). Is it the case that such a 'win' meant that Ed Miliband could never establish a proper image of leadership legitimacy given the situation? I think the answer is, on balance, no, and for two reasons. First, addressing the issue of his legitimacy head-on would have 'filled out' his persona and character. Second, if a powerful economic and leadership narrative had developed the legitimacy issue would have had less salience. Nevertheless, the singular nature of a younger brother beating the expected winner marked from the start the question of the legitimation and elaboration of leadership character.

From the psychological perspective, with all the caveats of my non-specialism in this area, I can make several points, bearing in mind that I am interested in the psychoanalytical aspects only as regards the projection of the persona and not the person: Ed Miliband – as I said in the Acknowledgements – I deliberately did not meet, although I attended many of his 'performances'. I am, therefore, not trying to psychoanalyse but to elicit the semiological implications and effects of the nature of Ed's win upon his persona and upon the overall political process. And, as I have said, there was something consequential about this 'brothers' aspect to the 2010 leadership election, not only because they were brothers but because they, as well as the media, made rather an issue of it, particularly David, as if this were indeed a contest between two famous sons of a famous father. And the media exploited this angle. In fact, at the time, and since – to a dramatic degree taken up by few political commentators – this resembled a vanity project (or rather two vanity projects) that went very wrong. All attention was on the two brothers and *none* on anyone else, even on the only black, only female candidate, Diane Abbott.

One other fundamental issue related to the fraternal nature of the competition has also been largely overlooked, namely, that because Ed's candidacy in 2010 claimed legitimacy from its repudiation of New Labour, it was not just a rejection of Blair but of his brother too. He did not just beat his brother, semiologically, he stood *in order to* beat him. This *became* the (unspoken) narrative significance of the sibling clash. This meant that the rhetorical/narrative/discursive reconciliation with the Third Way later on was itself highly problematic given that the 'fratricide' was based upon – justified by – an apparently ideological rejection (particularly in hindsight) of the Third Way by the 'frère cadet', rather than upon 'just' sibling rivalry. This meant that a later embracing of New Labour would involve a capitulation within a *personalized* conflict, and a repudiation of the only justification for the younger brother standing against the older one.

The defeat of the older brother by the younger did generate interest in Ed Miliband as a character: who was he to have achieved this? At one level of course he had done nothing except stand for the leadership as any aspiring MP and ex-minister might. And he did represent and reflect, if not a single Labour tradition/doctrinal pedigree – no contenders for leadership do, they all mix genres (even Jeremy Corbyn) – an arguably more leftist or activist view of government than the other candidates, apart from Diane Abbott. But the relationship to his older brother marked this election and his election victory. One might go as far as to say that if it did not haunt his 5-year leadership, it at least made it much more complicated as regards both narrative and persona. It was a topic constantly avoided rather than confronted. There is also the intriguing notion of whether the *ideological* differences between the brothers bore any relationship to their respective views of their father's radicalism – or their anticipation of what his (*outre-tombe*) view may have been of theirs. Did this issue impinge upon Ed Miliband's narrative and upon his persona? I have no idea what the answer to this is – whether Ralph Miliband was a factor in all this – but the question, or rather the posing of the question, has value. Someone else may be qualified to comment. But the sibling nature of the contest was formative of the subsequent development of *both* narrative and persona.

Miliband's leadership was deeply marked by the 2010 leadership contest. This was in part the 'fault' of the brothers themselves, who either subscribed or were constrained to allow the depiction of their sibling status as one of the interesting aspects of the contest. Declarations of their love for one another despite their differences were frequent and, as we mentioned above, they depicted themselves overtly as protagonists from a famous, intellectual, London political family, as if this contest illustrated their pedigree. None of the other three candidates had this media exposure, so there were immediate comparisons made with that other famous family of brothers, and even the suspicion that these brothers would possibly go on to dominate Labour as the Kennedys had the Democrats. The assumption was that David would lead with Ed in a prominent role, and that this would be even more so the case because David would come first and Ed – way out ahead of Burnham, Balls, and Abbott – second. If Ed had done a Bobby Kennedy rather than an Ed Miliband perhaps the history of the UK left might have been very different (although perhaps not, we should add).

The focus was on the brothers in great part because one of the two, David, the older brother, was largely the favourite to win. It would have been very different if, say, Andy Burnham had been the favourite, or even the second favourite. It had been assumed for several years that David Miliband, former Foreign Secretary, would be the successor to

Gordon Brown. David Miliband, moreover, gave an impression of himself orchestrating the leadership context. The impression was given that it was he who encouraged Diane Abbott to stand – to represent the left, and gender and ethnic diversity and thus 'illustrate' the party – yet the impression was also one of confident and generous regality, as was David's overall style at the many hustings and interviews (a lot of them using the Miliband family angle as a source of humour). He had a more assured and suave manner than Ed but the growing feeling of 'entitlement' began to negatively inform David's campaign, giving a further boost to Ed's, and not only among the trade unions and those activists who wanted to move on from New Labour, or perhaps back towards Old Labour. As with Corbyn's campaign in 2015, there was real vigour in Ed's. Towards the end of the long campaign, relations between the Milibands' two support teams began to deteriorate seriously as it became clear that it would be a photo-finish. Ed Miliband's campaign was by far the most intense and his team saw support grow and grow among activists. In the end he came second in both the members' (Constituency Labour Parties) and MPs' 'college', but crossed the finishing line with the trade union vote. The result therefore was perfectly fair and legal, but there was an air of illegitimacy about the win – pushed over the line by the 'union bosses' (who it was alleged had stuffed their campaign material with publicity for Ed...), and the rightful 'heir' defeated, the older brother humiliated. Into this then played, now extremely negatively, the family aspect. There was an air not just of the crown usurped, but of family drama.

All this took place in the new world of social media and 24/7 news. David's wife's anger was more than hearsay, the anguish and sadness of their mother the received view. The press, particularly the right-wing press, delighted in it all, the picture of the brothers hugging after the result becoming *the* picture of the event (the mark of Cain, '*je l'embrasse pour mieux l'étouffer*', the Judas kiss, a man may smile and be a villain; all these ancient myths and dispositions teem within our popular culture). The media then, and people generally, did the *next* ominous thing – *compared* the two brothers: the one more experienced, more suave, more assured, better looking, older, and a good speaker; the other, less experienced, less glamorous, more 'nerdy', more awkward, slightly adenoidal, and the winner. These 'trivial' perceived differences would go on to dramatically inform Ed's leadership image and style. The pro-Conservative press of course insisted on the comparisons, and clearly gave the impression that the Conservative Party itself was delighted with the result; and gradually the 'Wallace' depictions began to take hold. David eventually left to work in New York in a kind of self-imposed exile. We can see, therefore, that one of the central conditions of Ed's leadership performance was a very negative one, and to a certain degree he compounded the 'persona difficulties' through his performance of himself. Read on.

DESERT ISLAND DISCOVERIES: FRIGHTFULLY POTENT CHEAP MUSIC

In November 2013 Ed Miliband appeared on *Desert Island Discs* on BBC Radio 4. Let me stress at the outset, given the family issues involved, it is my view he should never have done this. The programme was strangely revealing of if not his character then at least a 'character' called Ed Miliband. *Desert Island Discs* has an estimated audience of around 3 million weekly, and is one of the most downloaded/listened to podcasts from radio (and the first broadcast (it is broadcast twice) goes out immediately after the omnibus edition of *The Archers*!). Kirsty Young, the presenter, later said that she thought Miliband's team had had a hand in his choices, as she suspected was the case with all politicians (doubtless true). My own view is that if he were helped it was more because he probably had little interest in music, which seemed clear from the programme. The choices, however, were themselves both bizarre and painfully revealing of 'a persona'. Three politically correct pieces were chosen (*Jerusalem*, the South African National Anthem, and Paul Robeson (*The Ballad of Joe Hill*)). Then there were some inane songs: *Take on Me* by A-Ha, Robbie Williams' *Angels*, and *Sweet Caroline* by Neil Diamond. (I quite like Neil Diamond, but I'm not sure I would publicize it). But there was no Dylan, no Tom Waits, no Madeleine Peyroux, no Radiohead, no Bach, no Pogues, no Blondie, no Keith Jarrett, no Chopin, no Natalie Merchant, no Tom Robinson, no Miles Davis....

It also has to be said that Kirsty Young was throughout persistent with Ed ('acerbic' was one expression used; *International Business Times*, 30 November 2013); the programme was more like *Hard Talk* than Roy Plomley's old programme: he followed his brother to the same Oxford college, did exactly the same degree (got a 2:i to David's 1st) and so on, then followed his brother into politics; went to work for Gordon Brown, Tony Blair's rival for whom David worked.... In its questioning, this was not like a *Desert Island Discs* we usually listen to; Young was suggesting a fraternal obsession/jealousy which in turn might shed light on the leadership contest itself. There was, therefore, the dull choice of 'the personal' songs alongside a developing conversation of acutely personal issues. He had talked a great deal previously about his father (including here quite movingly to Kirsty Young), never about his brother, nor mother, an impressive and intellectual woman. Who, one wonders, was the favourite son? In classical psychoanalysis it is, of course, the older son…, as is the idea that overcoming an older brother is linked to the psychological need for paternal recognition.

The nature of the conversation seemed to be throwing up questions of this nature. In overall 'trait theory'-type leadership terms, Miliband came across as decent, friendly, self-deprecating, honest and straightforward, unpretentious, an *ingénu*, uncool, clever but uncultivated, yet underneath all that with an implied problematic possible unconscious jealousy of his brother. The conversation also teemed with discussions of 'family': when he was a boy, his own boys, his father, his wife; more 'absent' from the exchanges were his mother, and from him though not from Young, his brother. This probing was much more intrusive than is usually the case on *Desert Island Discs*, as if Young was trying to understand or discover something. The listener also had the impression that the guest was not picking up on the deeper significance of her questioning (one assumes he did but the persona acted as if he did not). Ed Miliband also strongly gave – or allowed Kirsty Young to give – the impression of being a real nerd with the girls, etc. Kirsty Young oddly enough evoked these very private responses very easily – he was of the purple-jumper-white-trousers-at-the-party brigade; his chances of walking a girl home after the party thus significantly reduced. There was an allusion in fact to his having no girlfriend at all at university; and none of this general 'anorak-ness' being countered. Indeed, Ed seemed happy to come across as such from Young's questions. This in itself could have been exploited and justified; the performing persona could have *explained himself* to advantage. The earlier claims of Nick Clegg to 30 conquests to *GQ Magazine* in 2008 had indeed been regarded generally (the publicizing of it) as somewhat distasteful, even vulgar. But Miliband's not responding decisively to Young's questioning, and she an attractive woman of the same age – a year older – implying such a lack of interest in the fair sex was, in part, because he gave the impression he did not know what she was getting at, at the least a trifle puzzling. I want to make one final semiotic point about the final choice of music.

The last disc made this author gasp in disbelief. Ed's final choice – perhaps it was a bold Zola-like *J'assume*! of 'taking responsibility' – was

Edith Piaf's *Je ne regrette rien*, sung in her most heart-rending but defiant tones. The title in English (I mean the use of the French title in English) has become an amusing cliché, but the kind of *acte manqué* suggested by the choice – I regret nothing *in spite of the damage done* – was the implication. There was a kind of bravado in the choice (surely not deliberate). Given the earlier conversation which was much more about family than politics, the choice of song implied that it was not the leadership contest he 'did not regret' but the upset caused, and thwarting of his brother's prime ministerial ambitions, suggesting in the closing minutes of the programme a kind of emotional violence at odds with how he had come across until then. Paradoxically, the subjects of which Piaf sings and the manner in which she does so suggest the enormous emotional toll of not regretting.

Over the following period, the issue of Ed's relationship to his brother (and sometimes to the wider family) would grow rather than fade and (as with Kirtsy Young) the scale of the personal effects were admitted to more and more. He also – more and more – justified his choice in 2010 as a *political* one: he thought his 'project' was 'better for Britain' and so on, but the sense that somewhere a monumental mistake had been made pervaded the *non-dit* of political exchange, even on the part of Ed's own now declared intention, as if *post facto* he was searching for an acceptable reason – that is, his was an ideological not personal attack (this would indeed have been semiologically persuasive and politically fruitful if he had come second). The sense that, for many, Ed was the wrong leader became a stronger and stronger feeling (as reflected in the perfidious polls) and added to the negative accumulation of character traits, joining a whole collection of evolving views, and culminating in the 'not prime ministerial material' trait that he carried with him throughout the period and into the 2015 General Election campaign. The implication, and media and social media speculation, was that he was strong in one way – the ruthless elimination of his brother's desire to be the next Prime Minister; the strength of a Macbeth or Francis Underwood. In this way, the said and unspoken comparison with his (arguably prime ministerial) older brother had a continuous undermining effect. And it was, as Collins pointed out (*The Times*, 10 April 2015) 'a political fact' that had to be dealt with, rather than avoided. A final anecdotal although not insignificant point to make here is that 'celebrity politics', with its illusions of insights into private lives and feelings, had become by this time an extremely consequential phenomenon, suggesting here that the narrative that Miliband and his team gradually and then persistently screened out from his own – that is, the narrative of New Labour, in order to give 'Milibandism' a *voice* – was not just the narrative of New Labour but was also, by definition, the narrative of his older brother, David.

CONCLUSION

I hope I have demonstrated the interrelationship of the political and the personal and its complexity in this period in Labour Party history, as well as the interrelationship of narrative and performance in the political party in the contemporary period. That said, I need to focus here in this 'Conclusion of the Conclusion' as much upon Jeremy Corbyn as upon Ed Miliband; this not because I am writing an Afterword or a Postscript to this study, as a kind of catch-up with the aftermath of Labour's 2015 defeat and its 'failure' of leadership. The developments of the summer of 2015 and the election of Jeremy Corbyn as the leader of the Labour Party on 12 September were a startling confirmation of the approach adopted in this book, and of the much ignored existence of chance, the unexpected, the serendipitous for some (and serendipity's negative counterpart: 'shit happens' for others), and the creative role of narrative as a formative condition of political performance.

Few saw the possibility, let alone the likelihood, of Ed Miliband's victory over his brother David until very late in the day in the 2010 leadership campaign. And even fewer then reflected upon the reasons for this outcome, outside notions of the older Miliband's sense of 'entitlement' (I would rather emphasize his poor performance). Few dwelt upon the younger Ed's performance in the contest and the alternative narrative of renewal and youth elaborated by his vigorous supporters. When the changes to leadership selection and election were introduced at the Canning Town Special Conference in March 2014, few reflected upon the possible consequences of such changes. And yet there had been a recent and arguably ominous precedent. In 2006, in the French Socialist Party, Jack Lang, hoping it would benefit him, brought in a 20 euro membership fee which saw a surge in membership. In the ensuing election for the party's 2007 presidential candidate the result was a runaway victory for the outsider, Ségolène Royal, who took 60 % of the vote on the first round. (Sounds familiar?) Labour might have reflected upon this.

Few saw the Labour Party losing by such a margin to the Conservatives in May 2015. With few exceptions (e.g., Philip Collins in *The Times*) most (including me) were stunned by the scale of Labour's defeat. Once again, however, few went on to reflect upon the narrative and performative reasons for One Nation Labour's loss of dynamism in 2014, and how this contributed to Labour's 2015 General Election performance becoming almost a non-event, apart from some spirited performances by Miliband himself. The main comments in the shocked aftermath that followed concerned the party's lack of an 'economic narrative' and the 'uncharismatic', 'un-prime ministerial' image of the party leader. Little was made of the relationship between these two phenomena concerning narrative and image. And again, few (though see Stephen Bush in *New Statesman* from the beginning of the campaign) saw the surge in support for Jeremy Corbyn in the summer of 2015 (and that doubtless included Corbyn himself); nor were there any parallels drawn between the 2015 and the 2010 leadership elections, where narrative and performance also played such decisive roles. Each was about renewal, youth – perhaps an irony given Corbyn was 66 in 2015 – and the demand by an imagined 'unheard' to have 'a hearing'.

Political parties invariably experience membership surges after defeat. This happened with the French PS after Jean-Marie Le Pen beat Lionel Jospin to go through to the run-off of the French presidential election of 2002. In 2015, Lib Dem membership in the UK rose by 10,000 in the wake of their defeat, and more still after Corbyn's election. The Labour Party increase, however – if we include the £3 'supporters' and the 'opt-in' trade union members (both categories eligible to vote in the leadership election), as well as the new party members – reached a staggering (albeit contested) near-600,000 by September 2015: that is, a tripling of its numbers in 4 months. This is the fantasy mass membership dreamed of today in European political parties. It raises questions of the first importance regarding what I referred to earlier as 'rally politics'. So let us reflect upon this development in UK politics (I also have an untested theory that the 'Philosophy' part of the the PPE degree studied by so many in the upper echelons of the Labour Party barely exists next to the Politics and the Economics parts – a little more of the first and I suspect there would be more wisdom in party reflection upon the political process...).

When the 2015 leadership race began in May, there were few voices urging the infinitely more pressing need for reflection upon and debate about such an overwhelming defeat, and what might be done next before embarking on a new leadership contest. The party moved immediately on to the business of election of a new leader, even in its state of disbelief, leaving all the things it should have done not done. Moving straight on to the new process of choosing a successor to Ed Miliband meant that all three of the initial candidates, moreover, were members of the Shadow Cabinet (Andy Burnham, Yvette Cooper, and Liz Kendall; three other potential candidates – Tristram Hunt, Mary Creagh, and Chuka Umunna – ruled themselves out), thus 'carrying over' the notion of recent – and unreflected upon – defeat into the new contest. Initially, little was debated; whether Labour had been pro-business enough was perhaps the only topic of substance. Miliband seemed to have written himself out of the party narrative, almost instantly out of the party memory (he kept this silence throughout the leadership campaign and beyond); but this need not have happened. He could have 'overseen' a transition of sorts and an ideational debate of some kind. Other options were also available – Harman could have taken a more 'caretaker' role, or been joined by the ever-popular Alan Johnson, while the party 'rethought' itself, or at least re-thought the General Election. Anything but what took place: yet another non-event, into which the Corbyn candidacy exploded (and the 'drama' was added to by his getting his 35 nominations 2 minutes before the deadline). Narrative like nature abhors a vacuum.

It is true that the party membership had been moving somewhat to the left between 2010 and 2015; and there was a fun element of 'Syriza-Podemos' to Corbyn's candidacy (fun is a much underestimated motivator in politics (Lynch 2010; Provine 2000; Strick et al. 2012)), but this really reflected only a party in search of at least 'a conversation'. The scale, however, of the incomprehension/s and all the 'few saw' I mentioned above dragged the party over the summer of 2015 not fundamentally in a left or right direction but from incoherence and incomprehension towards at least a debate. Corbyn – a reluctant candidate – had been pushed by his friends and patronizingly invited by some party grandees to stand for the leadership so 'the left' of the party could have some voice. But the first piece of farce, the fracas over the party's response to the government's welfare proposals in July, brought Corbyn's narrative to the centre of the debate; because of Cabinet responsibility (acting leader Harriet Harman had spoken – and very publicly – on the *Sunday Politics* programme with Andrew Neil), the Shadow Cabinet contenders, Kendall, Burnham, and Cooper, were unable to vote against some of the government welfare proposals, and could not join the 48 MPs who did rebel, including one Jeremy Corbyn, turning his campaign into an anti-establishment and per-sonalized rally (regardless of his views on 'personality').

Another of Corbyn's advantages was not only that he seemed to be injecting fun and life into the debate; none of his opponents was per-ceived as a political figure of stature. We shall come back to this below as one of the strange legacies of Blairism and post-Blairism itself. So, until Corbyn started filling the halls, there were two 'old' faces (Burnham and

Cooper) and a 'new' one (Kendall, elected in 2010 but unknown beyond the Shadow Cabinet). So it seemed to be simply (almost) business as usual. We should not, therefore, underestimate the 'ludic' arrival of Corbyn's T-shirts, badges, and 'Jez we can'. His popularity was not only a rejection of the post-Blair/Miliband business as usual approach, it marked early on the humiliation of the three mainstream candidates who had seen only one another as their real rivals. Suddenly, all three and the party itself were overtaken by 'Corbynmania', once again underlining one of the main symbolic failings of the Miliband period, the failure to anticipate developments.

On the question of the alternatives to 'Milibandism' and this question of narratives abhorring a vacuum we should pause here, particularly as I have referred throughout this book to Blairism and New Labour. I should stress this point here about Blairism: one of the problems for the 'new' Kendall and many others on her 'wing' of the party was that they failed to understand the nature of narrative; 'change' did not mean the 'return' of the Modernizers in a kind of flip-flop once Miliband had lost. But much more fundamentally, New Labour, The Third Way, Blairism, the Modernizers *had no narrative*. Even Liz Kendall's discourse was 'a few home truths' and a call to realism; you cannot 'see' realism. And interventions by Tony Blair (at least two), Peter Mandelson and many other 'old' New Labour figures, demonstrated New Labour's lack of a new narrative in 2015, and arguably their own historic failure to renew The Third Way itself in the 2000s (a Fourth perhaps – one of the far-reaching rhetorical tricks was that the Third Way imprinted the idea that there were only Three 'Ways'...). The Modernizers assumed, with Miliband down and out, that 'the party' would just fall back towards them. Here too was a fundamental lack of sensitivity to and, as we have seen, understanding of the nature of narrative (and by extension to the rhetoric and the ideas they express and are in turn expressed by). In his second intervention (*The Observer*, 30 August 2015) Blair even admitted that he did not know what was going on. The 1994–1997 narrative of the Third Way should have given them a clue (especially him, see Chapter 2 on Blair's narrative). The party's success in London, where the Labour vote remained buoyant in 2015 was, surely, a clue to the potential for a revitalized party in search of a redefinition of its identity, potential, and direction. And the more the grandees came out against Corbyn, the more his popularity rose. Blairism and the Modernizers were offering nothing rhetorically; they were in fact now 'Old Labour'; and Milibandism had, as we have seen, lost its rhetoric. And we have also seen throughout this book that on a range of issues – the economy, welfare, immigration – it was never clear whether 'Milibandism' itself was left or right (see Bale in Clarke and James 2015). It could have blended a 'left' and 'right' narrative, but did not do this either.

Tom Lehrer, the American satirical lyricist, sang of the Spanish republican struggle against Franco 'He may have won all the battles, but we had all the good songs'. By June 2015, Jeremy Corbyn seemed to have all the good songs and was winning all the battles too. He turned the leadership election upside down; his meetings were filled to overflowing.

So what began as a spectacularly ill-judged scramble for Ed's fallen crown (and reliable rumour had it there was manoeuvring even before it fell) became a 'stop the ultra-left candidate'. The initial televised debates started off with the three front runners as if unaware of the tsunami gathering behind the radical 'lefty' from the 1980s, who then rode a rhetorical coach and horses through the contest. How did this happen? Let us get one thing clear: it had little or nothing to do with being left wing or right wing. Jeremy Corbyn made such a strong media showing because of his style and language, and his opponents' mediocre rhetorical 'offer'. Essentially – unlike Corbyn – Burnham, Cooper, and Kendall talked about little: did Labour overspend in the last Labour government? Yes it did (Burnham). No it didn't (Cooper). Cooper knew about women's issues and families because she was a mum (Cooper camp…. and Kendall had no children…). To stop Corbyn, Kendall should step down (Burnham's team). That's sexist (Kendall). Cooper should too (Burnham's camp). That's also sexist (Cooper's team). I'm not a Westminster insider, I regularly go back to the North to see my old football friends (Burnham). All dire stuff.

What was Corbyn talking about meanwhile? Everything. Moreover, Corbyn embodied a wide and deep tradition in the UK left (although perhaps not as wide and deep as he would claim) that could be recognized and engaged with (and in spite of the attacks upon him, his economic policy was – broadly – Old Left Keynesian rather than Marxist). In July the largest trade union, Unite, came out in favour of him followed by the CWU and Unison. His 'camp' was still active within the party, even though marginalized. There were also real and imagined connections between Corbyn and what we might call the 'problematic' hard left (sharing platforms over the years with Hezbollah, Sinn Fein, and so on). But throughout the summer campaign Corbyn quietly refuted, justified, or ignored these accusations, and I should stress that his rival candidates also avoided these areas. And it was clear that there was a mutual bond of affection between the lefty Corbyn and the Blairite Kendall which benefited Corbyn's image. More importantly still, Corbyn put forward his proposals with elegance, conviction, modesty, and intellectual coherence. And he at all times concertedly avoided personal criticism of his opponents (a brilliant rhetorical device to enhance one's own persona), and gave only measured responses to media attacks (because of 'Hillsborough', he simply refused any interviews with *The Sun* newspaper, again an astute rhetorical device – silence). The 'main' candidates 'embodied' nothing. As Corbyn's popularity began to climb, no image of the other candidates was retained after any performance. And Corbyn wanted to talk about all the things that made people want to vote Labour or not or join Labour or not or consider joining Labour, and so on.[8] Corbyn utterly transformed the debate and the stakes, and then prompted the greater doctrinal involvement and policy discussion of the other three candidates in the hustings, essentially from August so for only the last month. Corbyn gave a very old lesson in politics: leaders have to represent something, have to embody a political view or tradition, narrate it and 'perform' it to rhetorical effect, and be – or at least seem – authentic and sincere. And if you can fake sincerity....

We can make six concluding remarks which correspond more or less to each of the chapters. First, adapting and applying the Aristotelian categories of rhetoric is helpful in understanding contemporary political leadership rhetoric; conversely, Weber's definition of 'charisma' raises more problems than it solves. I have replaced it with the idea of leadership as an 'event' in which a narrative is 'performed'; notions of charisma today, however, abound in the wider celebrity culture, and this is a formative condition of performance itself. Second, previous Labour Party leaders have created a range, not necessarily of leadership 'types', but of characteristics, traits, and perceptions which inform the way the party understands and responds to leadership. Third, a party narrative is not simply a story the party wishes to tell about itself; it has to correspond to the doctrinal issues, legitimating structures, ideas of origins, trials, journeys, fortitude, deliverance, and so on that underlie most, if not all, 'stories'. Fourth, this narrative is 'told' by leaders and becomes a defining part of their leadership identity; they even become the 'protagonist' of the story as well as the 'teller of the tale'. Fifth, narrative and performance are necessary to one another and the leader falters if the narrative is weak, not sufficiently adhered to, or is abandoned. Sixth, there is a semiotics to leadership persona, and narrative performance of leadership points to meanings, implications, and significances that are not always intended but which have consequences.

---

[8] Corbyn's catalogue of leadership mistakes would only begin after he was elected leader, beginning with his first mediocre speech, his victory speech itself.

BIBLIOGRAPHY

Abrams, F. (1997) 'Blair: "I think I'm a pretty straight sort of guy"', *The Independent*, 17 November. http://www.independent.co.uk/news/blair-i-think-im-a-pretty-straight-sort-of-guy-1294593.html

Adonis, A. (2013) *5 Days in May: The Coalition and Beyond* (London: Biteback Publishing).

Allan, J.P. (1993) '1983–92: Neil Kinnock and the "New Model Party"'. http://scholar.lib.vt.edu/theses/available/etd-454016449701231/unrestricted/Etd5.pdf

Anderson, B. (1983) *Imagined Communities* (London: Verso).

Annesley, C. (2013) 'Men, Women and Gender Equality', paper presented at one-day conference, The Politics of One Nation Labour, Queen Mary, University of London, 18 April.

Aristotle (1991) *The Art of Rhetoric*, transl. Hugh Lawson-Tancred (London: Penguin Classics).

Assinder, N. (2007) 'How Blair Recreated Labour', BBC, http://news.bbc.co.uk/1/hi/uk_politics/6129844.stm

Atkins, J. (2011) *Justifying New Labour Policy* (Basingstoke: Palgrave).

Atkinson, M. (1984) *Our Masters' Voices* (London: Methuen).

Atkinson, M. (2004) *Lend Me Your Ears* (London: Random House).

Attlee, C. (1945) 'The Election Scene Landslide for Socialists', https://www.youtube.com/watch?v=oBnbXgl-_pU

Austin, J.L. (1975) *How to Do Things with Words* (Oxford: Clarendon Press).

Baldwin, S. (1933) *On England* [1924] (London: Philip Allan).

Bale, T. (2013, April 18). *One Nation Labour and the Welfare State*. Paper presented at one-day conference, The Politics of One Nation Labour, Queen Mary, University of London.

© The Author(s) 2017

J. Gaffney, *Leadership and the Labour Party*, Palgrave Studies in Political Leadership, DOI 10.1057/978-1-137-50498-2

Bale, T. (2015) *Five Year Mission* (Oxford: Oxford University Press).

Barthes, R. (1957) *Mythologies* (Paris: Seuil).

Baxter, J. (ed.) (2006) *Speaking Out: The Female Voice in Public Context* (Basingstoke: Palgrave).

BBC (1970) 'BBC Election 1970 David Dimbleby Harold Wilson', https://www.youtube.com/watch?v=TwAhWeb3-RY

BBC (1987) '1987GenElec: Neil Kinnock Reacts on Labour Losing Election', https://www.youtube.com/watch?v=YBiGz1q2AAM

BBC (1995) 'The Wilderness Years', BBC 2.

BBC (1997) 'Labour's Old Romantic: A Film Portrait of Michael Foot'. https://www.youtube.com/watch?v=ZFQDPXqf-80

BBC (1999) *Blair's Conference Speech* (full text). http://news.bbc.co.uk/1/hi/uk_politics/46000.stm

BBC (2000) 'Crisis? What Crisis?', http://news.bbc.co.uk/1/hi/uk_politics/921524.stm

BBC (2007) 'Brown Will Enter No 10 Unopposed', http://news.bbc.co.uk/1/hi/uk_politics/6660565.stm

BBC (2009) 'No 10 Official Quits Over Emails', http://news.bbc.co.uk/1/hi/uk_politics/7995044.stm

BBC Radio 4 (2011), 'Blue Labour', *Analysis*, transcript, 21 March, available at: http://news.bbc.co.uk/nol/shared/spl/hi/programmes/analysis/transcripts/21_03_11.txt

BBC Radio 4 (2013) 'Labour's New New Jerusalem', *Analysis*, 27 May, http://www.bbc.co.uk/programmes/b01sm2g0

Beattie, J. (2012) 'Game Changer: Opinion Poll Shows Huge Boost for Ed Miliband After Labour Conference Speech', *Mirror News*, 4 October, www.mirror.co.uk/news/uk-news/ed-miliband-opinion-poll-labour-1359120

Beattie, J. (2012a) 'One Nation', *The Daily Mirror*, 3 October, p. 6.

Beckett, F. (2014) 'Neil Kinnock, the Man Who Saved Labour', *New Statesman*, http://www.newstatesman.com/politics/2014/09/neil-kinnock-man-who-saved-labour

Beech, M. and Page, R.M. (2014) 'Blue Labour and Purple Labour: Alternate Futures for the Welfare State?', British Politics Group, http://britishpoliticsgroup.blogspot.co.uk/2014/11/blue-labour-and-purple-labour-alternate.html

Beech, M., Hickson, K. and Plant, R. (2004) *The Struggle for Labour's Soul: Understanding Labour's Political Thought Since 1945* (London: Routledge).

Behr, R. (2012) 'Project "Ed's Charisma" – The Mission to Help Miliband Loosen Up', *New Statesman*, 28 September – 4 October.

Bennett, W. (2014) *The Logic of Connective Action: Digital Media and the Personalization of Contentious Politics* (Cambridge: Cambridge University Press).

Blair, T. (1996) 'Leader's Speech, Blackpool 1996', http://www.britishpolitical-speech.org/speech-archive.htm?speech=202

Blair, T. (1997) 'Blair: I Think I Am a Pretty Straight Sort of Guy', *The Independent*, 17 November. http://www.independent.co.uk/news/blair-i-think-im-a-pretty-straight-sort-of-guy-1294593.html

Blair, T. (2006) 'Leader's Speech, Manchester 2006', http://www.britishpoliti-calspeech.org/speech-archive.html?speech=2

Blair, T. (2011) *A Journey* (London: Arrow Books).

Blair, T. (2013) 'Labour Must Search for Answers and not Merely Aspire to Be a Repository for People's Anger', *New Statesman*, 12 April.

Blond, P. (2010) *Red Tory: How Left and Right Have Broken Britain and How We Can Fix It* (London: Faber and Faber).

Blond, P. (2013) 'One Nation and the Conservative Tradition', paper presented at one-day conference, The Politics of One Nation Labour, Queen Mary, University of London, 18 April.

Blumer, J.G., Kavanagh, D. and Nossiter, T.J. (1996) 'Modern Communications Versus Traditional Politics in Britain: Unstable Marriage of Convenience' in P.Mancini and D.Swanson (eds) *Politics, Media, and Modern Democracy: An International Study of Innovations in Electoral Campaigning and Their Consequences* (Westport: Praeger).

Bogdanor, V. (2012) 'Half-Echoes of the Past', *New Statesman*, 28 September.

Bogdanor, V. (2013) 'The One Nation Labour Debate: Labour and the New Era in Politics', Labour Policy Review organized with Progress at the House of Commons, 19 March, Committee Room 10.

Bragg, B. (2011) 'Labour Is Already Too Blue', *The Guardian*, http://www.guardian.co.uk/commentisfree/2011/apr/07/blue-labour-globalised-capitalism

Brivati, B. (1997) 'Earthquake or Watershed? Conclusions on New Labour in Power', in B. Brivati and T. Bale (eds) *New Labour in Power: Precedents and Prospects* (London: Routledge).

Brivati, B. (2007) *The End of Decline: Blair and Brown in Power* (London: Politico's).

Brown, G. (2009) 'MPs' Expenses', Downing Street, https://www.youtube.com/watch?v=sBXj5l6ShpA&feature=channel_page

Brown, G. (2010) *A Future Fair for All: Labour Party Manifesto 2010* (Eastbourne: Gardners Books Ltd).

Buller, J. and Toby, J. (2011) 'Statecraft and the Assessment of National Political Leaders: The Case of New Labour and Tony Blair', *British Journal of Politics and International Relations*, 14, 4, 534–555, http://eprints.whiterose.ac.uk/65896/1/bjpi_471.pdf

Callaghan, J. (1978) 'Leader's Speech, Blackpool 1978', http://www.britishpo-liticalspeech.org/speech-archive.htm?speech=176

Callaghan, J. (1980) 'Leader's Speech, Blackpool 1980', http://www.britishpo-liticalspeech.org/speech-archive.htm?speech=178

Campbell, A. (2008) *The Blair Years* (London: Arrow Books).

Carr, R. (2014) *One Nation Britain* (Farnham: Ashgate).

Cesarani, D. (2014) 'Ed, There's Nothing Wrong with Being a Hampstead Socialist', *Jewish Chronicle*, http://www.thejc.com/comment-and-debate/comment/125522/ed-theres-nothing-wrong-being-a-hampstead-socialist

Channel 4 (2007a) 'The Last Days of Tony Blair', https://www.youtube.com/watch?v=WHPhobeyVI8

Channel 4 (2007b) 'The Rise and Fall of Tony Blair', www.youtube.com/watch?v=n_twlH_AG0A

Channel 4 (2008) 'Gordon Brown – Where Did It All Go Wrong?', https://www.youtube.com/watch?v=lRTg13dwttc

Clarke, C. and James, T. (eds) (2015) *British Labour Leaders* (London: Biteback Publishing).

Cooke, G. and Muir, R. (eds) (2012) *The Relational State* (London: IPPR), http://www.ippr.org/images/media/files/publication/2012/11/relational-state_Nov2012_9888.pdf

Corner, J. (2000) 'Mediated Persona and Political Culture: Dimensions of Structure and Process', *European Journal of Cultural Studies*, 3, 3, 386–402.

Corner, J. and Pels, D. (eds) (2003) *Media and the Restyling of Politics* (London: Sage).

Cowley, J. (2012) 'Ed Miliband. He's Not for Turning', *New Statesman*, 7 September.

Cowley, P. and Kavanagh, D. (2016). *The British General Election of 2015*. London: Palgrave.

Crace, J. (2015) 'Ed Miliband's Carved Pledges Could Sink Like a Stone', *The Guardian*, http://www.theguardian.com/politics/2015/may/03/ed-milibands-carved-pledges-could-sink-like-a-stone

Crines, A.S. (2011) *Michael Foot and the Labour Leadership* (Cambridge: Cambridge Scholars Publishing).

Crines, A.S. and Hayton, R. (eds) (2015) *Labour Orators from Bevan to Miliband* (Manchester: Manchester University Press).

Cruddas, J. (2012a) 'Jon Cruddas – The Maverick MP Trying to Lead Labour Out of the Wilderness', *The Guardian*, http://www.guardian.co.uk/politics/2012/jun/16/jon-cruddas-mp-labour

Cruddas, J. (2012b) 'Building the New Jerusalem', *New Statesman*, 28 September.

Cruddas, J. (ed.) (2013a) *One Nation Labour – Debating the Future*, http://labourlist.org/wp-content/uploads/2013/01/One-Nation-Labour-debating-the-future.pdf

Cruddas, J. (2013b) *Speech to Resolution Foundation on 'Earning and Belonging'*, http://www.newstatesman.com/politics/2013/02/jon-cruddass-speechresolution-foundation-full-text

Cruddas, J. (2013c) *The Condition of Britain*, http://www.ippr.org/press-releases/111/10331/jon-cruddas-mp-speech-on-the-condition-of-britain

Cruddas, J. (2013d) *One Nation Statecraft* (Speech), Local Government Association, http://www.joncruddas.org.uk/sites/joncruddas.org.uk/files/speech%20on%20statecraft.pdf

Davis, R. (2011) *Tangled Up in Blue* (London: Ruskin Publishing).

Deedes, H. (2012) 'Labour Has the Wrong Leader. But Not the Wrong Miliband', *Mail Online*, 24 January. www.dailymail.co.uk/debate/article-2091073/Ed-Miliband-Labour-wrong-leader.html#ixzz28nn6K46a

Denver, D. and Garnett, M. (2012) 'The Popularity of British Prime Ministers'. *British Journal of Politics and International Relations*, 14, 1, 57–73.

Demos (2010) We mean power: Ideas for the future of the left, http://www.demos.co.uk/files/Open_left_-_web.pdf?1266489744

Drake, P. and Higgins, M. (2012) 'Lights, Camera, Election: Celebrity, Performance and the 2010 UK General Election Leadership Debates', *British Journal of Politics and International Relations*, 14, 3, 375–91.

Drower, G.M.F. (1984) *Neil Kinnock: The Path to Leadership* (London: George Weidenfeld and Nicolson).

Dunn, T. (2012) 'We're Ed-ing in One Direction', *The Sun*, 3 October.

Dyer, R. (2003) *Heavenly Bodies: Film Stars and Society* (London: Routledge).

Dyer, R. and McDonald, P. (1998) *Stars* (London: BFI Publishing).

Elliott, L. and White, M. (1998) 'Brown's Grand Coalition: Prudence with a Purpose Is Budget Keynote', http://www.theguardian.com/politics/1998/mar/18/economy.welfare

Fairclough, N. (2000) *New Labour, New Language?* (London: Routledge).

Faucher, F. (2005) *Changing Parties: An Anthropology of British Party Conferences* (Basingstoke: Palgrave).

Fielding, S. (2013) 'White Heat and Low Politics', University of Nottingham, http://nottspolitics.org/2013/06/27/white-heat-and-low-politics/

Finlayson, A. (2002) 'Elements of the Blairite Image of Leadership', *Parliamentary Affairs*, 55, 3, 586–599.

Finlayson, A. (2004) 'Political Science, Political Ideas and Rhetoric', *Economy and Society*, 33, 4, 528–549.

Finlayson, A. (2007) 'From Beliefs to Arguments: Interpretive Methodology and Rhetorical Political Analysis', *The British Journal of Politics and International Relations*, 9, 4, 545–563.

Finlayson, A. (2012) 'Rhetoric and the Political Theory of Ideologies', *Political Studies*, 60, 4, 751–767.

Finlayson, A. (2014) 'Proving, Pleasing and Persuading? Rhetoric in Contemporary British Politics', *The Political Quarterly*, 85, 4, 428–431.

Foley, M. (2000) *The British Presidency* (Manchester: Manchester University Press).

Foot, P. (2005) *The Vote* (London: Viking).

Freeden, M. (1998) *Ideologies and Political Theory* (Oxford: Oxford University Press).

Freedland, J. (1998) 'A Portrait of Michael Foot, a Lesson for Labour', *The Guardian*, http://www.theguardian.com/commentisfree/2013/jul/23/archive-portrait-michael-foot-labour

Freedland, J. (2010) 'Ed Miliband Won Because He Was Neither Blair Nor Brown', *The Guardian*, http://www.guardian.co.uk/commentisfree/2010/sep/25/ed-miliband-labour-leader-conference

Gaffney, J. (1989) *The French Left and the Fifth Republic. The Discourses of Communism and Socialism in Contemporary France* (Basingstoke: Macmillan).

Gaffney, J. (1991) *The Language of Political Leadership in Contemporary Britain* (New York: St. Martin's Press).

Gaffney, J. (2001) 'Imagined Relationships; Political Leadership in Contemporary Democracies', *Parliamentary Affairs*, 54, 1, 120–133.

Gaffney, J. (2012) *Political Leadership in France: From Charles de Gaulle to Nicolas Sarkozy* (Basingstoke: Palgrave).

Gaffney, J. (2014). 'Political Leadership and the Politics of Performance: France, Syria and the Chemical Weapons Crisis of 2013'. *Journal of French Politics*, 12, 3, 218–234.

Gaffney, J. (2015) 'Why Is Jeremy Corbyn Stealing the Show?', *The Conversation*, http://theconversation.com/why-is-jeremy-corbyn-stealing-the-show-because-hes-the-only-labour-candidate-saying-anything-at-all-45120

Gaffney, J. (2016) 'Performative Political Leadership', in 't Hart, P. and Rhodes, R. (eds) *The Oxford Handbook of Political Leadership* (Oxford: Oxford University Press).

Gaffney, J. and Holmes, D. (eds) (2011) *Stardom in Post-war France* (Oxford: Berghahn Books).

Gaffney, J. and Lahel, A. (2013) 'Political Performance and Leadership Persona: The UK Labour Party Conference of 2012', *Government and Opposition*, 48, 4, 481–505.

Gaitskell, H. (1960) 'Hugh Gaitskell Giving a Speech Against Unilateral Disarmament', https://www.youtube.com/watch?v=1o1JWPrtdlg

Gaitskell, H. (1962) 'Speech by Hugh Gaitskell Against UK Membership of the Common Market', http://www.cvce.eu/en/obj/speech_by_hugh_gaitskell_against_uk_membership_of_the_common_market_3_october_1962-en-05f2996b-000b-4576-8b42-8069033a16f9.html

Garrigues, J. (2012) *Les Hommes providentiels: Histoire d'une fascination française* (Paris: Seuil).

Garzia, D. (2014) *Personalization of Politics and Electoral Change* (Basingstoke: Palgrave).

Giddens, A. (1994) *Beyond Left and Right: The Future of Radical Politics* (Cambridge: Polity).

Glasman, M. (2011) 'My Blue Labour Vision Can Defeat the Coalition', *The Observer*, 24 April, http://www.guardian.co.uk/politics/2011/apr/24/blue-labour-maurice-glasman

Glasman, M. (2013) 'One Nation and Blue Labour', paper presented at one-day conference, The Politics of One Nation Labour, Queen Mary, University of London, 18 April.

Glasman, M., Rutherford, J., Stears, M. and White, S. (eds) (2011) *The Labour Tradition and the Politics of Paradox* (London: The Oxford London Seminars).

Goldie, P. (2002) *The Emotions: A Philosophical Exploration* (Oxford: Oxford University Press).

Goodman, G. (1995) 'Harold Wilson', *The Guardian*, http://www.theguardian.com/politics/1995/may/25/obituaries

Gould, P. (2010) *The Unfinished Revolution* [1998] (London: Abacus).

Green, J. and Prosser, C. (2015) 'Learning the Right Lessons from Labour's 2015 Defeat' (London: IPPR *Juncture*), http://www.ippr.org/juncture/learning-the-right-lessons-from-labours-2015-defeat

Grice, A. (2012) 'Miliband Seizes Initiative with One Nation Labour', *The Independent*, 3 October.

Groves, J. and Shipman, T. (2012) 'Two in Three Labour Voters Want to Ditch Leader Ed Miliband for His Brother David', *Mail Online*, http://www.dailymail.co.uk/news/article-2210278/Two-Labour-voters-want-ditch-Ed-Miliband-brother-David.html#ixzz2A2702WPm

Harman, H. (2012) 'Harriet Harman: Emboldened Labour Have Fighting Chance', *BBC News Online*, 4 October, www.bbc.co.uk/news/uk-politics-19826546

Hasan, M. (2012) 'Come on Ed, You Don't Need Tony to Win', *Huffington Post UK Online*, 11 July, www.huffingtonpost.co.uk/mehdi-hasan/come-on-ed-youdont-needtony_b_1665129.html

Hasan, M. and Macintyre, J. (2011) *Ed: The Milibands and the Making of a Labour Leader* (London: Biteback Publishing).

Haworth, A. and Hayter, D. (2006) *Men Who Made Labour* (London: Routledge).

Heffernan, R. (2005) 'Exploring (and Explaining) the British Prime Minister', *British Journal of Politics and International Relations*, 7, 4, 605–20.

Hellmann, J. (1997) *The Kennedy Obsession: The American Myth of JFK* (New York: Columbia University Press).

Helm, T. and Hinsliff, G. (2009) 'Hazel Blears Savages Gordon Brown Over "Lamentable" Failures', *The Guardian*, http://www.theguardian.com/politics/2009/may/02/gordon-brown-hazelblears

Heppell, T. (2012) *Leaders of the Opposition: From Churchill to Cameron* (Basingstoke: Palgrave).

Hershman, G. (2015) *North London Geeks* (Amazon: CreateSpace).

Hodges, D. (2011) 'Just Who Is Refounding Labour?', *New Statesman*, 2 June, http://www.newstatesman.com/blogs/dan-hodges/2011/06/labour-party-zentrum

Hodges, D. (2011a) 'Refounding Labour Has Changed Nothing – But Tells Us a Lot', *The Guardian*, 21 September, http://www.guardian.co.uk/commentisfree/2011/sep/21/refounding-labour-changed-nothing-ed-miliband

Hodges, D. (2015). *One Minute to Ten* (London: Penguin).

Hoggart, S. (2012) 'Simon Hoggart's Sketch: Finally Ed Miliband Looked like he was in Command, *The Guardian*, 2 October, https://www.theguardian.com/commentisfree/2012/sep/26/ed-miliband-prime-minister-manchester

Hughes, C. (ed.) (2010) *What Went Wrong, Gordon Brown?* (London: Guardian Books).

Jago, M. (2014) *Clement Attlee: The Inevitable Prime Minister* (London: Biteback Publishing).

Jeffreys, K. (1993) *The Labour Party Since 1945* (London: Macmillan Press).

Jeffreys, K. (ed.) (1999) *Leading Labour: From Keir Hardie to Tony Blair* (London: I.B. Tauris) (including Laybourn; Wrigley; Riddell; Thorpe; Pearce; Brivati; Bale; Morgan; Shaw; Westlake; McSmith; Rentoul).

Jenkins, P. (1964) 'Edwardian or Jet Age?', *The Guardian*, 20 January, http://www.theguardian.com/century/1960-1969/Story/0,,105651,00.html

Jobson, R. (2014) 'Blue Labour and Nostalgia: the politics of tradition', *Renewal*, 22, 1–2, 102–117.

Jobson, R. and Wickham-Jones, M. (2010) 'Gripped by the Past: Nostalgia and the 2010 Labour Party Leadership Contest', *British Politics*, 5, 4, 525–48.

Johnson, B. (1995) 'Who *Are* All These People?', *Spectator*, 30 September, http://archive.spectator.co.uk/article/30th-september-1995/10/who-are-all

Johnson, A. (2012) 'Ed Miliband, Show Us You Have What It Takes to Be Prime Minister', *The Guardian*, 26 September, http://www.guardian.co.uk/commentisfree/2012/sep/26/ed-miliband-prime-minister-manchester

Jones, T. (1996) *Remaking the Labour Party: From Gaitskell to Blair* (London: Routledge).

Jones, T. (1997) '"Taking Genesis out of the Bible": Hugh Gaitskell, Clause IV, and Labour's Socialist Myth', *Contemporary British History*, 11, 2, 1–23.

Kellner, P. (2013) 'Ed Miliband Must Get Match-Fit'. (YouGov).

Kenny, M. (2013) 'Labour, England and One Nation', paper presented at one-day conference, The Politics of One Nation Labour, Queen Mary, University of London, 18 April.

Kinnock, N. (1983) 'Neil Kinnock Giving His Election Speech About Life Under Thatcher', https://www.youtube.com/watch?v=-QPhMVbleU0

Kinnock, N. (1985) 'Leader's Speech, Bournemouth 1985', http://www.britishpoliticalspeech.org/speech-archive.htm?speech=191; https://www.youtube.com/watch?v=bWLN7rIby9s)

Kinnock, N. (2000) 'Bitter Fight to a New Dawn', BBC News, http://news.bbc.co.uk/1/hi/in_depth/uk_politics/2000/labour_centenary/645202.stm

Kite, M. (2010) 'Ed Miliband: Self-Confessed Maths "Geek" with a Talent for Diplomacy', *The Telegraph*, http://www.telegraph.co.uk/news/politics/labour/8025055/Ed-Miliband-Self-confessed-maths-geek-with-a-talent-fordiplomacy.html

Krebs, R.R. and Jackson, P.T. (2007) 'Twisting Tongues and Twisting Arms: The Power of Political Rhetoric', *European Journal of International Relations*, 13, 1, 35–66.

Labour Party (2010) *New Politics. Fresh Ideas* (London: Labour Party).

Labour Party (2011) *A Better Future for Britain* (London: Labour Party).

Labour Party (2011a) *Refounding Labour to Win: A Party for the New Generation* (London: Labour Party).

Landale, J. (2012) 'Where Do Labour Stand After the 2012 Conference?', *BBC News*, http://www.bbc.co.uk/news/uk-politics-19829503

Lawton, K., Cooke, G., and Pearce, N. (eds) (2014) *The Condition of Britain* [Interim Report 2013] (London: IPPR).

Leapman, M. (1995) '"Rush of Blood" Was Kinnock's Downfall', *The Independent*, http://www.independent.co.uk/news/uk/home-news/rush-of-blood-was-kinnocks-downfall-1583723.html

Lemon, L.T. and Rees, R.J. (eds) (1965) *Russian Formalist Criticism: Four Essays* (Lincoln: University of Nebraska Press).

Lynch, R. (2010) 'It's Funny Because We Think It's True: Laughter Is Augmented by Implicit Preferences', *Evolution and Human Behaviour*, 31, 141–8.

MacDonald, J.R. (1924) 'Leader's Speech, London 1924', http://www.british-politicalspeech.org/speech-archive.htm?speech=155

MacDonald, J.R. (1931) '1931 Film Clip: Ramsay MacDonald's Election Appeal', National Archives, https://www.nationalarchives.gov.uk/cabinetpapers/alevelstudies/1931-film-clip.htm

Mandelson, P. (2010) *The Third Man: Life at the Heart of New Labour* (London: Harper Collins).

Marcus, G.E. (2002) *The Sentimental Citizen: Emotion in Democratic Politics* (University Park: Pennsylvania State University Press).

Marquand, D. (1977) *Ramsay MacDonald* (London: Jonathan Cape).

Marr, A. (2012) *The Andrew Marr Show*, BBC broadcast, 30 September.

Martin, W. (1986) *Recent Theories of Narrative* (Ithaca: Cornell University Press).

Martin, J. (2014) *Politics and Rhetoric: A Critical Introduction.* (London: Routledge).

Martin, J. (2015) 'Situating Speech: A Rhetorical Approach to Political Strategy', *Political Studies*, 63, 1, 25–42.

Massie, A. (2009) 'Gordon Brown: The Wrong Man in the Wrong Job at the Wrong Time', *The Telegraph*, http://www.telegraph.co.uk/news/politics/gordon-brown/6562795/Gordon-Brown-The-wrong-man-in-the-wrong-job-at-the-wrong-time.html

McCluskey, L. (2013) 'If Ed Miliband Is Seduced by the Blairites, He'll Be Defeated', *New Statesman*, 24 April.

McKie, D. (2005) 'Lord Callaghan', *The Guardian*, http://www.theguardian.com/news/2005/mar/28/guardianobituaries.politics

McQuillan, M. (2000) *The Narrative Reader* (London: Routledge).

Miliband, E. (2012) 'Ed Miliband's Speech to Labour Party Annual Conference 2012', http://www.labour.org.uk/ed-miliband-speech-conf-2012

Miliband, E. (2013) *One Nation Labour: The Party of Change*. Labour.org.uk, http://www.labour.org.uk/ed-miliband-speech-fabian-one-nation-labour-change

Miliband, E. (2013a) 'One Nation Labour: Britain Can Prevent a Lost Decade. Speech to People's Policy Forum', 23 March, http://www.labour.org.uk/one-nation-labour-britain-can-prevent-a-lost-decade,2013-03-23

Miliband, E. (2013b) Speech to Progress Annual Conference, 13 May, http://www.progressonline.org.uk/2013/05/13/speech-to-progress-annual-conference-2013/

Miliband, E. (2013c) *A One Nation Plan for Social Security Reform*, http://www.labour.org.uk/one-nation-social-security-reform-miliband-speech

Milne, S. (2012) 'Ed Miliband Must Move Further and Faster from New Labour', *The Guardian*, 3 October, https://www.theguardian.com/commentisfree/2012/oct/02/miliband-further-from-new-labour

Minkin, L. (1980) *The Labour Party Conference* (Manchester: Manchester University Press).

Morgan, K. (2006) *Ramsay MacDonald* (London: Haus).

Morgan, K.O. (2008) 'Labour's Greatest Hero: Keir Hardie', *The Guardian*, http://www.theguardian.com/commentisfree/2008/sep/19/labour.labourconference1

Morris, P. (ed.) (2003) *The Bakhtin Reader*. London: Arnold.

Mounier, E. (1947) *Qu'est-ce que le personnalisme?* (Paris: Seuil).

Muir, R. and Parker, I. (2014) *Many to Many: How the Relational State Will Transform Public Services* (London: IPPR).

Mulholland, H. (2010) 'Ed Miliband Defeats Older Brother in Race to Be Labour Leader', *The Guardian*, https://www.theguardian.com/politics/2010/sep/25/ed-miliband-labour-leader

Naughtie, J. (2002) *Rivals* (London: Fourth Estate).

Oborne, P. and Walters, S. (2004) *Alastair Campbell* (London: Aurum Press).

Pettitt, R. (2012) 'Me, Myself and I: Self Referencing in Labour Party Conference Leaders' Speeches', *British Politics*, 7, 1, 111–34.

Philpot, R. (ed.) (2011) *The Purple Book: A Progressive Future for Labour* (London: Biteback Publishing).

PMQs (2011) *Wallace & Gromit & Planet Vulcan jibes – David Cameron vs Ed Miliband* (PMQs, 12.1.11), http://www.youtube.com/watch?v=yy14xHBO98c

Porter, A. and Prince, R. (2010) General Election 2010: Gordon Brown's Gillian Duffy "Bigot" Gaffe May Cost Labour, *The Telegraph*, http://www.telegraph.co.uk/news/election-2010/7648327/General-Election-2010-Gordon-Browns-Gillian-Duffy-bigot-gaffe-may-cost-Labour.html

Propp, V. (1968) *Morphology of the Folktale*, 2nd edn (Austin and London: University of Texas Press).

Provine, R. (2000) *Laughter: A Scientific Investigation* (New York: Penguin).

Pugh, M. (2010). *Speak for Britain! A New History of the Labour Party* (London: Bodley Head).

Rémond, R (1983) *1958: Le Retour du Général* (Brussels:Complexe).

Richards, S. (2012) 'Ed's Display of Style – And Substance – Will Worry the Tories', *The Independent*, 3 October.

Riddell, M. (2011) 'Labour Must Not Be Airbrushed from History', *The Telegraph*, http://www.telegraph.co.uk/comment/columnists/maryriddell/8488658/Labour-must-not-be-airbrushed-from-history.html

Robinson, E. (2013) 'Recapturing Labour's Traditions? History, Nostalgia and the Re-Writing of Clause IV', Political Studies Association Annual Conference, Cardiff, 25–27 March.

Ross, T. (2015). *Why the Tories Won* (London: Biteback Publishing).

Rutherford, J. (2011) 'The Future Is Conservative', in M. Glasman, J. Rutherford, M. Stears and S. White (eds) *The Labour Tradition and the Politics of Paradox* (London: The Oxford London Seminars).

Rutherford, J. (2013) 'The Labour Party and the New Left', *Renewal*, 2, 1, 9–14.

Rutherford, J. and Lockey, A. (2010) *Labour's Future* (London: Lawrence and Wishart).

Sandbrook, D. (2010) *White Heat: A History of Britain in the Swinging Sixties* (London: Abacus).

Sandel, M. (2012) 'Labour Conference 2012: A Cerebral Address on Moral Limits of Markets', *The Guardian*, 30 September, https://www.theguardian.com/politics/2012/sep/30/labour-conference-2012-markets

Sartre, J.-P. (1960) *Questions de méthode* (Paris: Gallimard).

Schneer, J. (1990) *George Lansbury* (Manchester: Manchester University Press).

Seldon, A. and Lodge, G. (2011) *Brown at 10* (London: Biteback Publishing).

Seyd, P. (1999) 'New Parties/New Politics? A Case Study of the British Labour Party', *Party Politics*, 5, 3, 383–405.

Shipton, M. (2014) '"I Felt Helpless During Miners' Strike" Admits Former Labour Leader Neil Kinnock', *Western Mail*, http://www.walesonline.co.uk/news/wales-news/i-felt-helpless-during-miners-7891594

Smith, O. and Reeves, R. (eds) (2013) *One Nation. Power, Hope, Community* (London: One Nation Register).

Smith, M., Richards, D. and Diamond, P. (2013) 'Politicians Often Claim Commitment to Decentralising the State, but Once in Government They Are Unwilling to Relinquish Their Own Power', LSE British Politics and Policy blog, http://blogs.lse.ac.uk/politicsandpolicy/visions-of-subsidiarity-and-the-curse-of-the-british-political-tradition/

Sopel, J. (1995) *Tony Blair: The Moderniser.* (London: Bantam Books).

Street, J. (2004) 'Celebrity Politicians: Popular Culture and Political Representation', *British Journal of Politics and International Relations*, 6, 4, 435–52.

Street, J. (2012) 'Do Celebrity Politics and Celebrity Politicians Matter?', *British Journal of Politics and International Relations*, 14, 3, 346–56.

Strick, M., Holland, R.W., van Baaren, R.B. and van Knippenberg, A. (2012) 'Those Who Laugh Are Defenceless: How Humour Breaks Resistance to Influence', *Journal of Experimental Psychology: Applied*, 18, 2, 213–23.

Stuart, M. (2013) 'Hugh Gaitskell: What Is the Labour Leader's Legacy?', *Ballots & Bullets* (University of Nottingham), http://nottspolitics.org/2013/01/18/hugh-gaitskell-what-is-the-labour-leaders-legacy/

Suphi, S. (2012) 'He's a Real Showman', *Daily Mirror*, 3 October.

Sylvester, R. and Thomson, A. (2013) 'Was This the Week Miliband Finally Headed for Number 10?', *The Times*, 23 March, http://www.thetimes.co.uk/tto/news/politics/article3721001.ece

The Economist (2005) 'Obituary: Jim Callaghan', http://www.economist.com/node/3809548

The Guardian (1985) 'Excerpts from the Manchester Guardian 1960', February 23, 1985.

The Guardian (2000) 'Boring Old Blokes on TV – An A to Z', http://www.theguardian.com/theguardian/2000/nov/11/dumb6

The Guardian (2009) 'Gordon Brown Must Rediscover His Moral Compass', http://www.theguardian.com/commentisfree/2009/apr/19/gordon-brown-damian-macbride-draper

The Sun (1992) 'If Kinnock Wins Today Will the Last Person to Leave Britain Please Turn Out the Lights', http://www.bl.uk/learning/histcitizen/fpage/elections/election.html

Theakston, K. (2011) 'Gordon Brown as Prime Minister: Political Skills and Leadership Style', *British Politics*, 6, 1, 78–100.

Thorpe, A. (1988) 'Arthur Henderson and the British Political Crisis of 1931', *The Historical Journal*, 31, 1, 117–139.

Thorpe, A. (2008) *A History of the British Labour* Party, 3rd edn (Basingstoke: Palgrave).

Toye, R. (2011) 'The Rhetorical Premiership: A New Perspective on Prime Ministerial Power Since 1945', *Parliamentary History*, 30, 2, 175–92.

Treneman, A. (2012) 'Geek-tastic Ed Triumphs by Nicking a Tory Mantra', *The Times*, 3 October.

van Gennep, A. (1961) *The Rites of Passage* (London: Routledge and Kegan Paul).

Watson, I. (2015). *Five Million Conversations*. Edinburgh: Luath Press.

Watt, N. (2012) 'And Now It's Personal – Miliband the Leader Steps Into the Limelight', *The Guardian*, 3 October.

Watt, N. and Wintour, P. (2009) 'Gordon Brown Ordered to Repay £12,000 of Expenses', *The Guardian*, http://www.theguardian.com/politics/2009/oct/12/gordon-brown-repay-mps-expenses

Weber, M. (1964) *The Theory of Social and Economic Organization* (New York: Free Press).

Weber, M. (2004) *The Vocation Lectures* (Indianapolis: Hackett Publishing Co., Inc.).

Weiler, P. (1993) *Ernest Bevin* (Manchester: Manchester University Press).

Westen, D. (2008) *The Political Brain: The Role of Emotion in Deciding the Fate of the Nation* (New York: PublicAffairs).

Wheeler, B. (2006) 'Wilson "Plot": The Secret Tapes', BBC, http://news.bbc.co.uk/1/hi/uk_politics/4789060.stm

Wheeler, B. (2007) 'The Gordon Brown Story', BBC, http://news.bbc.co.uk/1/hi/uk_politics/6743875.stm

Wheeler, M. (2012) 'The Democratic Worth of Celebrity Politics in an Era of Late Modernity', *British Journal of Politics and International Relations*, 14, 3, 407–22.

Wickham-Jones, M. (2013) 'The Historical Origins of One Nation Labour', paper presented at one-day conference, the Politics of One Nation Labour, Queen Mary, University of London, 18 April.

Wickham-Jones, M. (2013a) 'History, Memory and the Social Democratic Project', Political Studies Association Annual Conference, Cardiff, 25–27 March.

Williams, P.M. (1979) *Hugh Gaitskell: A Political Biography* (London: Jonathan Cape).

Williams, R. (1987) *Culture and Society* (London: Hogarth Press).

Willner, A.R. (1984) *The Spellbinders: Charismatic Political Leadership* (New Haven: Yale University Press).

Wilson, H. (1963) 'Labour's Plan for Science', Labour Annual Conference, Scarborough, http://nottspolitics.org/wp-content/uploads/2013/06/Labours-Plan-for-science.pdf

Wilson, H. (1968) 'Leader's Speech, Blackpool 1968', http://www.britishpoliticalspeech.org/speech-archive.htm?speech=166

Windt, T. and Ingold, B. (eds) (1992) *Essays in Presidential Rhetoric* (Dubuque: Kendall).

Wintour, P. (2012) 'Labour Leader Vows to Unite Country as He Claims "One Nation" Mantle', *The Guardian*, 3 October.

Wodak, R. (2009) *The Discourse of Politics in Action: Politics as Usual* (Basingstoke: Palgrave Macmillan).

Wodak, R., Khosvavinik, M. and Mral, B. (eds) (2013) *Right-Wing Populism in Europe: Politics and Discourse* (London: Bloomsbury).

Wood, S. (2013) 'Explaining One Nation Labour', *Political Quarterly*, 84, 3, 317–320.

INDEX[1]

---

[1] Note: Page number followed by 'n' refers to footnotes.

© The Author(s) 2017
J. Gaffney, *Leadership and the Labour Party*, Palgrave Studies
in Political Leadership, DOI 10.1057/978-1-137-50498-2

Blair, Tony, 8, 16, 24, 29, 34, 36, 40,
49, 52, 56–66, 68–72, 74–9, 83,
88, 114, 118–19, 123, 125, 126,
128, 147, 148, 157, 164, 172,
176, 180, 181, 187, 189, 192,
194, 197, 200, 205–8, 211, 212,
214, 216, 217, 219, 231, 232,
234, 237, 243
Clause IV reform, 212
conception of leadership, 59–60
decision to support the US in Iraq,
62, 69
early years as leader, 60, 63
final Conference speech as Prime
Minister in 2006, 63
'forces of Conservatism' speech,
60, 77
formative political experience, 57–8
moderniser during 1990s, 57
oratorical abilities, 60–1
premiership, 8, 62
self-presentation of, 118
speeches as leader, 58
speech in Labour campaign,
2015, 176
unpopularity, 63, 64
Blears, Hazel, 77, 86
Blue Labour, 32, 73, 84, 86–7,
90–7, 101, 104–9, 112–13,
149, 208–9, 215–17, 220,
221, 222, 225, 230
Bogdanor, Vernon, 108n11, 204,
204n1, 205
Boyle, Danny, 96
Brand, Russell, 191–4
Brighton 2013 Party Conference, 153
Brown, George, 38
Brown, Gordon, 9–10, 24, 56, 59,
61–7, 68, 69, 70, 72, 75, 77,
81–2, 83, 86, 123, 124, 125,
138, 147, 156, 203, 204, 231,
232, 236, 237

chancellorship of, 62, 64, 65
premiership of, 65, 123–4
Brownism, 203, 231
Burley, Kay, 170, 171
Burnham, Andy, 25, 124n2, 147,
218n6, 223, 225, 226, 233,
235, 242, 244
Bush, George, 62, 173
Byrne, Liam, 89, 91–5, 97, 99, 102,
109, 155, 194

C
Cable, Vince, 65
Callaghan, Jim, 24, 41, 43–5, 49, 57,
65, 68, 69, 71, 72, 74–6, 79,
147, 206
Cameron, David, 124–5, 138,
146, 147, 156–8, 161–2,
166–9, 173–4, 176, 178, 180,
182, 186, 189, 191, 192, 194,
228, 233
Campaign Strategy Committee, 71
Capital in the 21st Century (Piketty),
162
celebrity politics, 7, 12, 48, 59, 78,
118–23
charisma, 12, 17–19
Weber's definition of, 245
charismatic leadership, 12, 19
Clause IV, 36–7, 40, 70, 71, 74,
152–3, 211–12, 214
Clegg, Nick, 166, 173, 174, 238
Cole, G.D.H., 109, 208, 225, 229
communication techniques, changing,
76–7
Conservative campaign, 2015,
174, 191
contemporary leadership, 83
Cooper, Yvette, 25, 142n7, 148, 218,
218n6, 266, 242–4
Corbyn 'insurgency' of 2015, 71

Lightning Source UK Ltd.
Milton Keynes UK
UKOW05n0042010617

302386UK00009B/48/P